"*Exploring Cusco* is not only the best guide to Cusco and the Sacred Valley, it is arguably the most insightful, intelligent and useful such book ever written about any major cultural centre of the world. A highly accomplished archaeologist, National Geographic explorer, and resident of Cusco for more than 40 years, Peter Frost wastes few words on the mundane challenges of travel. Rather he takes you beneath the surface of every major site you are likely to explore and then some, providing explanations for all of the mysteries that enchant true travellers to the region, even as he lays the history of the Inca and the Conquest before you as a gift. I own every edition of Exploring Cusco, which for me has always been as much a research tool as a guidebook, and I am delighted that a new updated edition is now available to fire the hearts of a new generation of scholars and travellers, adventurers all."

Wade Davis, National Geographic Explorer, anthropologist, author of *The Serpent and the Rainbow*, *One River* and *Into the Silence*.

"*Exploring Cusco* is the definitive guide to Cusco and its surroundings. Peter Frost has lived much of his life in the former capital of the Incas, has been walking the Inca Trail since 1976, has a profound knowledge and love of both Inca and colonial art and architecture, writes delightfully, and caters for both first-time visitors and experts, young and old. I thoroughly recommend it."

John Hemming, author of *The Conquest of the Incas*, *Monuments of the Incas* and *Tree of Rivers: the Story of the Amazon*, and director emeritus of Britain's Royal Geographical Society.

"*Exploring Cusco* has always been a 'must read' for anyone visiting Cusco and its surrounding region. The latest edition continues to provide the most important and up-to-date information based on Peter Frost's decades of experience. It is a pleasure to see this invaluable guidebook once again in print."

Johan Reinhard, National Geographic Explorer, pioneer of high altitude archaeology and author of *The Ice Maiden*, and *Machu Picchu, the Sacred Center*.

Exploring Cusco – 6th edition
Author-Publisher © Peter Frost 2018
www.peterfrost.org

First published by Lima 2000 in 1979, 2nd edition 1980; 3rd edition 1984;
4th edition 1989; 5th edition 1999.

Front cover: composite from photos of the Inca Trail to Machu Picchu
and Maukallacta (Paruro) by the author
Rear cover map © King of Maps, 2017

Illustrations by the author, maps by the author and Leo Duncan
Research, Design and Production Assistant: Leo Duncan
Research Assistant: Hannah Porst
Design and Layout: Nuria Urquiza

Printed by CreateSpace, Charleston SC

Hecho el depósito legal en la Biblioteca Nacional del Perú N° 2017-17611
ISBN: 978-612-00-3072-1

EXPLORING CUSCO

Peter Frost

The Classic Guide to
Cusco, Machu Picchu and Peru's Most Famous Region

6th Revised Edition

ABOUT THE BOOK

Peter Frost's *Exploring Cusco* was first published in 1979 and is now in its sixth edition, having been revised and updated repeatedly since then. His book is now known as the essential guide to Peru's most famous region for visitors: Cusco, Machu Picchu and the former Inca heartland. Every page is infused with the author's personal knowledge and experience, which includes many years of exploration and discovery in remote areas of the Andes. Exploring the region with this book is like having a private guide at your side.

Exploring Cusco focuses on the fascinating history, archaeology and folklore of the Cusco region. It also features numerous walking tours of Inca sites, both famous and obscure, along with many local hikes. You'll find countless recommendations for hotels, restaurants and tour operators, plus information and suggestions on how to get around. Much of the book is dedicated to the city of Cusco and the Sacred Valley, including Machu Picchu, the main areas of interest to tourists; but the complete book covers an area ranging from the city of Sicuani to Espiritu Pampa – the last refuge of the Incas – a distance of some 265km (166mi). (See back cover for a full map.) Those seeking pre-trip insights, those curious about Inca history or simply inclined to wander and explore, will find no better companion. Additional information and resources are available on the author's website at **www.peterfrost.org**

ABOUT THE AUTHOR

Peter Frost has been traveling in Peru since 1971 and has lived in Cusco for more than 30 years. In addition to *Exploring Cusco*, he is the author of *Machu Picchu Historical Sanctuary*, the Insight Compact Guide to Peru and Ecuador, and numerous articles about the Cusco area. His archaeological investigations and discoveries in the remote Vilcabamba region of Peru have been supported by the National Geographic Expeditions Council, and he now works for National Geographic as a local expert. He is also a freelance writer, lecturer, photographer and adventure travel guide.

ABOUT THE CONTRIBUTORS

Dr. Brian Bauer is an archaeologist with U. Illinois at Chicago, specializing in the Andes. A prolific author and field researcher, his output includes works on the Cusco ceque system, Inca astronomy, pilgrimage and state formation, as well as studies of the Chanka polity and the archaeology of the Inca resistance.

Dr. Gary Urton is Dumbarton Oaks Professor of Pre-Columbian Studies at Harvard U. and holder of a MacArthur fellowship. His seminal work on Quechua astronomy influenced a generation of Andean scholars, while his later focus on the Inca quipu has placed important milestones on the path to deciphering this enigmatic record-keeping device.

Dr. Holly Wissler is an ethnomusicologist and Quechua scholar with many years of traveling and exploring in the Andes. She has worked extensively recording the songs, music and folkways of the highland Q'eros nation and the Amazonian Wachipaeri.

Dr. Jorge Flores Ochoa is an anthropologist on the faculty of the University of San Antonio de Abad in Cusco. He is noted for his work on camelids and the culture of Andean herders, and is a founder of Cusco's Inka Museum.

Carol Stewart is an itinerant gourmet, psychologist and tarot reader whose sojourn in Cusco during the 1980s taught her that the way to Cusco's heart was through its stomach.

Leo Duncan is Peter Frost's son and assistant and an avid Andean explorer. He has made integral contributions to the researching and writing of this edition and currently calls Cusco home.

Table of Contents

Maps

ACKNOWLEDGEMENTS
To the Sixth Edition

The Quechua people of the Andes must feature first. Their ways, their ancestors, their heritage, their world – so often generously shared – have been this book's essence from the beginning. I thank them all.

Next, *The Conquest of the Incas* and its author, John Hemming. Chatting with him during a recent visit to Cusco, I told him, "You know, without your book I wouldn't have stayed here." It was true. More than 40 years ago his seminal work on late Inca history launched me on a quest that never really ended, hiking over mountain and through forest, sniffing out Inca remains (they were everywhere), and combing through written works and documents for clues about those extraordinary people.

It's not just me. I have heard Brian Bauer, another valuable ally and major influence of mine, refer to Hemming's opus as "the bible". So once again I begin with a wave to that book and its author, without which this one would never have been written.

Countless others have contributed in small and large ways to these pages. I am especially grateful to my old friend Jean-Jacques Decoster for his advice and support over the years. And I must thank both my son Leo Duncan and Hannah Porst for their vital assistance in bringing this new edition into the world. Vincent R. Lee, for his knowledge of Vilcabamba and his work on Inca stonework, Ruth and Kenneth Wright for their numerous hydrological studies, and Holly Wissler for her insights on Andean music and the Q'eros people – their data shared without hesitation. Stella Nair's research on Chinchero added much value to that section, as did Alexei Vranich to the Cusco city chapter, with his records on Inca Cusco. Donato Amado has been a valuable source on the Inca road system. Joseph Hollowell had provocative new thoughts about Ollantaytambo, while Rainer Hostnig contributed for both the latter and the area around Espinar. Nilda Callañaupa, Timoteo Ccarita and Andrea Heckman were go-to informants on the Andean textile tradition. Thibault Saintenoy, Tiburcio Waranqa and Matt Waugh were mines of information on Choquequirao and its hinterland, and thanks go to Javier Fonseca for new archaeology at Vilcabamba the Old. Fernando Astete, the late Alfredo Valencia and Marius Ziolkowski have all supplied additional information on Machu Picchu over the years. Vera Tyuleneva has been my default consultant on anything concerning Paititi, while Olly of King of Maps created excellent new cartography for the rear cover.

The vast General Information section has too many sources to mention, but special thanks go to Paul Cripps, Barry Walker and Roger Valencia for information on many topics. Maureen Santucci, Scott Lite, Javier Regueiro, Lesley Myburgh and Joey Greenstone all gave valuable input for the new Medicinal Plants section. Jimmy McSparron suggested medical services and helped with other details, while Claire Dean supplied transportation and guiding information.

My research in Vilcabamba, which informs much of this text directly or indirectly, has been supported by the National Geographic Expeditions Council, Enrique Velasco and Coltur, Jack Daulton and Roz Ho, and numerous individual sponsors. Of the many who have suffered there with me, special thanks go to Scott Gorsuch, Kevin Floerke and David Beresford-Jones.

INTRODUCTION TO THE SIXTH EDITION

This edition of *Exploring Cusco* continues a venerable tradition of allowing enormous stretches of time to pass between the publication of new editions, even establishing a new record for time elapsed during which it was out of print altogether. But here, at last, is the latest-new-improved edition.

What's new since the last edition in 1999? An awful lot. Tourism to Cusco has boomed and double boomed since then, and Machu Picchu is now on everyone's bucket list while more people are realizing that there actually are other astonishing things in Peru besides Machu Picchu.

Both Machu Picchu and the Inca Trail are more heavily regulated than ever, and Machu Picchu bulges at the seams with visitors yet somehow continues to receive more each year. On the up side, restrictions, waiting lists and huge entry lines have prompted tour operators to seek the roads less traveled and authorities to add new infrastructure, so there are plenty of revelations to talk about in these pages, along with new discoveries, theories and perspectives for well-known places. A superb condor-viewing site on the Apurimac Canyon, the inspiring "Rainbow Mountain" hike near Ausangate, newly opened trekking routes all over the region, new discoveries which greatly expand our understanding and range of interesting features at Choquequirao (seldom visited in 1999), hiking routes to the spectacular Inca site of Huajra Pucara, the transformation of Moray from an obscure brush-covered afterthought into one of the region's great attractions – all of this has occurred since the last edition.

This mountain of new information is tackled without adding a whole lot more pages by deploying technology; basically, you will find the essential information in the book and a heap more at **www.peterfrost.org** An attempt has also been made to distinguish between information you will definitely want from the book in your hand and details you can reference on the website and/ or download from the cloud, such as additional city services, trekking routes and so forth. And by the way, it's not *all* on the website so you gotta buy the book, OK?

As in previous editions, many sections include an *Explorer's Note*, intended to point adventurous travelers with time to spare towards the little-known routes, remoter areas and spontaneous surprises that still abound in this region and can add so much to the experience of exploring Cusco.

To clarify what is meant by "the Cusco region": Cusco is both a city *and* a region, the latter a political subdivision of 71,986km^2 (27,794mi^2), with the city of Cusco as its capital. (According to the 2015 data from the National Statistics Office (INEI), there are about 1.3 million people in the entire region, with about 450,000 in the city and outlying towns.) The "Cusco" of this guide, however, lies partway between these two entities – larger than the city, but smaller than the whole political region.

The aim is to avoid covering areas where neither interesting destinations nor basic services are available, while including lots of options within reach of the city for both soft adventurers and hardcore backpackers. Thus readers will find hotel accommodations that are rustic but tolerable, resorts where some can enjoy comforts equal to anything in Cusco, and trail/camping information for others.

How to Use This Book

To maintain the focus on the region's background, all recommended businesses and logistical details, such as hotels, restaurants, transportation, and tour operators, have been consolidated into the "General Information" section at the beginning of the book and cross referenced as necessary. All businesses within the boundaries of the Cusco city map (p.78) and a few of the more obscure streets have been given a coordinate, such as "B3", to correspond to their location on the map grid. Businesses Off the Map are labeled "OM". Very long website addresses have been shortened to TinyURLs, which look like this: tinyurl.com/j6at9zc Use them as you would a normal URL.

The main book chapters are arranged by geographical location and their relative popularity with visitors. Distances beside section headings [e.g. CHINCHERO (27km / 17mi)] are road distances measured from the Plaza de Armas in Cusco. The book can be read in any order, and curious visitors will learn much by reading the chapters for places they don't visit. There are lots of interesting tidbits and descriptions of remote places to explore for people with more time.

And here, a plea: if you follow paths to unknown places, if you come across unexpected delights, or something just plain interesting, if there is anything you feel should be in this book but isn't, *Exploring Cusco* would be grateful to hear from you. Such feedback, and any detected errors, are welcome on the "Contact" page of **www.peterfrost.org** There is an "Exploring Cusco Corrections" page to right all wrongs and a "Reader Feedback" page for your comments.

Quechuas and Incas

Previous editions stated: "Pre-hispanic history in Peru – as any candid authority will admit – is about 60% speculation, 30% probability, and 10% established fact, without counting that portion which is totally unknown." Well, the percentages have changed since then. Now 12% is established fact! Maybe. And most of that percentage concerns the Incas, those Andean latecomers for whom we have the most reliable record. Our knowledge of the Andean past remains abysmally sketchy when compared to what we know of Old World civilizations. Thus, much of what has been written even about the Incas is open to dispute.

To avoid cluttering these lines with qualifiers and academic asides, I have adopted the following heresy: wherever a historical or archaeological assertion comes from a respected source, seems reasonable, and is not contradicted by other plausible theories, I cite it as fact. On the other hand, where a popularly held belief is doubtful (as in the case of Moray) or demonstrably mistaken, I try to expose it.

My intention in these matters is to chart a course between the timid reductionism of so much academic interpretation of Inca history and the extreme flights of fact-free fantasy that are even more common; a wide enough strait to sail through, surely, without getting beached on either shore.

The language of the Inca empire was Quechua. Millions still speak this language, and in modern times this is the generic name for all of them: the Quechua people. Quechua place names are often graphic and colorful; frequently they describe the history or geography of a location. So wherever possible I have included a translation. Spellings of the names of some Inca ruins and other Quechua words vary wildly depending on the writer's preferences and first language, the time of day, and the alignment of the stars. Is it "Sacsaywaman" or "Saqsayhuaman"? "Pachacutec" or "Pachacuti"? "Cusco," "Cuzco" or even "Qosqo"? Blame Quechua for being unwritten and the Roman alphabet for its phonetic mismatch. Be aware that in the lawless world of Andean spelling, c's become q's and w's become hu's with disorienting randomness. Where possible, spellings are consistent and correspond to local signage. Otherwise, spellings that help anglophones correctly pronounce the word have been used.

Finally, concerning Quechua and other arcana, if you come across a strange word or an abbreviation you don't understand, check the glossary or the list of abbreviations at the back of the book.

Authors run into another problem when writing about "the Incas." The vast agglomeration of peoples under rule from Cusco in the years preceding the Spanish invasion had no collective name that has survived, other than *runa*, meaning simply "people." "Inca" was the Quechua term used to describe just one person, the ruling emperor himself – the Sapa Inca. We have a word for the nobles who ruled under him: *orejones* – big ears – a Spanish word alluding to the huge gold earplugs worn by the aristocracy. But one is stuck for a word to describe the culture as a whole, and so most writing about ancient Peru mingles the correct and incorrect use of the word Inca shamelessly. What follows here is no exception.

One thing is certain – it is wrong to call the modern Quechua people "Incas." The broadest possible use of that term includes only the ruling elite of Cusco before the Conquest, a group thought to have numbered around 30-40,000. Today, some say the Quechua-speaking Q'eros people from the remote mountains east of Cusco (*see p.276*) are descended from refugees of the Inca nobility. And a group of families in the town of San Jerónimo near Cusco claim descent from Huayna Capac and wield some supporting genealogical evidence. Aside from these outliers, most modern Quechua people are not, and never were, Incas.

Any mention of the early chronicles in these pages refers, of course, to post-Conquest Spanish accounts – along with a few mestizo and indigenous documents – transcribed from a multitude of sources. The Incas only had an oral history, plus their method of record-keeping on colored knots and cords (*quipus*), as far as we know for sure. Most of the quipus were destroyed, either deliberately or by neglect, during the colonial era, and today only some 800 survive. Even the majority of these lack archaeological context, and so are very difficult to interpret. That said, some extremely smart people are working on this challenging problem today, much new understanding has been teased out of the extant quipus in recent times, and every new archaeological quipu find adds a new piece to the puzzle. Some day important new revelations may emerge from this source.

GENERAL INFORMATION

ABBREVIATIONS

a.k.a.   also known as
BF   Serves breakfast
BTC   *Boleto Turistico del Cusco*, the
         various Cusco tourist tickets
         (*see p. 18*)
CRA   *Circuito Religioso Arzobispal*
         (religious circuit) ticket. (*see p. 19*)
crnr   corner
DRC   *Dirección Regional Desconcentrada de
         Cultura de Cusco*, the local culture
         ministry in charge of the ruins sites.
IGN   *Instituto Geográfico Nacional*, the
         national cartographic agency res-
         ponsible for mapping the country
LM   Live music
LM&D   Live music and dance
GV   Great View
NE   northeast
NW   northwest

OM   Off Map, when an address is off the
         Cusco city map on p.78
Pl.   Plaza
RBA   *Ruta Barroco Andino* (Andean
         Baroque Route) ticket (*see p. 19*)
s/n   *sin numero*, an address with no
         exact street number
SE   southeast
SL   a Set Lunch is served at a
         restaurant
SPS   Social Project Support. Supports
         worthy social causes and/or NGOs
SST   Separate Site Ticket, for a tourist
         site selling its own individual ticket
SW   southwest
TT   *Terminal Terrestre*, Cusco's main bus
         station. (*see p. 20*)
UNSAAC   *Universidad Nacional San Antonio
         Abad de Cusco*, Cusco's main
         university, located on Avenida
         la Cultura a short taxi ride from the
         city center

A CUSCO OVERVIEW

Population

According to 2015 estimates, the city of Cusco (including some nearby towns) has about 450,000 inhabitants; the total for the department of Cusco is about 1.3 million. (See the *Exploring Cusco Museum* **www.peterfrost.org** for how Cusco's population and many other things have changed since 1979.)

Climate

During the May-September dry season the weather is generally sunny, with spells of overcast or showers. From October to April the weather is far more variable, with a tendency to sunshine in the morning with rain later. January and February are the wettest months. Annual rainfall is 29in (73.7cm). The Andean seasonal variation seems to have become less reliable in recent years, and the weather less predictable.

Tourism Season

The busiest season is May through September. A severe crunch occurs in the latter part of June (due to *Inti Raymi*, *see Festivals p. 51*), and between July 28

15

and August 10, when Peruvian national vacationing peaks and all services are overloaded. This is a good time to avoid Cusco; if you can't, then double-reconfirm your plane, train, and hotel reservations. Christmas is also a busy time. Also note that, conversely, in the low tourist season, especially February and March, some of the services mentioned below are cut back or closed altogether.

Altitude

Cusco sits at 3,400m (11,150ft) above sea level. At high elevation air pressure is lower. Each lungful of air captures fewer oxygen molecules. Curb your enthusiasm for the first couple of hours when arriving by plane from Lima. Relax, lie down, adjust. Avoid respiratory depressants, such as alcohol, sedatives and sleeping pills. (For better sleep, take acetazolamide [*see below*] instead.) Eat lightly for a day or so. Dehydration occurs very rapidly at high altitude, thus it is vital to drink plenty of fluids. All this will speed acclimatization. In a day you will feel better, and in two days you should be fine.

Hypoxia or AMS (acute mountain sickness), known locally as *soroche*, can be hard to shake off once it starts. Symptoms: shortness of breath, headache, nausea, dizziness, insomnia, loss of appetite, vomiting in bad cases. Descent is the infallible cure for altitude problems. The Sacred Valley, only 45 minutes from Cusco by the most direct route, is about 500m lower, and this is enough to cure or greatly improve most cases of AMS. However, various remedies and preventatives can help. The local remedy is tea made from coca leaves *(mate de coca)*. This is helpful, but by no means

a cure. Chewing is even better. (*See* p. 48) Peripheral edema (fluid retention, puffiness) is common at high altitude. Any diuretic, such as coca tea, will help alleviate this.

Pharmaceuticals. As with any prescription medicines, consult a physician. Acetazolamide has shown good results as prophylaxis and treatment of AMS; it is also used in the treatment of glaucoma and is a diuretic. It acts as a respiratory stimulant and also counteracts the blood alkalosis associated with AMS. Taking the drug at night before sleep is particularly helpful. It is available over the counter at Peruvian pharmacies (*see p. 46*). Most people experience a slight tingling in their extremities as a side effect, some feel drowsy, and a few have more serious adverse reactions. (One extremely serious side effect: it ruins the taste of beer.) It is a sulfa drug, and the usual precautions apply. Dexamethasone is an alternative for the sulfa-intolerant.

Most *controlled* medical conditions show little or no extra risk at high altitude. Young and old, fit and unfit, normal pregnancies, those with diabetes, heart disease, even mild lung disease – all are welcomed by the mountain gods. Consult your medic, nonetheless.

Altitude for Hikers. If you are hiking one of the region's trails, some of which go to 5,000m (16,400ft) or more, you will be ascending far higher than Cusco. This requires extra acclimatization and precautions. Do a light hike or two before the big one. Note that a low sleeping altitude is more important than how high you go during the day.

Very high altitude can produce extremely dangerous conditions known as High Altitude Pulmonary Edema (HAPE) and High Altitude Cerebral Edema (HACE), which can even be fatal if not treated. Taking time for acclimatization, and gradual ascent, are the keys to prevention. To set off for the Inca Trail the day you fly into Cusco from sea level is asking for trouble.

Early recognition of symptoms of progression from AMS to HAPE/HACE is vital to treatment. These are: labored breathing while at rest, ataxia (loss of physical coordination), mental confusion, extreme lassitude, cyanosis (purple lips and fingernails), persistent dry coughing, audible congestion in the chest. Coma, then death, are the ultimate consequences.

Treatment for HAPE/HACE: Descend! Immediately! Descending 500-1000m is usually sufficient. If this cannot be accomplished immediately, administer oxygen if available, and dexamethasone. Nifedipine or another vasodilator is also helpful. Keep patient warm, and encourage to purse lips on exhalation (improves oxygen absorption). Note that HAPE/ HACE or severe cases of AMS can also be treated using a hyperbaric chamber. These are available at SOS Medical Clinic, Clínica Cima, and O2 Medical Network (*see p. 46*).

Robbery and Safety

Cusco is safe as far as big South American cities go, but be careful nonetheless: a tourist is still a thief's favorite lunch. Favorite theft locations are crowded streets and railway stations, on trains and buses, anywhere that confusion reigns. Streets notorious for pickpocketing are *Nueva*, *Teqte* and *Belen* (C4-D4). In these situations, wear your backpack in front, have a money belt, hold on to your camera, and pay attention. Thieves work in pairs or groups, so be suspicious of attempts to disorient you (throwing soap or condiments on your clothes, money on the ground in front of you, etc). Use the safe-deposit if your hotel has one.

Late night choke-hold or knife muggings can also happen, especially in the approaches to Pl. Nazarenas and in the San Blas district. Be careful on *Tandapata* in San Blas (D1-F2) after dark and anywhere higher up from there towards the road to Cristo Blanco. Try to stick to the main roads there after dark: *Choquechaca, Carmen Alto and Bajo*, and *Cuesta San Blas*. Take an official, marked taxi back to your hotel at night. Robberies and rapes are occasionally reported at Qenqo, Sacsaywaman, Amaru Marcawasi (a.k.a Temple of the Moon) and environs. It is wise to be clear of them before dusk, unless with a group.

Muggings via date rape drugs have also happened in clubs and some hostels. Thieves operate in groups where one of them, often an attractive local, will start a conversation and drug your drink while you are distracted. Their friends will be waiting to rob you as you stumble out the door. Don't accept drinks from strangers, watch your drink and go in a group of safe people. If you are assaulted, make a report to the Tourist Police *(see below)*. For assaults in progress, call 105 on any phone for emergency dispatch. See p. 41 for hiking safety tips.

TOURIST INFORMATION AND SUPPORT CENTERS

iPerú, 3 locations in Cusco: Velasco Astete airport (OM); Pl. de Armas, Portal de Harinas 177 (D2) and beside La Compañia church (D3). In Aguas Calientes: Av. Pachacutec, 1st block, Of. 4, www.peru.travel/iperu Official info center present in most major cities. Maps, general info and helpful staff. If you have a complaint against a business they can help mediate (for punitive, binding action see INDECOPI below).

Dircetur, Mantas 117A (D3), tel. 222032 and Plaza Tupac Amaru, Wanchaq (OM). The regional tourism development office. Good source for maps, transportation info, and general questions. Helpful staff. Sells the BTC tickets.

Cosituc, Av. El Sol 103 Galerías Turísticas (D3), tel. 261465 Sells the various BTCs.

Tourist Police, Pl. Túpac Amaru, Wanchaq (OM), tel. 235123 If you are robbed or assaulted, file a report (*denuncia)* here for insurance purposes. This also helps police know where greatest concentrations of thefts occur. For emergencies, including those in the mountains, call 105 on any phone (Spanish only).

INDECOPI, Pasaje Constanza A-11-2, Urb. Constancia (OM), tel. 252987, www.indecopi.gob.pe If you've been screwed by a travel agency, hotel, restaurant, etc., this government agency is there to prevent abuses against tourists. They can enforce fines and other punitive actions.

Immigration. Av. Sol 612 (F4). Mon-Fri 08:00-16:00, Sat 9:00-12:00, tel. 222741 You can currently renew your tourist visa up to 183 days per year by crossing the Bolivian or Chilean border.

CONSULATES

These are the main ones. For others, see: **www.cuscoconsulates.org/en/**

British, Jr. Los Geranios 2-G, Urb. Mariscal Gamarra, 1st floor (OM), tel. 224135, Barry.Walker-HonCon@fconet.fco.gov.uk
French, Nueva Baja 560 (B3), tel. 249737, consulatdefrance.cusco@gmail.com
German, San Agustín 307 (E3), tel. 235459, cusco@hk-diplo.de
USA, Av. el Sol 449, of. #201 (E4), tel. 231474, CuscoACS@state.gov, Mon-Fri 8am-2pm

TOURIST TICKETS

Different tickets grant entry to museums and ruins in Cusco and vicinity. The Cusco tourist tickets, 1) and 2) below, are abbreviated BTC *(Boleto Turistico del Cusco).* Students with ISIC cards usually qualify for discounts (carry the card with you).

1) *Complete BTC:* For 16 major sites in the region. Lasts 10 days.
2) *Partial BTC:* There are three of these; each includes some of the 16 major sites.
    A) The four major ruins near Cusco. Lasts one day.
    B) Tipón, Pikillacta, and 6 cultural sites/museums. Two days.
    C) The four main ruins in and around the Sacred Valley. Two days.

For current BTC pricing and a complete list of sites, see the tariffs on **www.cosituc.gob.pe** (Spanish only. For this information in English see **www.peterfrost.org**). The BTCs can be purchased at Dircetur, Cosituc (*see above*), or any of the sites included in

18

the tickets. You must buy either a complete or partial BTC to enter these sites; one-site tickets are not available.

3) *Machu Picchu:* Separate from all other tickets. Two timeslots: 6am-12pm, 12pm-5:30pm. Entrance to Huayna Picchu or Machu Picchu Mountain is extra. Tickets available electronically at **www.machupicchu.gob.pe** (note that you can only *reserve* tickets online, not actually *pay* for them. Pay at one of the authorized offices mentioned on the site or in person at Dirección Regional de Cultura in Cusco (Garcilaso s/n (C3), Mon-Sat 7:00am-7:30pm) or in Aguas Calientes at the Centro Cultural de Machu Picchu. *Important!* Bring your original passport with you to Machu Picchu, as this is a requirement for entry.

4) *Circuito Religioso Arzobispal (CRA):* The Cathedral, San Cristobal and San Blas churches, and the Museum of Religious Art. See **www.cra.org.pe** (Spanish only)
5) *Ruta del Barroco Andino (RBA):* La Compañía in Cusco plus three churches on the valley road southeast *(see Chapter 7).* See **www.rutadelbarrocoandino.com**

The CRA and RBA tickets can be purchased at their individual sites.

6) *Inca Trail to Machu Picchu:* These will be purchased for you by your travel agency or independent, authorized guide.

Other locations have their own separate site tickets (SST) and can be purchased on site.

COMMUNICATIONS

E-mail and Internet
Travelers with their own computer, tablet or smart phone will find wifi at most lodgings and cafes. There will often be a desktop computer available for use at hotels. Many streets in the Cusco center have internet cafes.

Telephone
Peru country code: 51. Lima / Cusco prefixes: 01 / 084 within Peru, 1 / 84 from overseas. Landline calls within the department of Cusco (e.g. Sacred Valley) are local and carry no prefix. Cell #'s begin with 9. To call Peru cell phones from overseas, dial country code followed by the 3-digit prefix and 6-digit number.

A *locutorio* is a call centre for national and international calls; they are often paired with internet cafes. (Making international calls was a Herculean task in 1979 – see the *Exploring Cusco Museum* **www. peterfrost.org** to learn how easy you have it now.)

Satellite Phones
For extended expeditions, satellite phones are available to rent from the Crees Foundation (**www.crees-manu.org**).

Mail
Serpost, the post office, crnr of Av. Sol and Av. Garcilazo (F4).

Courier Services
DHL, Av. Sol 608 (E4), tel. 244167
Olva Courier, Av. Pardo 575B, (E4), tel. 235292

AIR TRANSPORTATION

Local airlines offer online ticket purchase and check-in. Non-residents/non-citizens of Peru pay substantially higher prices than locals on LATAM & Avianca. Flights are sometimes delayed or cancelled during the rainy season (Dec. through Mar.).

Visitors arriving at Cusco airport are advised to take one of the official taxis waiting at the exit. They cost more than the street taxis beyond the gates but are safer. The safest way to take a cheaper taxi is to wait for one to drop someone off at the airport and then take that one. If traveling light, you can also take the public bus line **C4M**, which passes in front of the airport and the San Pedro market in the center.

Airlines

LATAM (formerly LAN), Av. El Sol 840 (F4), www.latam.com The 600-pound gorilla, with very reliable service, most daily flights, highest prices and widest network of international connections. Hefty fare surcharge for non-Peruvian residents.

Avianca, Av. El Sol 602B (E4), www.avianca.com Also has international connections and service standards.

Star Peru, Av. El Sol 627 Of. 101 (E4), www.starperu.com **& Peruvian Airlines**, Av El Sol 627A (E4), www.peruvian.pe Significantly cheaper, domestic service only; delays and cancellations more likely, especially during the rainy season. Peruvian has daily flights to La Paz, Bolivia.

LC Peru, www.lcperu.pe Inexpensive, but flights are often canceled.

ROAD TRANSPORTATION

Cusco's bus terminal (*terminal terrestre* – TT) is on Calle Micaela Bastidas, a little ways south of Ovalo Pachacutec and the Inca monument there (OM). Numerous companies run buses from here to all major destinations, and most of them have a stand here. Many of the main line bus companies have websites and offer online ticket purchase, but in practice it is better to go to the TT or company office in person to get reliable schedule information and buy the ticket.

Small passenger van services run just about everywhere; their main stations are listed below.

Evening departures and nighttime travel are popular with local people, whereas visitors usually like to see the landscape. Morning departures are harder to find, but they exist. Check around.

Overland travel can be hazardous owing to poor road conditions and reckless drivers. The more reputable bus companies cost a bit more but have better safety records and are more comfortable.

Main Bus Lines

All of the following bus lines have booths in the TT except PeruHop.

Cruz del Sur, Av. Industrial 121 (OM – very close to TT), tel. 480010, www.cruzdelsur.com.pe Nationwide service, top-of-the-line.

Ormeño, tel. 261704, www.grupo-ormeno.com.pe Nationwide service.

Oltursa, tel. 608012, www.oltursa.pe Most main Peruvian cities.

PeruHop, 172 Meson de la Estrella (C4), tel. 228718, www.peruhop.com An on-off bus service, with stops in Lima, Paracas,

Huacachina, Nazca, Arequipa, Puno, Copacabana and La Paz. Well reviewed services; a convenient way to visit southern Peru and Bolivia.

How to Get There

Directions to various important destinations near Cusco are listed below, first by cardinal direction (clockwise around the compass) and second by increasing distance from Cusco.

North (Local ruins, Sacred Valley, Chinchero, Moray, Machu Picchu, Vilcabamba).

Sacsaywaman-Qenqo-Lanlakuyok-Puca Pucara-Tambomachay. Taxis will go to any of these sites. The public bus line Señor del Huerto travels from *Mercado Rosaspata* (OM – 100m east of Calle Puputi and Collasuyo) and goes past all of these, turning around at the last. For Sacsaywaman, ask to get off at Cristo Blanco. For Lanlakuyok (a.k.a. *Zona X* in Spanish), ask for it by name.

Pisac-Calca-Yucay-Urubamba. Vans to Pisac depart from all along *Puputi* (OM) and cheaper, slower public buses going as far as Urubamba depart from the nearby *Mercado Rosaspata (see above)*, which any taxi driver can take you to. Frequent departures from 2am-8pm. For transport to the ruins above Pisac, look out for minibuses or taxis just north of the main highway bridge into town.

Lares. Take one of the buses to Calca mentioned above. From there, vans depart to Lares from the main bus station when full. 3-4 hours from Cusco.

Maras, Salineras & Moray. Take the Chinchero-Urubamba *colectivo (see below)* and get off at the Maras turn-off (called *Ramal de Maras*), about 20km (12.5mi) after Chinchero. Taxis and *colectivos* waiting here will take you to Maras, Salineras or Moray.

Chinchero-Urubamba-Pachar-Ollantaytambo. *Colectivos* depart from the crnr of *Av. Grau* and *Pavitos* (OM - follow *Cuichipunco* (E4) south). Frequent departures from 2am to 8pm.

Santa María-Santa Teresa-Quillabamba. 4 hours to Santa Maria, 6 hours to Quillabamba. (For Santa Teresa, take a *colectivo* or taxi from Santa Maria – 1hr). Public vans depart between 4am-10pm from *Av. Antonio Lorena*, three blocks uphill (west) from *Almudena* in the Santiago district (OM); cars to Quillabamba leave a block or two east of *Almudena*. The public bus company C4M going west on *Santa Clara* (B4) can drop you off here. No buses at the TT. (*See below for tourist-quality transportation to Santa Teresa.*)

Aguas Calientes. There is no road leading into Aguas Calientes. After the train, *(see p. 24)* the most convenient option is to buy a round trip to the hydroelectric plant (*hidroeléctrica*) near Santa Teresa, available from innumerable tour agencies in the Cusco center. (*Warning*: The road from Cusco to Santa Teresa going over the Málaga Pass is a long, twisty and rough ride for those with motion sickness.) Then, walk beside the train tracks for two hours (11km/9.4mi) to arrive. There are plans to put a control point along this path charging walkers an entrance fee. Instead of walking, you can take the overpriced train heading east from *hidroeléctrica*. Confirm current train schedules and buy tickets at the PeruRail office at the Santa Teresa market (open daily 5-7:20am, 12-4pm) or take your chances by going directly to hidroeléctrica.

Huancacalle-Vilcabamba. Take a *colectivo* to Santa María *(see above)*. From there, take another *colectivo* to Huancacalle and onwards.

San Miguel (a.k.a. Chuanquiri). *Colectivos* leave from Quillabamba *(see above)*, about five hours. The road continues south and takes you to the trailhead, a 15-minute walk from Espiritu Pampa.

East (towards Madre de Dios and jungle).

Ocongate-Tinqui. *(See www.peterfrost.org)*
Paucartambo. Vans leave from the spot known as *El Control* in San Jeronimo just south of Cusco near the police station (OM – take a taxi). Reliable mid-morning departures, sometimes also in the afternoon if the van fills up.

Quincemil-Mazuko-Puerto Maldonado. Many buses leave from the TT. Private cars from City Tours Sr. de Huanca, Av. La Paz 407 (OM), crnr of *San Martín* and *Confraternidad*, tel. 982-041577. Vans from Apu Araza Camanti, Tomasa Tito Condemayta 1506 (OM - near the Coliseo Cerrado), tel. 987-400532.

Try to travel this road by day – there have been armed attacks on public transportation at night.

Southeast (towards Arequipa and Bolivia).

San Sebastian-Saylla-Tipón. The public bus company **Los Leones** signed "Saylla-Tipón" and passing through Pl. San Francisco will go past all of these towns. For the San Sebastian church, get off at the *primero paradero San Sebastian* and walk 500m down *Obispo Molinero*. Also, buses to Sicuani (*see below*) will pass by these towns and get there faster. For the ruins of Tipón,

get off at the town of the same name; it's a long walk or a short taxi ride to the ruins.

Pikillacta-Andahuaylillas-Urcos-Sicuani. About 1.5 hours to Urcos, 2.5 hours to Sicuani. Buses leave from *Av. de la Cultura* and *Pasaje Carrasco* in front of the Regional Hospital (OM). Take a taxi; any driver will know the place. *Colectivos* to Sicuani also leave from in front of Garcilaso stadium on *Av. Huayruropata* (OM).

Puno. Good highway, about 6-8 hours. Many options at the TT. TurismoMer (www.turismomer.com) and Inka Express (www.inkaexpress.com), neither of them with TT offices, offer this route as a one-day tour, visiting highlights such as the Inca Temple of Viracocha at Raqchi and the early site of Pucará along the way.

La Paz, Bolivia. Paved all the way, many options at the TT. Beyond Puno to La Paz, you may have to change buses. The Peru-Bolivia border crossings are closed between midnight and 8am and sometimes for lunch as well. Do *not* cross without receiving entry and exit stamps – this will cause problems and maybe a fine later when leaving or entering either country.

(Transportation between Peru and Bolivia has an interesting nautical history; read more in the *Exploring Cusco Museum* **www.peterfrost.org**)

Arequipa. About 10 hours. Many options at the TT, nightly departures, usually around 8pm.

South (towards the wild, lesser known backcountry of Chumbivilcas).

Maukallacta-Huanoquite (via Yaurisque). Unofficial taxis and *colectivos* leave from the west end of *Belenpampa* (OM - first left after crossing *Puente Belen*, south on *Belen*, D4). Departures are irregular; ask around. Taxis will take you directly to the trailhead for Maukallacta (about 1.5 hours); *colectivos* go to Yaurisque, where you can arrange further transport to the trailhead. The road from Cusco to Yaurisque is spectacular but sinuous.

Espinar. Empresa Real in the TT goes to Espinar, 3:30pm departures daily. You can also get here from the bus terminal in Sicuani (*see under "Southeast" above*).

Livitaca (via Yanaoca and Pongoña). Empresa Elegantes Korilazos, SE crnr of Hermanos Ayar and Tomasa Titto Condemayta (OM), tel. 984-307346. Daily 6:30am-2pm.

West (towards Lima and Cusco's backcountry).

Ccorca. (*See www.peterfrost.org*)

Mollepata. Two hours. *Colectivos* leave from the west side of *Arcopata* near the intersection with *Av. Alta* (A3).

Quillarumiyoc-Tarawasi-Saywite-Cachora (via Curahuasi). Take a Curahuasi *colectivo* (2.5 hours) departing from the south end of *Arcopata* (A3). For Quillarumiyoc, get off at the community of San Martín, walking distance from the ruins. For Tarawasi, ask to get off at the ruin site 1.5km (0.9mi) before the town of Limatambo. For the ruins of Saywite and the town of Cachora, take a taxi from Curahuasi directly to either location. *Colectivos* going to Abancay (also leaving from *Arcopata*) will pass by the turnoffs to all of these sites (without needing to transfer in Curahuasi for the latter two) but will likely charge you the full fare to Abancay.

Nazca-Lima (via Abancay). Paved highway. 20-24 hour journey to Lima. Many options at the TT, frequent departures. It is often not much more expensive to fly to Lima, especially for a round trip purchased in Cusco in advance.

Andahuaylas-Ayacucho-Lima. (*See www. peterfrost.org*)

Taxis

Taxis are a cheap and convenient way to get around. Within Cusco center, a flat fare is charged, around $1-2. Day and half-day rates for travel around Cusco are similarly low, and divided between three or four people a day out can be surprisingly economical. It is actually cheaper to hire a taxi with driver than to rent a car. Taxi drivers robbing their passengers is pretty rare, but the safest option is still to call a radio cab. Reliable ones include **Aló Cusco**, tel. 222222, **Ocarina**, tel. 255000, **Taxi Tours Florida**, tel. 251919, and **Taxi Turismo**, tel. 245000.

Vehicle Rentals

Hertz, Velasco Astete Airport (OM), tel. 4455716

Manu Rent a Car, Av. Sol 520 (E4), tel. 233382, www.manurentacar.com Rents 4x4's and vans.

Peru Moto Tours, Saphi 578 (C2), tel. 232742, www.perumototours.com 4x4 and motorcycle rentals.

Europcar, Saphi 639 (B2), tel. 262655, www.europcar.com Range of cars and 4x4 vehicles.

RAIL TRANSPORTATION

There are three destinations from Cusco: Machu Picchu (Aguas Calientes), Puno, and Arequipa.

Machu Picchu

For a description of the sights along the train journey, see p.225. Train services depart from either Poroy (30 minutes' drive from Cusco) or Ollantaytambo. From Jan through April, Cusco departures are "bimodal" (bus from Cusco, then train from Ollantaytambo). There are two operators: PeruRail and Inca Rail. The latter only runs its economy service from Poroy. Trains do not depart from stations in the city of Cusco (but they used to: see the *Exploring Cusco Museum* www.peterfrost.org for why they don't now and just how bad service was in 1999).

PeruRail, Velasco Astete airport (OM), Portal de Carnes 214 (D2) and Pl. Regocijo 202 (C3), tel. 581414, www.perurail.com Three levels of service:

Hiram Bingham service. High end, luxury, open bar, brunch and dinner on board, tea at the Belmond sanctuary lodge, dining car seating, and shuttle bus to ruins with entry ticket and guiding service included. The train has a bar/observation car with live music.

Vistadome service. Good visibility for landscape viewing, includes light meal and soft drinks, colorful (if somewhat noisy) folk dance and fashion show on board during return journey.

Expedition service. Simpler version of the above, with less visibility and no meals.

Inca Rail, Portal de Panes 105 (D2), tel. 581860, www.incarail.com *Inca service.* Fancy train with 3 levels: *Executive* (soft drinks included); *First Class* (gourmet meal included); *Presidential* (luxury table seating, exclusive, open bar, 5-course gourmet meal.)

Puno

A longish (10.5 hours) but superbly scenic journey. Operated by PeruRail: the luxury Belmond Andean Explorer train and more basic PeruRail Titicaca train. The Explorer is an overnight service including food and drink, live music and dance, alcohol, overnight accommodations, and guided tours of the ruins of Raqchi, and the main attractions in Lake Titicaca. There is also an overnight Explorer option without the guided tours. The Titicaca is a cheaper day service, with no guided tours, leaving Cusco around 7am and arriving around 5pm.

Arequipa

PeruRail's Belmond Andean Explorer train offers the same superb scenery and stops between Cusco and Puno but then extends it far southwest to Arequipa. Three-days / two-nights total. This is a luxury sleep-aboard train with several stops for guided tours: Raqchi, Lake Titicaca and the floating islands, and the ancient rock paintings of the Sumbay Caves. The train has luxury cabins, an observation car, bar and dining cars, a piano bar, and a spa opening in March 2018.

HOTELS

In recent years hotels and other services have proliferated in Cusco. There are now hundreds, without even counting guesthouses in private residences. Below is a limited selection of well established hotels, or ones well known to the author, in approximately descending order of price and quality (A) through (D) – based on "rack rate" prices, which may be negotiable, especially during low season (see p. 16). For more hotel recommendations see General Information, and to learn what a fancy hotel would run you back in 1979, see the Exploring Cusco Museum at **www.peterfrost.org**

Price Category A: $300-$2,000 per night

Hotel Monasterio & Palacio Nazarenas, Palacio 140 (D2), tel. 604000, and Pl. Nazarenas 144 (D2), tel. 582222, www.belmond.com Owned by Belmond Properties. Luxurious, 5-star hotels, both in historic buildings. Centrally located and among the best in the city.

Inkaterra La Casona, Pl. Nazarenas 211 (D2), tel. 234010, www.inkaterra.com Very high end and exclusive converted colonial mansion. Just 11 spacious rooms with all the trimmings.

Palacio del Inka, Pl. Santo Domingo 259 (E3), tel. 231961, www.libertador.com.pe Colonial building, pleasant staff and good service. 212 Rooms.

Marriott, Ruinas 432 (E2), tel. 582200, www.marriott.com Colonial building in the city center.

Price Category B: $80-$300

Hotel Plaza de Armas, Av. Portal de Mantas 114 (D3), tel. 225959, www.cuscoplazadearmas.com Friendly, privately-owned and comfortable in great location. Rooftop terrace with astounding views of the historic center.

Novotel, San Augustin 239 (E3), tel. 581033, www.novotel.com Centrally located, contemporary design inside of colonial building.

Antigua Casona San Blas, Carmen Bajo 243 (F2), tel. 200700, www.antiguacusco.com 14 rooms in a renovated 19th century mansion right in San Blas. Nicely decorated.

La Posada del Inca, Portal Espinar 108 (D3), tel. 277061, www.sonesta.com Comfortable hotel, very centrally located.

Casa Andina, www.casa-andina.com Two quality levels, five locations close to the city center.

Hotel Ruinas, Ruinas 472 (E2), tel. 260644, www.hotelruinas.com Pleasant, central, in-house restaurant, buffet breakfast included. 54 rooms.

Eco Inn, Av. El Sol 1010 (OM), tel. 581270, www.ecoinnhotels.com.pe Not in the city's heart, but modern and convenient with good spa.

Price Category C: $40-$130

El Arqueólogo, Pumacurco 408 (D1), tel. 232522, www.hotelarqueologo.com Quiet, garden setting. 20 rooms. In-house restaurant with weekly jazz and opera music.

El Balcón, Tambo de Montero 222 (B2), tel. 236738, www.balconcusco.com Remodelled colonial building in very central location, intimate, terrific view.

T'ika Wasi, Tandapata 491 (E1), San Blas, tel. 231609, www.tikawasi.com Pleasant and cozy, outside terraces, GV.

Pensión Alemana, Tandapata 260 (E1), tel. 226861, www.hotel-cuzco.com/en Pleasant small hotel w/ garden, in San Blas. Spa, adjacent "Café 7&7" on 3rd floor w/ GV of Cusco center.

Cusco Plaza I and II, Pl. Nazarenas 181 (D2), tel. 246161 and Calle Saphi 486 (B2), tel. 263000, www.cuscoplazahotels.com Friendly, both centrally-located.

Hostal Corihuasi, Suecia 561 (C2), tel. 232233, www.corihuasi.com Nicely decorated and centrally located. GV from the southern rooms. Breakfast included.

Niños Hotel, Meloc 442 (B3), tel. 231424 and Fierro 476 (A3), tel. 254611, www.ninoshotel.com A pleasant, modest hotel in a converted colonial mansion. Recommended. SPS.

Hostal Suecia, Suecia 332 (D2), tel. 233282, www.hostalsuecia1.com Colonial building, simple rooms, very central.

Andenes de Saphi, Saphi 848 (B1), tel. 227561, www.andenesdesaphi.com Small, central, comfortable, personable atmosphere.

Price Category D: $10-$40

Hostal Quipu, Fierro 495 (A3), tel. 236179, www.hostalquipu.com Clean, economical, friendly management, somewhat away from center. Use official taxis at night in this area.

Ecopackers, Santa Teresa 375 (C2), tel. 226505, www.ecopackersperu.com Centrally located budget hostel for backpackers.

Pariwana Hostel, Meson de la Estrella 136 (C4), tel. 233751, www.pariwana-hostel.com Clean, friendly, centrally-located backpackers hostel.

Supertramp, Sapantiana 424B (D1), tel. 225783, www.supertramphostel.com Clean, new facilities using recycled materials. Dorms and private rooms. Frequent events, plus volunteer stays.

Hitchhikers Backpackers Hostels, Saphi 440 (C2), tel. 260079, www.hhikersperu.com Simple backpackers hostel located two blocks from main square.

RESTAURANTS

On Cusco's dynamic food scene restaurants frequently open, change location and go out of business. Many restaurants are cookie-cutter affairs. Don't settle for mediocrity! Countless gems in all price ranges deserve your dining dollars. Recommendations are based on quality, location, social project support, uniqueness, price range and longevity. Many locales serve an inexpensive set lunch menu. Within categories, listings are approximately in descending order of price. Most places can be found online. For more recommendations, see www.peterfrost.org

By law, menu prices must include sales tax. Some restaurants add a service charge. If not, tipping is usual at mid- to high-end restaurants. See Abbreviations (p. 15) for meanings such as VO.

Fine Dining

MAP Café, Pl. Nazarenas 231 (D2), tel. 242476 Novel glass-box dining atmosphere in colonial patio in the Museo de Arte Precolombino; fancy novoandino cuisine.

Cicciolina, Triunfo 393 (E2), 2nd floor, tel. 239510 Great atmosphere, great cocktails and great Peruvian/mediterranean cuisine in lovely old colonial building. Tapas bar. Dinner by reservation. BF.

Limo, Portal de Carnes 236 (D2), 2nd floor, tel. 240668 One of the top Cusco restaurants, with novoandino menu. GV.

Baco, Ruinas 465 (E2), tel. 242808 From the inspired Australian-Peruvian partnership that created Cicciolina (see above); big selection of South American wines.

Incanto, Santa Catalina Angosta 135 (D3) tel. 254753 Good Italian, Peruvian & Fusion food, within glorious walls of former Inca palace.

Traditional Peruvian

Pachapapa, Pl. San Blas 120 (E2), tel. 241318 Open air patio & indoor dining, traditional Andean & fusion cuisine plus good pizza.

La Feria, Portal de Panes 123 (D2), tel. 286198 A classy take on traditional Peruvian dishes, weighted towards highland food. Nicely decorated, GV. VO.

Barrio Ceviche, Portal Harinas 181 (D2), tel. 266334 Traditional Peruvian coastal dishes with fitting marine ambience. Fresh fish daily from Lima.

Kusikuy, Amargura 140 (C2), tel. 262870 Highly rated. Excellent place to try guinea pig and highland food. Reserve at least 1hr in advance for the former. VO.

El Paisa, Av. Sol 819 (F4), tel. 501717 Northern Peruvian food. Big, popular and recommended by locals. Very loud LM.

Yola, Av. Pardo 789 (E4), tel. 973-585555 *Criollo* food, *anticuchos* at night; local crowd, inexpensive.

Pl. San Francisco outdoor food bazaar (C3), Sundays 8am-3pm. Great selection of food styles, inexpensive.

General Food Styles

Morena Peruvian Kitchen, Plateros 348B, tel. 437832 A modern take on Peruvian food, plus burgers, pastas, and good smoothies. Service is attentive and the decor is welcoming. The best tables are downstairs. VO.

Greens Organic, Santa Catalina Angosta 135 (D3), 2nd floor, tel. 254753 Emphasis on organic food from local providers. Wide variety of options, with excellent juices. VO. BF.

Yuraq, Av. Pardo 1036 (OM), tel. 222591 Small, nice decor. Predominantly Peruvian food plus pastas and pizzas.

Pucara, Plateros 309 (C2), tel. 222027

Good national and international cuisine served with fresh vegetables at reasonable prices. Pleasant atmosphere. Chocolate desserts recommended. SL. VO.

Coffee Museum, Espaderos 136 (C3), tel. 263264 Good coffee, alcoholic drinks and meals in a historic colonial house. Display of the history of coffee production in Peru. BF.

Café Tinku, (see p.30)

Pankracio, Recoleta 500 (E2), tel. 260034. A good sandwich joint.

Mr. Soup, Garcilaso 210 (C3), 2nd floor, tel. 253806 International soups, typical Peruvian soups and vegetable creams. Big portions. VO.

Antojitos, Marquez 284 (C3), tel. 225353 Inexpensive SL, fried chicken at night.

Carnivores

Uchu, Palacio 135 (D2), tel. 246598 Peruvian-inspired steak house in an old hacienda. Steaks are served on hot stones for you to prepare to your liking. Some VOs available.

Fallen Angel, Pl. Nazarenas 221 (D2), tel. 258184 Specialty tenderloin steaks; flamboyant decor; famous for wild seasonal parties. LM.

Los Toldos, Almagro 171 (D3), tel. 229829 Rotisserie chicken, salad bar, big portions. Delivery.

Pasta & Pizza

La Cantina, (see p.28)

Bodega 138, Herrajes 138 (E2), tel. 260272 Warm atmosphere, good pizza & pasta. No reservations, gets crowded, go early. Extensive craft beer selection.

Justina, Palacio 110 (E2), tel. 255475 Small, funky pizza and wine bar.

La Pizza Carlo, Maruri 381 (E3), tel. 247777 Tiny place, excellent pizza.

Vegetarian

Organika, Resbalosa 410 (C2), tel. 237216 Organic produce from their farm in Urubamba, handmade pasta, goat cheese, beet lemonade and reasonable prices.

Prasada Templo Vegano, Choquechaca 425 (D1), tel. 946-871435 Great veggie burgers, curries and huge juices.

Salud De Luz, Nueva Alta 458 (B3), tel. 236587 Vegan food and SL in a nicely decorated setting. Gluten- and soy-free.

Shaman Vegan Raw Restaurant, Santa Catalina Ancha 366B (E2), tel. 261419 Tables lavishly decorated with crystals. Juices, salads, and vegan takes on Peruvian dishes.

El Encuentro, Santa Catalina Ancha 384 (E2) and Tigre 130 (C2), tel. 247977 Salads, sandwiches, soups, juices, inexpensive. SL.

Govinda Lila's, SW crnr of the San Blas market (F2). Big portions, delicious, inexpensive. SL only.

Ethnic

Kion, Triunfo 370 (D2), tel. 431862 High-end Peruvian-Chinese restaurant. Probably the best dumplings in the city. VO.

La Cantina, Saphi 554 (C2), tel. 242075 Best Italian food in the city, with good Italian wine, pizza and cheeses.

Supayshi, Santa Teresa 383 (C2), second floor, tel. 941-363215 Andean-inspired sushi. VO.

Tacomania, Teatro 394 (C3), tel. 597608 Good Mexican food. Dinner only. VO.

Bojosan, San Agustin 275 (E3), tel. 246502 Japanese *udon* noodle dishes: beef, duck, chicken, pork, algae. Sapporo beer and sake. Clean, simple interior. Cash only.

Sa Rang Che, Procuradores 341 (D2), tel. 235877 Kimchi and other Korean food. Run by Koreans. Lunch and dinner.

Paloma Imbis Greek, Plateros 369 (C2), tel. 991-362425 Falafel, shawarma, hummus. The go-to spot for Middle Eastern food. VO.

Quintas and Picanterías

Traditional highland cooking, weighted towards meat, serving chicha, guinea pig (*cuy*), organ meats, stews and soups; sometimes LM&D. *Picanterías* are traditionally the low-rent version of a *quinta*. Usually lunch only.

Quinta Eulalia, Choquechaca 384 (D1), tel. 224951 Delightful open-air eating on a sunny day; inexpensive regional food. A local institution. Lunch only. LM.

La Chomba, Tullumayo 339 (E3), tel. 272702 Traditional picantería. Lunch and dinner. Spanish-only menu. Rustic.

Tradiciones Cusqueñas, Belen 835 (D4), tel. 231988 Indoor quinta, funky local flavor. LM.

Picantería María Angola, Choquechaca 292 (E2), tel. 223547 Traditional *Cusqueño* food served at reasonable prices.

Cuatro Suyus, Fierro 471, opens at 5pm. Popular with locals, rarely visited by tourists.

Cafés and Desserts

Deli Monasterio, Palacio 136 (D2), tel. 604000 Fresh baked bread, sandwiches, pastries.

Coffee Museum, see p. 27, good for coffee all day.

La Valeriana, Av El Sol 576 (E4) and Plazoleta Espinar 180-184 (D3), tel. 506941 Lasagnas, sandwiches, cakes, donuts, brownies, breads, juices. Comfortable seating area.

FOODS OF CUSCO

There are three basic places to support your food habit in Cusco: restaurants, street vendors and the *mercado* – the public market where *campesinos* sell their produce. There are, of course, conventional corner stores and supermarkets, but unless you are homesick you will find the other options more fun.

There is much to choose from in Cusco's restaurants: beef (*carne* or *lomo*); chicken (*pollo* or *gallina*); pork (*cerdo* or *chancho*); fish (*pescado*), such as local freshwater whitefish (*pejerrey*) or trout (*trucha*), prawns (*camarones*) and shrimp (*langostinos*). All are cooked in myriad ways. The rich sauces are usually beef- or chicken-stock based, with vegetables cooked in. Dishes are generally served with either white rice (*arroz*) or potatoes (*papas*), with a bit of lettuce or tomato on the side. (But beware: lettuce harbors microbes as does no other vegetable; even hardened travelers avoid it.)

Suggestions for some good restaurant dishes: *ají de gallina* (spicy chicken); *rocoto relleno* (stuffed chili, often very spicy); *adobo* (pork in a spicy broth, served only in the mornings); *lomo saltado* (chopped beef with rice and vegetables); and *chupe de camarones* (prawn soup).

Soups in particular are often very good. I recommend *locro* (corn-based, with chunks of meat and vegetables); *chairo* (similar, but with potato and *chuño*, the Andean freeze-dried potato, instead of corn); *caldillo de huevo* (egg soup); and *sopa a la criolla* (chopped beef with noodles and mild chilis).

Street vendors offer a variety of meals and snacks, some of which can be sampled without fear - the ones which are not served on the vendor's dishes and are thoroughly cooked before your eyes. Try *anticuchos* (beefhearts on bamboo skewers, with a potato) or *tamales*, usually reliably well-cooked, which come *dulce* (sweet) or *salado* (salted/savory). Fresh-baked *empanadas* (flaky pastries stuffed with cheese, chicken or beef) are good, as are the many varieties of bread and sweet pastries.

The San Pedro market (city map #22 - see p. 108) is a must-visit, especially for the exotic fruits: *pepino dulce* (a yellow, purple-streaked fruit that tastes something like a melon); *chirimoya* a.k.a. *custard apple* (a green, knobby, soft-skinned fruit with sweet and delicious white pulp); *granadilla* and its cousin *maracuyá*, the passion fruits with egg-like shells containing a white bag of tasty seeds, which are both gelatinous and crunchy; and several varieties of banana – the small ones about the size of frankfurters and the fat ones with reddish skin and pink pulp inside are the best. Then there are the usual tropical favorites: papaya, mango, and avocado, all at a low price and high quality that – if you choose carefully – will knock your socks off.

Buen provecho!

– Carol Stewart

Café Ayllu, Almagro 133 (D3), tel. 255078 and Marqués 263 (C3), tel. 255078 Good pastries, homemade fruit yogurt, classical music, snacks; fast service; opens early. A classic Cusco institution. BF.

The Meeting Place, Pl. San Blas 630 (F2), tel. 952-729564 Famous for their waffles and milkshakes. Serves teas, coffee and other sweets. Run by volunteers; profits support local NGOs.

Café Tinku, Nueva Baja 560 (B3), tel. 249737 Light meals with varied menus and good coffee in a relaxing colonial patio. Breakfast/lunch only.

Qucharitas, Procuradores 372 (D2), tel. 226019 Hand-made ice cream: select your ingredients and the server combines them on a cooled metal plate. Crepes, brownies, juices and coffee. Gluten- and lactose-free options.

Cafe Ricchary, Concevidayoc 116 (C4), tel. 984-305571 Lots of coffee, with all organic products. Cozy. Friendly owners will explain the coffee brewing process if they are around.

La Esencia, Limacpampa Chico 400 (F3), courtyard, 2nd floor, tel. 984-169134, tinyurl.com/zjx4mq2 Light snacks and teas prepared from the essence. Theatre, music and storytelling by local artists (see web page).

Picarones Ruinas, crnr of Ruinas and Tullumayo (E2) Serves *picarones* (Andean donuts made with sweet potato flour), a traditional night time treat. Follow the smell of fried dough.

Breakfast Spots

Cicciolina, Greens Organic, The Coffee Museum, Café Ayllu.

Bar/Restaurant

Museo del Pisco, Santa Catalina Ancha 398 (E2), tel. 262709 Upscale pisco and cocktails, tapas. Nightly LM.

Calle del Medio, Calle del Medio 113 (D3), tel. 248340 Novoandino/fusion style menu. Dislocating decor. LM.

Paddy Flaherty's Irish Pub, Triunfo 124 (D2), 2nd floor, tel. 225361 Pleasant, friendly watering hole. Cable TV. Broadcasts sports and will even record them for you.

Norton's Tavern, Santa Catalina Angosta 116 (D3), 2nd floor Great location, nice feel and motorcycle-themed decor. Hamburgers, grill. Dart boards. GV.

Limbus, Pasñapakana 133 (E1), tel. 431282 Eclectic food menu. Cocktails. Good prices on local craft beer. Steep climb. GV.

Cholo's, Calle Palacio 110 (E2), tel. 987-885080 Large selection of local, national and international craft beer. Small, but with a courtyard patio. Light snacks and burgers.

Qosqo Beer House, Pl. Regocijo 169 (C3), tel. 242504 Centrally located beerhouse. Stocks most of the local craft breweries and has a selection of snacks.

See www.peterfrost.org for local craft beer breweries.

Chicherías

Serve the traditional corn beer *chicha* in large glasses called *caporales*. In the countryside, these bars are often marked by a red plastic bag on a stick.

La Chomba, *see Quintas and Pictanterias, p. 28*

Las Manuelitas, 433 Jr. Atahuallpa (OM), just north of the intersection with *Tupac Yupanqui*.

La Lunareja, 420 San Jose (OM), near Pl. Santiago.

DANCE BARS AND LIVE MUSIC

Ukukus, Plateros 316 (C2), 2nd floor, tel. 254911 Funky, good-sized dance space, often with live local bands. A venue much appreciated by Cusco musicians for its commitment to giving local bands a chance to perform.

Mama Africa, Portal de Panes 109 (D2), 2nd floor, tel. 246544 Rock, reggae, usually packed with a teen to twenties crowd.

Mythology (tel. 255770) and **Inka Team** (tel. 974-791282), Portal de Carnes 298 (D2) Always crowded with locals and foreigners, mix of music. Both bars are next to each other.

Km 0, Tandapata 100 (E1), tel. 998-516720 LM every night, small space.

El Huarique, Tandapata 909 (E2), second floor. Small retro-decorated bar with live music.

La Esencia, (*see p.30*)

Traditional Peruvian Dance and Music

Tunupa, Portal de Confituria 233A (D2), 2nd floor, tel. 252936 Buffet restaurant with nightly LM&D in a large, well decorated space.

Centro Qosqo, Av. Sol 604 (E4), tel. 227901 Nightly music and dance shows in a large theatre space. Doors at 6:30pm.

Municipal Theatre, Mesón de la Estrella 149 (C4), tel. 972-998880 Variety of performances, including international artists. See schedule at **tinyurl.com/j9bplcm**

FOOD MARKETS

For those looking to cook their own food. Markets in tourist areas tend to be high-priced.

Gato's, Santa Catalina Ancha 377 (E2) High-priced American products.

Casa Market, Portal Mantas 120 (D3) Expensive, but good products.

Orion, Union 117 (B4), Meloq 417 (B3), and Matara 271 (D4) American-style supermarket. Fresh fruit, vegetables, meat. American products: peanut butter, granola bars, hygiene items.

San Pedro Market, crnr Santa Clara and Tupac Amaru (#22 city map) The biggest food market in the center. See p. 108.

NATURAL AND SPECIALTY FOODS

Choco Museum, Garcilaso 210 (C3), tel. 244765, and Hatunrumiyoc 480 (E2) Workshops, tours, chocolate, truffles, hot chocolate.

Misky, Maruri 265 (E3) and Tupac Amaru 155B (C4), tel. 262888 Peruvian coffee, chocolate, tea, peanut butter, honey, marmalades.

La Rabona, Herrajes 146 (E2), tel. 241305 Excellent locally made bread (definitely the best for leagues around); also chocolate and natural snacks.

Green Stop, Carmen Bajo 235 (F2), tel. 236955 Kimchi, kombucha, bread, snacks, unpasteurized fruit vinegars, and many other healthy products.

San Pedro Market, (*see above*) Many local products (honey, chocolate, salt, *maca*, coca, etc.). The best prices on dried fruit and nuts: **Frutas Secas Emilia**, Kiosk 1077, along the SW edge of the market next to one of the entrances.

Cafe y Chocolates Cusqueño, Concevidayoc 155 (C4) Well-priced local chocolate, coffee and honey. Also, see the even lower-priced market in the parking lot next door at 153.

LEARNING AND COURSES

Cooking and Gastronomy

Marcelo Batata, www.cuscocookingworkshop.com High-end, well reviewed. Explanation of Peruvian gastronomy, exotic fruit tasting, and a tour of their mini replica of San Pedro market in addition to the cooking.

Rooftop Kitchen, www.rooftopkitchenperu.com A tour of San Pedro Market, then a cooking class in their rooftop kitchen with a great view of downtown Cusco.

Museo del Pisco, *(see Bars, p. 30)* Drink making classes.

Choco Museum, *(see Natural and Specialty Foods, p. 31)* Chocolate making courses.

Spanish

Academia Latinoamericana, Pl. Limacpampa Grande 565 (F3), tel. 243364, www.latinoschools.com

Amauta, San Agustin 249 (E3), tel. 242998, www.amautaspanish.com

Amigos, Zaguan del Cielo B-23 (OM), tel. 242292, www.spanishcusco.com Also does Quechua. SPS.

Centro Tinku, Nueva Baja 560 (B3), tel. 249737, www.centrotinku.com Also does Quechua.

FairServices, Pasaje Zavaleta C-5, Urb. Wanchaq (OM), tel. 984-789252, www.fairservices-peru.org SPS.

Mundo Antiguo, Triunfo 374, int. 6 (D2), tel. 225974, www.learnspanishinperu.net

Proyecto Peru, Siete Cuartones 290 (B3), tel. 240278, www.proyectoperucentre.org SPS.

Dance

Many Spanish schools (*see above*) also offer salsa classes, among them Amauta, FairServices, and Proyecto Peru.

Salseros Cusco, Collacalle 480 (F3), tel. 984-956212, tinyurl.com/j3zkb2z

Astronomy

Cusco Planetarium, tel. 974-782692, www.planetariumcusco.com Family-run facility near Sacsaywaman (OM). Enthusiastic, English-speaking guides teach you about the southern hemisphere constellations and Inca astronomical beliefs. Has telescopes and a star projector. Reservations required.

Casa Andina in Yanahuara (*see p. 56*) has a planetarium in the Sacred Valley, well away from the light pollution in Cusco.

Miscellaneous

Center for Traditional Textiles, (*see Textiles, p. 35*) Traditional Andean weaving techniques and the use of natural fibers.

Julio Gutierrez (*see Artists p. 33*) and **Pablo Seminario** (*see p. 33*) offer pottery and ceramics courses.

ARTS, HANDCRAFTS AND SOUVENIR SHOPPING

Conservation note. Jaguar and ocelot skins, macaw-feather arrows and headdresses, collections of butterflies and insects etc. – buying any of these items sponsors destruction of the region's wildlife, and their export is illegal. Please don't buy them! Also, fake shamans claim magical powers for Andean condor feathers, and award or sell them to their mystical tourism clients. Condor feathers are obtained by hunting and killing the world's largest flying bird – formerly abundant in the Andes, but becoming rarer every year. *Don't buy these feathers, or accept them as "initiation" gifts!*

Cusco Artists

Cusco has some superb artists and craftspeople. Not all those listed below are from Cusco, and some are not even Peruvian, but all of them live and work in the Cusco region and have become part of the local scene.

Pablo Seminario, the region's most original ceramic artist with an international reputation, sells his work, along with other quality local handcrafts, at his pottery studio in Urubamba *(see p. 56)* and inside the Museo de Arte Precolombino, tel. 246093 (city map #9).

Carlos Olivera, sculptor, known locally for his antic surrealities in bronze and stone. Works and shows from his studio in Saylla (OM). tel. 964-363201, tinyurl.com/yacdvxt8

Miki Suzuki, Japanese expat, designs clothing, sweaters, cotton prints and many other items, and sells them, along with other interesting local handcrafts, at **Pedazo**, Plateros 334B (C2), tel. 242967

King of Maps, *(see p.39)* Artistic maps.

Renee Durand Chacón, Pumacurco 473 (D1) Contemporary Andean art: his paintings are a fusion of sacred plants, female metamorphosis, natural landscapes, and social commentary. A very distinctive style.

Julio Gutierrez is Cusco-based artist making pottery in the colonial style and offering courses at his workshop **Taller Inca**, Calle Inca 357, Santiago (OM), tel. 984-682709, www.kutiry.com

Lucho Soler, tinyurl.com/y793foz3 A Lima ceramic artist specializing in one-off fine art pieces at his pottery in Ollantaytambo. Also sold in Cusco at Cuesta San Blas 584 (E2).

Museo Maximo Laura, Santa Catalina Ancha 304 (E3), tel. 277383, www.museomaximolaura.com A well displayed collection of the award-winning tapestries of Máximo Laura. Brightly colored and intricate pieces. International shipping.

Sabino Huamán, Tandapata 370 (D1), tel. 984-296440, sabinohuaman@gmail.com Makes Andean instruments, including the *bandurria, chaccha, quena,* and *mosheño*. Also makes one-piece guitars and charangos. Does a *zampoña* workshop by reservation where you can custom build your own.

Mariana del Hoyo, tel. 984-237058, www.expandetuser.org Unusual and distinctive Andean and nature-themed, batik-style artwork on paper.

Longstanding local artists and artisans of renown in the San Blas district include:

Olave, Pl. San Blas 651 (E2). Quality ceramics, carvings and paintings.

Mendívil, the Cusco family famous for its giraffe-necked models of saints. Two stores: Pl. San Blas 619 (E2), and Hatunrumiyoc 486 (E2), tel. 233247

Mérida, Carmen Alto 133 (E2). Social commentary in the form of painfully contorted clay figurines. Edilberto Mérida died in 2009, but works by his daughter are still for sale.

Assorted Handcrafts

Arte Antropología, Ruinas 105 (E2), tel. 984-639666 High quality antique and modern textiles, ethnic clothing, ceramics, and wood carvings.

Cuesta de San Blas, Cuesta San Blas 584 (E2), tel. 246993 High-quality paintings, sculptures and pottery by Peruvian artists.

Xapiri, Garcilaso 210 (C3), tel. 596435, www.xapiri.com Fair-trade indigenous art gallery and cultural space focusing on the Amazon. Textiles, ceramics, jewelry, weapons, natural resins and more. SPS.

Mágica Arte, Triunfo 118 (D2), tel. 246493 Felt slippers, jewelry and fine alpaca wool coats.

Ollantay Shoes, Choquechaca 211 (E2) Handmade leather and suede boots with weaving details. Also does backpacks, wallets, belts, sweaters.

Bazaars

Three markets with a typical range of local handcrafts for one-stop shopping are **Yachay Wasi**, Calle Triunfo 374 (E2), **Feria Artesanal de Productores Plateros**, Plateros 334 (C2), and **Feria Artesanal de Productores Qoricancha**, Av. el Sol 608 (E4). On Saturdays there is an open-air handcraft market in Pl. San Blas (E2). San Pedro market also has a wide range of goods at its northern end and in the middle aisles towards the food court.

To hit just one good area for browsing and shopping, start at the Pl. de Armas and walk up *Triunfo*, along *Hatunrumiyoc*, and up *Cuesta San Blas* to Pl. San Blas; many of the shops mentioned are on this route. *Plateros* and Pl. Regocijo are also good.

Jewelry

Ilaria, Portal Carrizos 258 (D2), tel. 246253, www.ilariainternational.com Expensive, high quality jewelry. Also inside various high end hotels in Cusco.

Esma Joyas, Triunfo 393, interior 106 (E2), tel. 260824 Striking and original handmade jewelry, much different from other local fare.

Spondylus, Cuesta San Blas 505 (E2), tel. 232527, and Pl. San Blas 617 (E2), tel. 235227 Silver jewelry using precious stones and seashells, notably the spiny oyster shell.

Bethania de Ugarte, tinyurl.com/ycms784u. Makes very nice, distinctive ethnic-style silver jewelry.

Latin Stones, Av. Pachacutec 205 (OM), tel. 987-101619, tinyurl.com/y9dyqrj8 Huge selection of jewelry, stone beads, and carvings at cheaper prices than elsewhere.

Alpaca Wool Clothing

More options than we could possibly fit here. Below is just a sampling. **www.peterfrost.org** has many more choices.

Kuna, Portal de Belen 115 (D2) and Portal de Panes 127 (D2), and many other locations www.kuna.com.pe Fine baby alpaca clothing for both genders.

Sol Alpaca, Portal Mantas 134 (D3), and many other locations, www.solalpaca.com High quality alpaca knitted wear for men and women with a few select vicuña pieces as well.

La Casa de la Llama, Palacio 121 (E2), tel. 240813 Many items made from llama wool. Nice gifts for children.

Makipe, San Agustin 399 (E3), tel. 261408 Has 100% baby alpaca wool sweaters with original, stylish designs.

JK 100% Baby Alpaca, Garcilaso 292 (C3), tel. 941-095430. Uses natural wool colors (no dyes) to make sweaters, scarves, ponchos and accessories.

YOU FEEL! YOU FEEL!
Or, are they pulling the wool over your eyes?

Local guides like to say we have two kinds of alpaca clothing in Cusco: baby-alpaca and maybe-alpaca. Strolling vendors usually sell the latter. *You feel! You feel!* they cry – knowing that alpaca is soft to the touch...but so is brushed acrylic. Real baby alpaca wool ("wool" from now on) is the very soft first shearing from a young animal. Street merchandise is nearly always either a wool-acrylic blend or outright acrylic, no matter what the label or vendor says..

It can be difficult to tell the difference between wool and synthetic blends, but here are a few tips:

Wool sweaters feel soft and smooth on the inside and outside. They may also have a slick, soapy feel. Acrylic sweaters are often brushed on the outside to make them feel smooth like wool, but the inside is rougher. If there's a difference in texture from inside to out, it's not wool.

Hold the garment up to light. If the color is uniform, it's likely alpaca. If you see red, blue or green sparkles, this indicates synthetic fibres. More sparkles means more synthetic.

Wool feels cool to the touch when you first pick it up. Synthetic does not.

Hand-made, quality wool sweaters are usually knit in one piece with no seams inside. Synthetics are typically mass-produced and will have interior seams.

Bright, flashy colors indicate chemical dyes used on synthetic garments. Wool products are often left undyed or have softer, natural colors. That neon green scarf you're holding isn't wool.

Head to the expensive stores (Kuna, Sol Alpaca, etc.) and try these tests on their genuine wool garments. Note the prices. None of this is to say that you can't buy an attractive synthetic garment. You just won't get the benefits of alpaca wool: high warmth-to-weight ratio, the soft and not scratchy feel, and the fact that it won't eventually pill like synthetic does.

– Leo Duncan

Textiles

Tankar Gallery, Palacio 121 (E2), 2nd floor, tel. 228936 High quality weavings and tapestries.

Center for Traditional Textiles, Avenida El Sol 603 (E4), tel. 228117, and inside the Museo de Arte Precolombino (#9 city map), tel. 263446, www.textilescusco.org

Ponchos, vests, sweaters and accessories in traditional Andean style. Ongoing weaving demonstrations and excellent textile museum. SPS.

Inkakunaq Ruwaynin, Av. Tullumayo 274 inside Casa Campesina (E2), tel. 260942 Fair trade weaving store, each piece has the artist's name.

Mosqoy Peruvian Textiles, in The Meeting Place (*see Cafés and Desserts, p.30*), www.mosqoy.org Scarves, belts, coin purses, table runners, and more, with naturally dyed local wool. Proceeds support the weavers from Quechua communities.

Tiendas Museo, Portal de Comercio 173 (D3), tel. 227621 Quality traditional weavings by Josefina Olivera.

Benemerita Society of Cusco Artisans The market to the right of La Compañia church (city map #4) has a wide range of handcrafts and souvenirs. Of note are the weavings of Timoteo Ccarita and wife Benita, attending Mon-Sat 10am-1pm, 3-9pm.

Leather

Casa Mantay, Carmen Alto 141 (E1), tel. 5941112, Palacio del Inka hotel, Pl. Santo Domingo 259 (E3), Milhouse Hostel, Quera 270 (D4) Stylish leather accessories produced by abused teenage mothers. Fairtrade certified. SPS.

Art in Leather, Pl. San Blas 606 (E2), tel. 984-002080 Attractive leather purses, handbags, wallets and accessories with exclusive designs.

Musical Instruments

Sabino Huaman, See Cusco Artists, p. 33

Qosqo Instrumentos Musicales, Cabracancha 455 (E3), tel. 992-753003 Third-generation artisan Jorge del Castillo makes and sells guitars, charangos, mandolins, and wind instruments.

Taller Ayarachi, in the courtyard at Hatunrumiyoc 487 (E2), tel. 950-807426 Full of traditional Andean musical instruments.

PRACTICAL SHOPPING

English Books

SBS, Av. el Sol 864 (F4), tel. 248106 Has the newest releases.

Genesis, crnr of Santa Catalina Ancha and Angosta (D3), tel. 257971, and Calle del Medio 130A (D3), tel. 241016

Librería Jerusalen, Heladeros 143 (C3), tel. 235428 Guidebooks and book exchange.

Outdoor Equipment

(See the Exploring Cusco Museum www. peterfrost.org for how difficult it used to be to buy outdoor gear.)

The North Face, Portal de Comercio 195 (D3) and Pl. Espinar 188 (D3) One of the few vendors of genuine North Face gear.

Tatoo Adventure Gear, Portal Espinar 144 (D3), tel. 236703 High quality gear from well-known brands, plus their own house brand.

Himalaya Outdoor, Procuradores 398 (C2), tel. 286838 First- and second-hand gear sales, and rentals. Sells camping gas, both canisters and white gas (*bencina*). General equipment repair. English spoken. Sells topographic maps.

Cordillera "Live Outdoors", Calle Garcilaso 210 (C3), tel. 244133 Hiking clothing and shoes. Many big name brands.

Pirámide Outdoor, Santa Catalina Ancha 361 (E2), tel. 225463 Wide selection, especially backpacks.

Plateros: this street (C2 – just one block long) features numerous stores selling locally-made outdoor equipment. Price much lower than imports; quality varies, but some is not bad.

A SONG OF CUSCO

People in the Andes sometimes say that there are several kinds of music: sublime music, good music, ordinary music, bad music, and Mexican music. This unkind jibe arises from a certain natural pride in the Andean musical tradition. The music of the Quechua and Aymara people, descended from the Inca empire, has lodged itself deep in the souls of generations of musicians throughout Latin America. (Only Spain and Africa have had comparable impact here.)

The music is both sad and lively. Tunes like the *huayno* are charged with this paradox: the rhythm makes you want to dance, the melody tears your heart out. It is impossible to say now what the music played in Inca times sounded like. For example, the tragic quality underlying the piping of Andean flutes – was that present in the glory days before Pizarro, or was it born of the horror of the Conquest? No one can say.

We do know, however, what instruments Inca musicians used. Pre-Columbian peoples had not developed stringed instruments; there were only wind and percussion. The most common of the percussion instruments still in use today are the two types of drums, the *wankar* (also known as the *bombo*), a big side-drum that gives the bass-line to most Andean bands, and the *tinya*, a little hand-drum, traditionally played by women. For ritual and magic purposes the drum is played with seeds or chilis inside it. Also common are small cymbals and bells, and dried seed pods or sheep, llama or alpaca hooves (the latter known as the *chaccha*), worn around the wrists and ankles.

The ancient wind instrument most popular today is the *quena*, the ubiquitous Andean flute made of bone, wood or bamboo. It originally used a pentatonic scale but nowadays is tuned to the familiar western chromatic. Its heart-piercing sound first reached most Euro-American ears in Simon and Garfunkel's reworking of "El Condor Pasa," a famous tune in Peru (S & G made up the lyrics). There is also the lesser-known *mosheño*, the large flute traditionally played before ceremonial offerings.

Then there is the *antara* and the *zampoña* or *siku*, which are different versions of the familiar bundle of bamboo tubes that we call "panpipes." Examples of these made from ceramic and dating from early Peruvian prehistory have been found. It has a haunting and breathy sound. The *antara* is a solo instrument, tuned to the pentatonic scale. The *zampoña* is an intriguing example of Andean "dual complementarity" – in a traditional setting the complete instrument is two separate bundles, considered to be the male and female halves of the instrument, which must be played by two people to make the full scale. Thus the traditional *siku* melody is played as a dialogue between a pair, or many pairs, of musicians (to visualize this, imagine two pianos, one with only the black keys, and the other

37

with only the white, playing one piece of music). Modern city musicians "cheat" by holding both halves of the instrument together and playing them as one instrument.

Three of the most popular and characteristic instruments in Andean folk music – the guitar, harp and *charango* – are stringed, and therefore European imports. However, two of them have been completely transformed in their Andean incarnations. Instead of the massive frame of the European version, the Andean harp is light and portable. It can be played by a walking – or even a drunkenly staggering – musician. It has a sound-box to give it volume, and it is tuned to the diatonic scale.

The little *charango* is a hybrid of the mandolin and the *bandurria* (a 16 string lute). In the past, the sound-box was often made from the shell of some unfortunate armadillo. Let it be known! – the ones with a wooden sound-box are much better, both for the music and the armadillo.

Many Cusco bars and restaurants feature music from the Peruvian coast. It is easily distinguishable from the highland variety. The musicians use guitars and, for percussion, a *cajón* – simply, a box with a round hole – on which a player sits and beats out a greater variety of sound than you would believe possible.

Be aware that almost all the locally seen groups play a highly modified and commercialized form of Andean music. It is hard to hear authentic traditional music that has not been adapted to foreign tastes unless there is a performance by the group *Wiñay Taki Ayllu.*

In the local clubs, the group *Expresión* is noted for an adventurous approach to Andean folk; *Amerinka* and *Metáfora* are also good. Andean rock is played locally by the groups *Chintatá* and *Pueblo Andino. Amaru Pumac Kuntur* plays what has been called "Peruvian Tribal Fusion" at Ukukus (*see p.31*). Coastal music is played by *Son Peruano.*

Some places where you can hear local music are listed on p. 31. To purchase any of these instruments, see Musical Instruments, p. 36.

(Thanks to Román Vizcarra and Holly Wissler for information for this section.)

– P.F.

Outdoor Equipment Rentals and Repair

Quality of equipment available for rent varies enormously. Check and test everything (especially stoves) before you set off on a trip. Recommended are **Himalaya Outdoor** *(see above)* and **Speedy Gonzales** across the street. **Himalaya** is also good for all around repair. **Creaciones Noelia** (Chaparro 271 (B4), 944-048567) specializes in backpack repairs. For shoe repair, **Elmer Renovadora de Calzados**, Matara 270 (D4), tel. 246919.

Maps

Many bookstores *(see p. 36)* have maps for major trails, but often at low levels of detail.

King of Maps, Tandapata 100B (E1), tel. 953-448355, www.kingofmaps.com Prints of stylish, hand-drawn maps and illustrations, in a classic style, of South America, Machu Picchu, and other Andean/Pre-Columbian themes. *(See rear cover.)*

Himalaya Outdoor, *(see p. 36)* Central but more expensive and fewer maps than Maratón.

Maratón, Av. de la Cultura 1020 (OM), across the street from UNSAAC, tel. 225387 The cheapest and best-stocked place in Cusco to buy topographic maps; has all of southern Peru.

Camera Equipment and Repairs

Batteries, memory cards and film, if you still use it, are widely available in the center of Cusco. There is a string of photography supply stores on the first block of Av. el Sol.

Foto Nishiyama, Av. el Sol 130B (D3), tel. 231217 and Triunfo 346 (D2), tel. 242922

ADVENTURE TOURS AND EXPEDITIONS

Many of the following companies offer a variety of adventure tours and activities. Note that hard-core hiking and rafting trips shut down during the November-March rainy season. However, the Inca trail is hiked every month except February and the softer sections of the Urubamba River are rafted year round. (Since all necessary details are online, this section only cites travel agency websites.)

Trekking and Hiking

The Cusco region is fabulous terrain for everything from day-hikes to treks and backpacking. This is wide open country; no "Keep Out" signs and few barbed-wire fences. Very intrepid adventurers with compass, map or GPS could reach the Peruvian coast on foot from here if they wanted to (and it's been done.) The views are astounding and the countryside is endlessly varied. Hiking is a big part of exploring the region and its ruins, many of which can only be reached on foot. But since this is not primarily a hiking book, many of the routes mentioned have been described in detail in the Trekking section on **www.peterfrost.org**

The Inca Trail is justifiably famous but very heavily used, regulated and restricted. You must reserve as many as six months in advance for high season through a certified guiding agency. If you can manage it, the five-day version of the Inca Trail is well worth it as it allows you to escape the crowds and have more time for the highlights.

Meanwhile, there are dozens of other hikes and circuits in the area. Some less well known ones are suggested in the appropriate chapters. The six-day Ausangate Circuit is a rigorous gem of a high-altitude hike *(see p. 284)*, while the Salcantay route from Mollepata to Santa Teresa offers a combination of high mountain passes and cloud-forest environments *(see p. 207)*. New routes have opened up in the Machu Picchu area *(see p. 206)* as less-traveled alternatives to the Inca Trail. These routes are quite remote, and hikers must be competent and self-sufficient.

A general point about the hikes suggested in this book is that the Andes are rugged and rocky, and a good pair of hiking boots or shoes is a distinct asset. Sneakers will do in a pinch. Carry something waterproof, especially during the rainy season (November through March).

Etiquette. Campesinos (peasant farmers) don't have much, and if you trample their crops they will have even less. Take care about this, and watch out also for irrigation channels, which are easy to damage if you walk along their banks.

Gifts. Campesinos, especially children, will often ask for money or gifts. It's depressing when one's human contact routinely begins with an outstretched hand. I seldom give money, except in exchange for a photo. Candy is even worse; you feel like a jerk not giving it to kids when you have it in your pocket, but think what you're doing. If you do a hike, you may find that children come running up to you to demand imperiously, "*Dame dulce!*" ("Give me candy!") – and it's because people have been giving them candy.

Giving away food is more in keeping with the system of *ayni*, the reciprocity that traditionally underlies all material transactions in the Andes. After all, they grew the stuff (and sold it to you cheap, yes?). So to bring some cooked or baked food (e.g. bread) back to the countryside is to practice reciprocity, the way I see it. People will frequently offer you cooked potatoes or corn in exchange; try not to cause offence by refusing it.

Other extremely useful, if not exactly reciprocal, gifts are pencils and school notebooks. Campesinos crave a decent education for their children (it is one of the chief reasons for migration to the cities), and can often barely afford these simple items. If you can think up something their kids can do for you in exchange, you are reinforcing their most vital cultural tradition. For example, ask them to guide you along the trail a little way – say to the next turnoff (*desvío*). For adults, coca *(see p.48)* is cheap, light to carry, and easy to share, so carry extra when you hike. Cigarettes are popular gifts among adult males in the countryside (there is an odd folk myth that they cure headaches, when in fact the exact opposite seems to be true). For the giver, they have the advantage of being ultra light; for the receiver, all the well-known disadvantages – but you can take comfort in the knowledge that campesinos simply cannot afford to get addicted to them. Another suggestion is souvenirs from home – a picture of the Golden Gate Bridge or the Kremlin always goes down well. And of course, nothing beats a Polaroid camera *(see p. 39)*. What better gift than an instant photo for people who have never seen a picture of themselves?

Safety. In case of emergency, the High Mountain Police handle search and rescue operations. To initiate one, call the central emergency number "105" on any phone. Reception is patchy deep in the mountains, so either take a satellite phone or leave a detailed itinerary with a responsible person to call on your behalf if you're overdue. Sat phones rentable in Cusco from the Crees Foundation (**www.crees-manu.org**).

Dogs are the biggest hiking threat, especially if you get near their territory or the animals they are guarding. Most *campesinos* keep them and sometimes they rush at you in savage-looking packs. The barking is mostly for show, but bites are not unheard of, especially for cyclists. Picking up a rock and pretending to throw it normally deters them, but if they persist, actually throwing it will do the trick. If genuinely threatened, the business end of a hiking pole is also effective. Pepper spray can be purchased at Himalaya Outdoor (*see Outdoor Equipment, p. 39*), but that carries its own risk of blowback. Although rabies is uncommon in and around Cusco, you *must* seek medical attention if bitten, even if you're vaccinated. Effective treatment may be available locally, but rabies immunoglobulin, a component of some treatments, is unavailable in Peru; a trip home may be called for.

Women are advised not to hike alone. Rape is not common but has been reported, especially around or after dark near Amaru Marcawasi north of Cusco. Robbery is also rare on more remote hikes and will likely be a crime of opportunity if it does happen.

Trekking/Hiking Operators

You get what you pay for: cheap hiking agencies may put you in huge groups with poorly paid and minimally trained guides and porters. Environmental concern and social responsibility may be nonexistent. They may evade local taxes and health benefits for employees. Here are some reputable ones.

Mountain Lodges of Peru, www.mountainlodgesofperu.com This company has cornered the inn-to-inn market on the famous Salcantay Trek to Machu Picchu (*see p 207*) and Lares (*p. 164*) with a series of luxury lodges. SPS.

Auqui, www.auqui.travel Old, established and highly knowledgeable, specializing in high-end personalized itineraries. Operates **Andean Lodges** (www.andeanlodges.com) in partnership with local villagers, on a trekking circuit near Ausangate with comfortable lodges (*see p. 284*). Uses pack llamas instead of horses. SPS.

Amazonas Explorer, www.amazonas-explorer.com Many years of experience in hiking, mountain biking and rafting; well-established. Run by long-term expat Paul Cripps. SPS.

Enigma, www.enigmaperu.com High end operator. SPS.

Explorandes, www.explorandes.com The oldest established in the Peruvian adventure travel scene. Hikes and camping trips into the interior, rafting and kayaking. Not cheap, but experienced and reliable. SPS.

Manu Expeditions, www.manuexpeditions.com & www.Birding-In-Peru.com Highland trekking groups, horseback treks, and birdwatching, wildlife and photo safari expeditions to Manu National Park.

Apus Peru, www.apus-peru.com Does standard routes but specializes in off-the-beaten-path treks. Signature route is a nine-day Choquequirao- Vilcabamba-Machu Picchu hike. Well trained staff. SPS.

Ecoinka, ecoinka.com Long-established, reputable. Minimum-impact environmental and cultural practices. Has a unique 5-day Inca Trail variation.

Andina Travel, www.andinatravel.com Variety of adventure tours: trekking, biking and rafting. Hikes to the little-known Quillarumiyoc ruins from its hotel in Zurite. SPS.

Andean Adventures, www.andeanadventuresperu.com Long-established company with wide range of adventure travel itineraries. SPS.

Wayki Trek, www.waykitrek.net Longstanding agency run by guides from indigenous communities; profits support development projects there. Holds ISO certifications for good management and environmental practices. SPS.

Travel and Healing, www.travelandhealing.com One of the only operators offering hikes integrated with traditional Andean shamanic ceremonies. *Ayahuasca* and *san pedro* (see p. 48).

Alternative Inca Trails, www.alternativeincatrails.com Local guide Alain Machaca does remote treks from 1-15 days around the Cusco countryside.

Xtreme Tourbulencia, www.x-tremetourbulencia.com Well-reviewed Inca Trail budget operator.

United Mice, www.unitedmice.com Another basic services company with good reviews. SPS.

Private Freelance Guides. See **www.peterfrost.org**

Trail Running and Bootcamps

These are relatively new sports here, and very few agencies offer them.

Peru Fitness Holidays, www.perufitnessholidays.com Trail running from one day to over two weeks; can integrate this with yoga and massages. Also offers boot camps in the Sacred Valley. SPS.

Rafting Operators

Cusco is an excellent base for kayaking and rafting on some of the wild Andean rivers. See **www.peterfrost.org** for some of the more popular local rafting routes and safety recommendations. Many companies sell rafting trips, but some merely take your booking and pass you on to the operator. It is best to go direct, such as with:

Amazonas Explorer, *(see Trekking, p. 41)* Wide range of river trips out of Cusco. Long-standing and highly reliable.

River Explorers, www.riverexplorers.com Rafting trips around Arequipa, Cusco, Lima, and Puno. Well reviewed.

Apumayo, www.apumayo.com Long-established, reliable company in all aspects of adventure tourism, owned and managed by founder Pepe Lopez. SPS.

Xtreme Tourbulencia *(see above)* Does the Apurimac River and the Chuquicahuana rapids.

Standup Paddle Boarding (SUP)

A calmer alternative to rafting, great for family outings. A few companies now offer this paddle-propelled surfboard option on local lakes (Huaypo and Piuray) and easier whitewater sections of the Urubamba. Offered by **Amazonas Explorer** *(see Trekking p. 41)* and **SUP Cusco**, www.supcusco.com

Kayaking

Few reputable commercial operators run whitewater kayaking trips here. For independent kayakers wanting logistical support and transportation. Amazonas Explorers (see Trekking, p. 41) may be able to help on an ad hoc basis.

Mountain Biking

The Cusco region is terrific for mountain biking and the Peruvian scene in general has exploded in recent years. There are innumerable bikeable trails close to the city and many more starting a day's drive away. It's easy to put your bike on the roof rack of almost any local bus (make sure they load it properly), and travel to trailheads around the region.

Beginner riders (if you just arrived at altitude, include yourself in this category no matter *how* fit you are!) can take some of the most spectacular downhill road-runs anywhere in the world. They go on for hours. *But beware:* Dog attacks! Homicidal drivers! Suicidal pedestrians! Broken glass! Highway soccer matches (usually on blind curves)! *Be alert!*

See Mountain Biking on **www.peterfrost. org** for a list of local routes.

Biking Operators

Many agencies offer the standard day tours of the local ruins. The ones listed below are also known for their good bikes and/or their technical, off-the-beaten-path trails.

Amazonas Explorer *(see Trekking, p. 41)* Experienced and reliable. Trips ranging from ½ day to a 12-day Lake Titicaca-Machu Picchu tour.

Aspiring Adventures, www. aspiringadventures.com Small agency with experienced local guides and expat owners. Trips of 1-12 days. Longer trips involve cultural encounters and homestays with locals.

Haku Expeditions and **Gravity,** www. hakuexpeditions.com, www.gravityperu. com Owners Bill and Nic are passionate about local mountain biking. Trips tailored to ability level and are 1-10 days. Most trips have cultural aspects. Has well reviewed Airbnb accommodations. **Gravity** focuses on shorter trips and a more general, mass-market audience.

Quechua Bikes, www.perubiking.com Offers a variety of bike routes for all ability levels.

Xtreme Tourbulencia, *(see Trekking, p. 42)* More economical bike trip operator.

Cusco Biking Tours, www. cuscobikingtours.com Free two hour bike tours of Cusco city (bike rental extra). Also has various single- and multi-day trips.

Bike Rentals

Check the brakes and tire pressure and inspect the frame for damage. The bike should come with a helmet, pump, basic tool kit and puncture repair kit.

Aita Peru, Plateros 392 (C2), tel. 246033, www.aitaperu.com Around 35 bikes available.

Intihuatana Bike and Trek, Saphi 635 (B2), tel.984-688922 Many bikes available. Bring your passport.

Bike Home, Tullumayo 438 (F3), tel. 224354 Four bikes available.

Bike Maintenance and Parts

Russo Bikes, Avenida Tacna 218B, Wanchaq (OM), tel. 221560

Bike Home, (*see Rentals above*)
Confraternidad Market, crnr of Confraternidad and San Martin, near Ovalo Martin Chambi (OM). On the first floor, there is an entire row of bike shops with inexpensive parts and accessories.

Horse Riding

People selling cheap, short, unregulated tours can easily be found by walking around Cristo Blanco and the pedestrian entrance and eastern edges of Sacsaywaman. Operators with qualified guides and more remote, interesting routes are listed below.

Manu Expeditions (*see Trekking, p. 41*) Rides from 1-4 days on their own specially-bred horses, with routes around Chinchero, Huchuy Cusco, Lamay and Lares.

Perol Chico, Urubamba, www.perolchico. com Trips with unique Peruvian *paso* (pacing) horses of 2-11 days. The 11-day trip through the Sacred Valley is recommended by National Geographic as one of the top 10 in the world. Trips geared towards intermediate-experienced riders.

Travel and Healing, www.horseridingcusco. com, (*see Trekking, p. 42*) One-day tours around Cusco, including the ruins of Moray. Also has *paso* horse rides. SPS.

Haku Expeditions (*see Biking Agencies above*). A half-day ride to remote Inca ruins above Cusco, plus tours of Maras/Moray.

Mountaineering

The region is ripe with potential for ice climbing on beautiful high peaks, but is largely neglected in favor of the Cordillera Blanca in northern Peru. There are three major Cordilleras: the Vilcanota (highest: Ausangate, 6338m/20,790 ft); the Vilcabamba (Salcantay,

6,273m/20, 575 ft); and the Urubamba (Verónica, 5,751m/18,865ft).

Auqui, (*see Trekking, p. 41*)
Enigma, (*see Trekking, p.41*)
Sky High Expeditions, www. skyhighandes.com Owner Nate Heald is an experienced mountaineer and has climbed most of the local peaks. In addition to the standard routes, he guides remote, infrequently summited mountains that other agencies don't.

Rock Climbing

Most people don't come to Cusco for the climbing, but there is a small climbing community, a gym, and a few nearby crags. The local crags include: a bouldering area called Los Techos, an easy walk from the Temple of the Moon in Cusco; a top-roping crag called Las Queuñas near Chacán (*see Walk*); a sport-climbing area near Lamay; another sport-climbing area in the vicinity of Pachar in the Sacred Valley; and a recently developed area called Ch'acco Huayllassca near the town of Pitumarca on the Valley Road Southeast.

Séptima Climbing School, Casa de la Juventud, Coliseo Cerrado (OM), basement #15, tel. 984-762295, www.7aescueladescalada.com The local climbing gym. They also maintain the local crags and post information, topo maps, and details on how to get there (mostly in Spanish).

Paragliding

Mountainous regions high above sea level are not ideal for beginners at this sport.
Flying Expedition, www.facebook.com/ flyingexpedition Owner Leo Infanta offers courses.

Action Valley, www.actionvalley.com Paragliding 45min outside of Cusco.

Ziplining, Via Ferrata, Bungee Jumping, Paintball, ATV

Most have heard of ziplining, but via ferrata (climbing cliffs via metal rungs in the rock) is less well known.

Natura Vive, www.naturavive.com Has a 400m via ferrata route plus ziplining down from the top. Also has suspended, transparent sleeping capsules near Ollantaytambo where you can spend the night dangling off the side of a cliff.

Action Valley, (*see Paragliding above*) Ziplining, bungee jumping and paintballing from their park on the road to Poroy.

Maras Adventure, Garcilaso 265 (C3), office 5, tel. 505797, www.marasadventure. com Ziplining, horseback riding, mountain biking and ATV around Maras. SPS.

Cola de Mono, www.canopyperu.com 6-stage zipline in Santa Teresa, about 2.5km (1.5mi) long in total. Also one of the highest in South America.

Peru Moto Tours, (*see Car Rentals, p. 23*) Quad bike and motorcycle tours, rentals, and lessons.

Fishing

The Vilcanota/Urubamba River is too polluted and overfished to be worth considering. (But it wasn't always. Check the Exploring Cusco Museum at **www. peterfrost.org**)

Peru Anglers, www.peruanglers.com 1-4 day trips around Cusco, Arequipa, and the Amazon from April to October. Provides all necessary equipment; uses catch and release practices.

Explorer's Inn, www.explorersinn.com Offers fishing trips in the rainforest on the La Torre and Tambopata Rivers. The best time is the rainy season between October and April when the rivers are high.

VOLUNTEERING AND EXPERIENTIAL TOURISM

Volunteer opportunities abound in Cusco, but not all organizations are reputable or beneficial to the communities they work in. For a list of recommended organizations, see Volunteering in Cusco on **www. peterfrost.org** Not all organizations will accept people on the spot, and prior application may be necessary.

Traditional Andean culture is profoundly different from the Western one in the way that people view time, money, spirituality, relationships, and the environment. Experiential tourism gives you house stays in remote rural villages where you experience their ways of life while hiking and taking in other activities; note that accommodations may be basic.

CBC Tupay, www.cbctupay.com Specializes in trips to six remote Quechua communities in the Sacred Valley area. Activities include workshops on traditional weaving, traditional medicine, Andean cooking, hiking, and learning about the local culture, spiritual practices, and language. Also offers a more relaxing two-day version of the Rainbow Mountain hike (see p.284) with an overnight stay in the community of Chari. SPS.

Wayki Trek, (see p.42)

Awamaki, (see Shopping, p.58) Tours, homestays and volunteer placements in Quechua communities near Ollantaytambo,

45

plus artisan workshops for dyeing, weaving and wood carving. Also has a shop in Ollantaytambo selling textiles. SPS.

Alternative Inca Trails, *(see Trekking, p. 42)* For a more rural experience, Alain Machaca teaches how to prepare *cuy* (guinea pig), *chicha* and bread in his family home in Paruro.

Qoricocha Lodge, www.qoricochalodge. com A variety of adventure sports and cultural activities from their lakeside lodge, including hiking, biking, horse riding, gastronomy, Andean ceremonies and farming.

Santos Machacca Apaza, tel.984-366790, tinyurl.com/y8jf6bpb santosmachacca2@ hotmail.com From Q'eros, now living in Cusco. A trained cook who regularly arranges trips into Q'eros (see p.276). Trilingual: English, Spanish, Quechua.

HEALTH AND MEDICAL

Exotic parasites and foodborne infections are easy to catch here. If you are sick, get checked out here instead of back home; local labs and doctors know the signs, symptoms and treatments better than their counterparts elsewhere. Medications also may be cheaper locally and available without prescription.

Medical Clinics and Doctors

SOS Medical Clinic, Av. las Gardenias, Urb. la Florida, Wanchaq (OM), tel. 984-662599, www.sos-mg.com

MAC Salud, Av. de la Cultura 1410 (OM), tel. 582060, www.macsalud.com

CIMA, Pardo 978 (OM), tel. 255550, www.cima-clinic.com

O2 Medical Network, Puputi 148 (OM), tel. 221213, www.o2medicalnetwork.com

Paredes, Lechugal 405 (D4), tel. 225265

Dr. Eduardo Luna, Humberto Luna 210 (OM), tel. 984-761277, eduardolunapr@ hotmail.com General medicine, speaks English, does house and hotel calls. Recommended.

Medical Labs

Laboratorio Clinico Fleming, Quera 235 (D4), tel. 224929. For tests on blood, urine, feces, etc. Reliable, with lower charges than the major clinics. 8am-12pm, 5-7pm.

Pharmacies

Botica Karilyn, Zetas 328 (F3), tel. 251376 Well-stocked, helpful owner, and better prices than the big chain pharmacies.

Dentists

Jenny Quintanilla, Av. La Cultura M-8b (OM), tel. 402803 Spanish only.

Solución Dental, Limacpampa Grande 587 (F3), tel. 254988 English spoken.

Natural Medicines

Inkalys, Hacienda Llaullipata (OM), tel. 993-235298, www.inkalys.com Phytotherapy, aromatherapy products and accessories, essential oils, natural soaps and cosmetics. Does aromatherapy and essential oil distillation workshops, plus plant identification walks.

Chiropractors

Dr. Howard Levine, Urb. Magisterio, Av. J. Gabriel Cosio 108 (OM), tel. 431983, www. centroquiropracticocanada.com

Dr. Ilya Gomon, Urb. Fideranda F-1-A (OM), Of. 201, tel. 507293, tinyurl.com/ gv9458z

Physiotherapy, Massage, Acupuncture

Innumerable young women offer inexpensive massages in the Plaza de Armas and on *Triunfo* and *Marques* streets; good for relaxation but not for therapy. The following are professionally trained therapists.

Cusco Therapeutic Massage, Pumamarca F-21, east down Lucrepata (F2), tel. 966-145697, www.cuscotherapeuticmassage. com Expat Dan Rowe is trained in neuromuscular and sports massage techniques and can come to your hotel.

Healing House, Qanchipata 555 (E1), tel. 241624, www.healinghousecusco.com Reiki, massage, acupuncture, reflexology. SPS.

Paramatma, Asnoqch'utun 279 (F2), tel. 987-138380, www.cuscoholistichealing. com Massage, acupuncture.

Centro de Terapia Alternativa Kauna, Pasaje Esmeralda 194-A (OM), tel. 262402. Homeopathy and vacuum cupping by Jens Laurits Soerensen. Natural medicines store. Lodging and meals for patients only.

Tikray Wasi, Urubamba, tel. 982-349861, tinyurl.com/y7l2dqj7 Massage, acupuncture, Chinese cupping, reiki.

Yoga

Inbound Yoga, Carmen Alto 111 (E2), tel. 945-876897, www.yogacusco.com

Healing House, *(see Massage above)*

Paramatma, *(see Massage above)*

Yoga Room, tel. 997-119812, www. yogaroomcusco.com Private lessons, immersions, retreats and training in the Sacred Valley and over Peru.

Vegetarian Peru Adventures, Limatambo, tel. 238390, www.veggieperu.com Yoga retreats near the town of Limatambo,

plus tours of the nearby ruins and condor lookout.

Gyms

Most Cusco gyms aren't up to North American standards, but they'll do for a dropin.

Premier Gym, Maruri 265, basement (E3), tel. 973-684012, tinyurl.com/y8ynu2q5 Small but central, good facilities and fun classes. Has day passes.

Smart Fit, Plaza Real mall, Av. Collasuyo 2964 (OM), www.smartfit.com.pe The best and biggest facilities, but only has monthly plans.

Spas and Saunas

Palacio del Inka, *(Inside the hotel - see p.25),* tinyurl.com/y9cwb34o Gorgeous facilities, reasonably priced and usually lightly attended.

Andina Spa, Tullumayo 112 (E2), tel. 252550, www.andinaspa.com Variety of sauna and spa treatments, close to the center. Well reviewed.

Oasis Sauna Spa, Quinto Paradero, San Sebastian (OM), tel. 270386, tinyurl. com/y8lnp2oo Locals' sauna far from the center, good value. Wet and dry saunas, pool. Jacuzzi extra. Take a taxi.

MEDICINAL PLANTS AND PRACTITIONERS

Peru has a long history of medicinal plant use, from the relatively mild stimulant coca leaf to the intense psychoactives of *ayahuasca, san pedro* cactus, and *willka* snuff. These plants are legal in Peru and are safe if used properly and with an experienced practitioner. (According to Article 299 of the Peruvian criminal code, up to eight grams of marijuana and two grams of cocaine are also legal. It is illegal to carry two different types of drugs – except the legal plants mentioned above – at the same time, no matter the quantity.) Powerful psychoactives are not recreational: they can provide intense, restorative, and sometimes life-changing experiences. Use with proper respect and preparation, following all pre-ceremony recommendations. Choose your practitioner carefully: a shady shaman could mean a bad trip or even rape or robbery during the session, so avoid quickie street propositions. Do not attempt to prepare these medicines by yourself: it requires skill and practice. The following are safe and come highly and widely recommended. The websites **www. retreat.guru** and **www.ayamundo.com** (truly trip advisors!) can be used to check shamans and retreat centers. **Scott Lite** (tel. 944-245254, farfromhere001@gmail. com) is an ethnobotanist who practices with and lectures on plant medicine. For brief overviews of ayahuasca, san pedro and willka, see the "Medicinal Plants" page on **www.peterfrost.org** . For in-depth book resources, see "Medicinal Plants" in the Bibliography.

Coca

Coca bushes (*Erythroxylum coca* and *E. novogranatense*) grow at the lower altitudes of the eastern slopes of the tropical Andes. The leaves have had ceremonial, social, nutritional and medicinal uses in the Andes since long before the Inca empire. Yet to most people, they are just the source of cocaine. Cocaine is to coca as ivory is to elephants: a small part of the whole

beast. Cocaine is obtained by chemically extracting one alkaloid from the coca leaf and dumping all the rest. The leaf, however, contains a complex of fourteen alkaloids, significant amounts of vitamins A & E, plus iron, potassium, calcium, lots of sodium, and various other minerals in trace amounts (source: *The Incredible Leaf* – Cochabamba 1992). Chewing coca leaves by themselves has no intoxicating effect, and the amount of cocaine in each leaf is minute. For more on coca and cocaine, see the coca leaf page on **www.peterfrost.org** (**The Coca Museum** [Pl. San Blas 618 (F2), tel. 501020] has interesting displays on the history and uses of coca leaves, plus a graphic on cocaine production.)

For chewing, the best leaves are fresh and soft, with a strong aroma. Vendors will let you smell and touch them. The best local place is Mercado Ccascaparo, down *General Buendia* (C4). This market is chaotic; ask where the coca vendors are. You can also find decent leaves at San Pedro market (city map #22). Don't forget to buy the *llipta* ("yeep-tah"), a small block of compressed plant ashes that activates the various alkaloids in the leaf; coca chewing has little effect without this. *Llipta* comes in various flavors depending on which plant is used. Beginners should avoid cacao and quinoa as they are highly caustic; stevia and *muña* (Andean mint) are milder. Baking soda (*bicarbonato de sodio*) works even better, is available in pharmacies, and is also less caustic. For coca chewing technique and storage, see **www.peterfrost.org**

Ayahuasca

Etnikas, www.etnikas.com Expensive, but good for first-timers. Sessions are small, safe and medically supervised: the shaman, a doctor, a nurse, a psychologist and an anthropologist all work with the participant. Sessions are done in their proper ceremonial and cultural context, with both Amazonian and Andean traditions. Authorized by the Ministry of Health. SPS.

Sapan Inka, Calca, tel. 984-698548, www. sapaninka.com Small ceremonies (max 4 people) at their retreat house. 3- or 6-day retreats. Vegetarian diet and post-ceremony integration sessions. Offers *san pedro* and a visit to Machu Picchu during the 6-day retreat.

Shaman Shop, Triunfo 393 (E2), tel. 226278, shamanshopcusco.com Many years of experience. Also offers *san pedro*, sweat lodges, and other spiritual services. Insist on Kush as your shaman; his apprentices get mixed reviews.

Sacred Valley Tribe, Pisac, tel. 968-055619, www.sacredvalleytribe.com Large ceremonies (up to 100 people) at regular intervals; better for the more experienced due to large groups and lack of individual attention. Excellent use of music enhances the experience. Has smaller 7-day retreats and *san pedro* ceremonies.

San Pedro

Another Planet Peru, tel. 241168, www. anotherplanetperu.org Owner Lesley Myburgh and her sons have been working with *san pedro* for decades. Ceremonies take place at her retreat just outside Cusco. Participants can tour the nearby Temple of the Moon or elect to stay in the garden. Overnight stays available.

Ubuntu Ayni, Huarán, tel. 958-194174, www.ubuntuayni.com Owners Bernhard and Liza-Marié combine elements of

Andean and African shamanism into their retreat center *san pedro* practice. Ceremonies are held regularly or on request. Lodging available.

Travel and Healing, *(see Trekking, p. 42)* Same owners as Etnikas *(see Ayahuasca above)*, with the same professionalism. Sessions are with Q'ero shamans.

Casa de Wow, Ollantaytambo, *(see hotels, p. 57)* A *san pedro* experience and cultural tour in one. The owner "Wow" takes participants to the ruins of three local temples, performing ceremonies at each and explaining their significance.

Willka

WachumAwaken, tel. 944-029500, tinyurl.com/js6hn5p Owner Joey Greenstone sometimes incorporates willka into his *san pedro* ceremonies but can also provide it by itself upon request.

Sofia Cottage Urubamba, *(see Hotels p. 55)* Owner Danielle and ceremony partner Jeronimo show you how to prepare willka and then perform the ceremony. Also offers *ayahuasca, san pedro* and temazcal sweat lodges.

MUSEUMS

BTC, CRA or SST indicate the entrance ticket required. See Tourist Tickets, p. 18 for more information. Some of these museums are described in more detail in Chapter 2: The City of Cusco.

Casa Concha Machu Picchu Museum, (city map #15) Mon-Sat 9am-5pm, (SST) Historic collection of material, taken by Hiram Bingham to Yale U. in 1912 and repatriated to Cusco in 2011-12. Classic exhibits, plus Bingham photos and memorabilia.

Center for Traditional Textiles, *(see Textiles p. 35)*, (suggested donation) A small but beautifully done display of traditional weaving techniques and pieces from the Andes.

Cusicancha, Mon-Fri 7:15am-1pm; 2-4pm (free) (city map #16) A series of Inca courtyards, formerly connected to the Qoricancha, which may have once held the mummies of royal Incas.

Inka Museum, Located in the Admiral's Palace (city map #9) Mon-Sat 8am-6:30pm, holidays 9am-4pm (SST). A large display of mainly Inca material; excellent relief models of Moray, the Qoricancha, the Q'eswachaka bridge and Choquequirao. Most descriptions have English translations.

Museo Inkariy, Calca-Urubamba road, Km 53, tel. 792819, tinyurl.com/y98avlam Daily 9am-5:30pm, (SST). (see p.163)

Museum of Contemporary Art - Municipal Town Hall, Pl. Regocijo (C3). Daily 9am-1pm, 2-6pm, (BTC). A permanent collection of work by contemporary Cusco artists, including paintings, statues and ceramics. Hosts special exhibitions from time to time.

Museum of Popular Art, Av. el Sol 103 (D3), basement. Daily 9am-6pm (BTC). A large display of ceramic figurines showing aspects of daily life and culture, including long-necked Mendívil saints, religious celebrations, and a nativity scene made from bent cutlery and bike parts.

Museum of pre-Columbian Art - Plaza Nazarenas (city map #9) daily 9am-10pm, (SST). A varied and excellent collection of pieces from the spectrum of Peru's pre-Columbian civilizations, displayed as outstanding works of art without much chronology or background.

Museum of Religious Art - crnr of Hatunrumiyoc and Palacio (city map #13), daily 8am-6pm (CRA). Many colonial paintings. The greatest treasure is a famous and fascinating series of twelve paintings depicting the Corpus Christi processions of 17th-century Cusco.

Puca Marka Site Museum, Maruri 314-5 (city map #16), Mon-Fri 9am-6pm, Sat 9am-1pm (free). Headquarters of Scotiabank. Excellent Inca walls and displays of the site's checkered history. 2nd floor exhibit of world-famous early 20th-century Cusco photographer Martin Chambi.

Qoricancha Archaeological Museum, Av. el Sol on the park adjacent to Santo Domingo church (E4), daily 9am-6pm (BTC). Some artifacts from excavations done when the park was being built, plus assorted displays on Inca history. Also provides access to the park.

Regional Historical Museum, Casa de Garcilaso (city map #26) Daily 8am-5pm, (BTC). Interesting collection of archaeological material and colonial paintings.

Santa Catalina Museum, Santa Catalina Angosta (D3) Mon-Sat 8:30am-5:30pm, Sun 2-5pm, (SST). A collection of colonial-era paintings and artifacts.

CHURCHES

Cathedral, Sagrada Familia, and El Triunfo, Pl. de Armas, Daily 10am-6pm, (CRA). (city map #2)

La Compañía, Pl. de Armas, Mon-Sat 9am-5:30pm, Sun 9-11:30am; 1-5:30pm (RBA). (city map #4)

Monastery of La Merced, Calle Mantas, Mon-Sat 08:00-12:30pm; 2-5:30pm (SST) (city map #19)

Qoricancha / Convent of Santo Domingo, Pl. Santo Domingo (city map #18), Mon-Sat 8am-5:30pm, Sun 2-5pm (SST).

San Blas, Pl. San Blas, Daily 8am-6pm (CRA) (city map #12)

San Cristobal, Calle Don Bosco, Daily 8am-6pm (CRA) (city map #6)

San Francisco, Pl. San Francisco, Daily 9:00am-6:00pm (SST) (city map #24)

Santa Clara, Calle Santa Clara, no regular hours. (free) (city map #21)

CUSCO REGION CALENDAR

There are innumerable small festivals and processions in the Plaza de Armas all year round, and it's an unusual week where something doesn't happen. The major festivals are:

Jan. 20, procession of saints in *San Sebastián*, near *Cusco*.

Carnival, February or March, 40 days before Easter.

Monday before Good Friday - *Cusco*: lively parade of the Lord of the Earthquakes, an important religious festival. Easter itself is interesting, but this is the day of Cusco's spiritual patron.

May 2/3 - on all mountaintops with a cross on them, and their adjacent towns: the Vigil of the Cross, a boisterous affair.

Pentecost Sat-Tues, 50 days after Easter. *Ollantaytambo*: costumed dancers; horseback games; bullfight. *Urubamba*: El Señor de Torrechayoc. Loud, colorful celebrations of the patron of Urubamba, with costumed dancers and processions.

Trinity Sun-Tues, First Sunday after Pentecost. *Qoyllur Rit'i*, the massive "Snow Star" festival in the remote *Sinakara Valley* near *Mawayani*, north of Ausangate.

Thursday after Trinity Sunday (May or June) - *Cusco*: Corpus Christi. Saint effigies from all the churches of Cusco are brought to the Cathedral to "sleep" with Christ and the other saints, and taken on parade next day; a very colorful and emotional event.

June 17 - *Raqchi*: a lively local festival to the old creator god, Viracocha. Lots of music.

Second weekend of June - *Q'eswachaka*: the 4-day reconstruction of a traditional Inca bridge (*see p. 289*).

June 24 (and ten days or so before that date) - *Cusco*: Cusco Week, a plethora of parades culminating in *Inti Raymi*, a pageant of the Inca festival of the winter solstice, vigorously celebrated to this day, and by no means staged only for tourists.

End of June - *Ollantaytambo*: Ollantay Raymi, a huge re-enactment of the Ollantay Drama, a story of forbidden love between an Inca princess and a commoner. Lots of food, music and dancing.

July 15-17 - *Paucartambo* (also *Pisac, Huarocondo* and *Quillabamba*): festival of the Virgin of Carmen. Costumed dancers enact rituals and folk tales in the streets.

July 28, Peruvian Independence Day. *Combapata*: *Yawar Fiesta* ("Blood Festival"), the famous ritual struggle between a condor and a bull, symbolizing the hoped-for triumph of the native people (the condor) over the invader (the bull). Stay away if you love animals.

August 14, *Tiobamba* (near Maras): major religious festival and market; well worth a visit. *Calca*: Virgin of the Assumption, major religious festival, market and parades.

Last Sunday in August - *Cusco*: *Huarachicoy*, a re-enactment of the traditional Inca manhood rite performed at Sacsaywaman by local schoolboys in period costumes.

September 14 - *Huanca*: religious pilgrimage to the shrine of *El Señor de Huanca*. Huge event in awe-inspiring mountain setting.

November 1-2, All Saints and All Souls days, celebrated everywhere with bread dolls, traditional cooking, remembering the dead and visiting cemeteries.

December 23-24 - *Cusco*: *Santorantikuy*, the "Buying of Saints." Traditionally (and still partly) a Christmas-eve market for figures and settings used in traditional Cusco nativity tableaux, but now also an orgy of Cusco-style Christmas shopping, including many handcrafts.

CULTURAL, FESTIVAL & ARCHAEOLOGICAL TOURS

Coltur Peru, www.colturperu.com One of the oldest Peruvian tour agencies. Conventional itineraries, plus wide selection of cultural and specialized tours, including family-oriented, gastronomic, weaving, Inca masonry, photography, deaf, blind and women-specific.

Aspiring Adventures, *(see Biking Agencies p. 43)* Tours of the festivals of *Inti Raymi, Virgin of Carmen and Qoyllur Rit'i*. This last is endorsed by National Geographic.

Apus Peru, *(see Trekking, p. 42)* Tours of *Qoyllur Rit'i, Q'eswachaka, Virgin of Carmen, Inti Raymi, Yawar Fiesta*. Also tours rural weaving and farming communities.

Milla Turismo, www.millaturismo. com Long-established local agency with customized tour itineraries.

Travel and Healing, *(see Trekking, p. 42)* Traditional Andean ceremonies, including coca leaf readings, cleansings, and offerings. Integrates trekking with these ceremonies.

Haku Expeditions, *(see Biking Agencies, p. 43)* Focus on one-on-one interactions with locals: help a shepherd tend his flock, hike to a local's home and eat lunch there, or do the comprehensive "day in the life" tour.

Tikray Wasi, *(see Health and Medical, p. 47) Despachos* available upon request by traditional Andean priests from Q'ero.

MISCELLANEOUS

Money Changing

Peru has two currencies officially in circulation: Peruvian Nuevos Soles and American dollars. For ordinary shopping for small items, you need Soles. Dollars work for larger purchases in handcraft stores or paying for hotels. Numerous exchange shops and individual money changers (*cambistas*), especially on Avenida el Sol, give a better rate than banks and save you time. Count your change carefully and watch out for fake bills, which are common in both U.S. and Peruvian currency. Cambistas won't accept torn or tattered U.S. bills, so don't accept them as change. (Peru has a tumultuous monetary history. See the Exploring Cusco Museum at **www.peterfrost.org** for recent tumult.)

Kodak Digital Developed Center, Av. el Sol 180 (D3) Trustworthy, good exchange rates.

Western Union, Av. el Sol 608 (E4), tel. 244167 For money transfers

Begging

Traditionally, Saturday is *Día de los Pobres* (Day of the Poor) and it's okay to beg. Giving on Saturdays is a way to distribute your alms if you feel sympathy for the innumerable beggars but overwhelmed by the constant demands.

Laundry
These are everywhere, but **Lavanderia Louis,** Choquechaca 264 (E2), tel. 243485 is central and reliable.

Dry cleaning
Lavanderia Inka, Ruinas 493 (E2), tel. 223421 The only one in the center.

THE SACRED VALLEY

The Valley is an excellent base for exploring the Cusco region, including Machu Picchu and the Inca Trail, with a better climate, lower altitude and calmer environment than Cusco. Some visitors go there straight off the plane from Lima. Independent visitors can easily travel the length of the valley between Ollantaytambo and Pisac on public transport, whose cheap and frequent buses can be flagged down anywhere. Urubamba is the most central location, Pisac is closest to Cusco, while Ollantaytambo is most convenient for Machu Picchu and has the most services. Both of the latter have interesting attractions of their own.
Note: telephone calls from Cusco to the numbers below are local and require no prefix.

Pisac
Hotels.
Allpawasi Pisac Lodge, eastern edge of town, tel. 984-727353, tinyurl.com/ybsba7hr Small, ecologically constructed hotel on a family farm. Does tours of their fields and dairy and quinoa production facilities. Adobe pizza oven, plus a jacuzzi in the largest suite.
Melissa Wasi, short taxi ride outside of Pisac, tel. 797589, www.melissa-wasi.com Cozy bed and breakfast, bungalows for rent with open second floor to enjoy mountain view. 20 minute walk from Pisac.
Hotel Royal Inka, just beyond outskirts of Pisac, on the way to the ruins; tel. 263276, www.royalinkahotel.pe Olympic-sized swimming pool open to general public, tennis court, sport fields.
Paz y Luz Hotel and Healing Center, 1 kilometer from Pisac bridge, tel. 910-598781, www.pazyluzperu.com Great for group workshops and events, individuals can rent bungalows. 20 minute walk from Pisac.
Pisac Inn, on Pisac main square, tel. 203062, www.pisacinn.com Sauna, nicely decorated (paintings), pleasant atmosphere, friendly management with owners Román & Fielding Vizcarra, shared and private bathrooms.
Chaska Pisac Hotel, Av. Amazonas s/n, tel. 973-109675, tinyurl.com/yal9yl2f Clean, simple hotel with meditation room and shared kitchen. Close to main square.
Hospedaje Inti, Calle Espinar s/n, tel. 509154, tinyurl.com/ychgzv6b Middle-range, family-run hostal. Clean, basic. Shared kitchen, sitting space.
IntiKilla Backpacker Pisac, Av. Amazonas 153, tel. 987-313559 Inexpensive dorms.

Restaurants.
Cuchara de Palo Bar & Restaurant, located inside Pisac Inn (*see above*), tel. 203062 Gourmet restaurant using local and organic ingredients. Creative novo Andean dishes and traditional plates. Wood burning oven pizza served on Sundays. VO.
Mullu Cafe, Pl. de Armas 352, tel. 203073 Asian cuisine and traditional Peruvian dishes, creative juices, great balcony view of plaza, modern art inside for sale. VO.
Blue Llama, Pl. de Armas, tel. 203135 Fun decor, view of plaza, kid friendly. Breakfast,

coffee, smoothies, soup, sandwiches. Small shop inside. VO.

Ulrike's Cafe, Pardo 613, tel. 203195 One block from main square, rooftop terrace, book exchange, kid friendly. Pizza, hamburgers, soups, sandwiches, excellent carrot cake and brownies. VO.

Sapos Lounge, Espinar s/n, tel. 994-647979 Good pizza and an ample drink menu. Produce from a local organic farm. One of the few nightlife spots. Owner Jaime is helpful, friendly and English-speaking.

Apu Organic, Grau 534, tel. 788959 Hearty vegetarian food with a wide array of options.

Shopping.

Pisac has a handcraft market every day, with Sunday being the biggest. The market has a huge selection of fairly standard items. There are also dozens of handcraft stores scattered around town.

Calca and Vicinity
Hotels.

Inkaterra Hacienda Urubamba, town center of Huayoccari near Yucay, www.inkaterra.com Beautiful, secluded, estate setting. Arranges local excursions for medicinal plants, birding and agriculture. Luxurious.

IFK Lodge, In Huarán near Calca, tel. 974-791456, www.ifk.pe A large estate on the banks of the Urubamba River, with stunning views of Mt. Pitusiray and the surrounding countryside. Organizes tours of the area.

The Green House Hotel, Huarán, tel. 941-299944, www.thegreenhouseperu.com Cozy hotel with outdoor gardens and communal space.

Yoga Mandala, In Arín near Calca, tel. 984-361955, www.yogamandalasacredvalley.com Rustic yoga and general retreat center: vegetarian meals, massages, hikes, sweat lodge.

Paucartika Hacienda Lodge, Near Lamay, tel. 981-235159, www.paucartika.com Great location at base of a cliff in a refurbished old hacienda. Camp site, restaurant, bike rentals and adventure tours, yoga and dance.

Restaurants.

Huayoccari, tel. 984-688036, reservas@huayoccari.com Family home of the Lambarri-Orihuela clan, nearest thing to royalty in the Urubamba Valley. Offers exclusive lunches, *paso* horse riding tours by prior reservation. They have a private museum collection of colonial and pre-Columbian art and artifacts.

Viva Peru, in Huarán, tel. 958-301214 Gourmet sandwiches, wraps, quiches, salads and juices. Try the unusual homemade ice cream flavors such as mango cardamom and coconut raspberry. Periodically hosts live music and guest chefs. SPS. VO.

La Quinta 8a, intersection of the main highway and Av. Garcilaso, tel. 202081 Huge portions of traditional Peruvian food. Come hungry.

Quinta El Carmen, Av. Vilcanota 848, tel. 771278 On the main road is a pleasant garden spot, serving tasty lunches at reasonable prices.

Yucay
Hotels and Restaurants.

Sonesta Posadas del Inca, Pl. Manco II 123, tel. 201107, www.sonesta.com Large, spacious hotel, colonial hacienda style, partly original, in pleasant grounds.

La Casona de Yucay, Pl. Manco II 104, tel. 201116, www.hotelcasonayucay. com Pleasant, personal, spacious gardens, colonial house surrounded by cornfields. 50 rooms.

Añañau, Garcilaso 155 Main Plaza, tel. 201623, www.ananauperu.com Traditional Peruvian food, pizzas, salads and homemade pastas. Very well reviewed. VO.

Urubamba
Hotels.

Tambo del Inka, Av. FerroCarril s/n, on the highway to Ollantaytambo, Tel. 581777, www.libertador.com.pe Modern, spacious riverside grounds with fine views, large auditorium/conference center, swimming pool, horses for rent, health spa, fitness center. Private railway station with departures to Machu Picchu.

Sol y Luna, Fundo Huincho lote A-5, tel. 608930, www.hotelsolyluna.com 43 bungalows, each individually painted and beautifully decorated. Spa, library, pool, sauna, gym. Beautiful grounds. SPS.

Willka T'ika, Paradero Rumichaca, outside Urubamba on the road to Ollantaytambo, tel. 201181, www.willkatika.com An intimate and comfortable hotel, in an exquisite garden setting, built by *Pachamama's Children* co-author Carol Cumes. Spirituality workshops.

Boutique Hotel Lizzy Wasi, Pisonayniyoc s/n, Urb. La Cantuta, tel. 994-207921, www.lizzywasi.com Charming, intimate bed and breakfast, spacious courtyard. American owner, Elizabeth, can help plan your trip.

Las Chullpas Eco Lodge, Querocancha s/n, a few kilometers from town, tel. 201568, www.chullpas.pe Lovely setting in forest, each room is decorated differently,

attention to detail, filling breakfast, great for retreats.

La Capilla Lodge, Rumichaca Km. 72, tel. 434627, www.capillalodge.com Small, friendly garden hideaway in the countryside near Urubamba.

Sofia Cottage Urubamba, Callejon Chico, tel. 987-466484, www.facebook.com/ sophiacottage On the outskirts of town. Dormitories and private rooms. Shared kitchen and living room, plus a garden. Organizes plant medicine ceremonies (*see p. 49*).

Hostal Ccatán, Paraje Ccatán on Av. Torrechayoc, 1km (0.6mi) from the Torrechayoc Church, tel. 984-948092 Inexpensive, simple rooms and campsites on the outskirts of town.

Campsites.

Camping Los Cedros, tel. 201416, www.travatools.com/loscedros Follow the road to Pumahuanca, about 0.5 km (0.3mi) past the Church of Torrechayoq. Swimming pool, bar, restaurant, hot showers. Spacious and pleasant camping areas, with showers and toilets. Rents tents and camping equipment. Hosts numerous parties – especially Full Moon ones – and caters to a young crowd.

Mystical Adventures Hostel and Campsite, 3km (1.9mi) west from Urubamba on the main road, tel. 974-373652, tinyurl.com/yass42v8 Another pleasant campsite with some inexpensive hotel accommodation. Shared kitchen, lounge and games room, arranges tours.

Restaurants.

The main streets of *Mariscal Castilla* (near the town center) and *Berriozabal* (near the bus terminal) have many interesting restaurants and cafes.

El Huacatay, Jr. Arica 620, tel. 201790
Gourmet, creative dining experience.
Lovely garden patio. Secluded atmosphere.
Reservations recommended during high
tourist season. Closed Sundays.

Paca Paca, Av. Mariscal Castilla 640, tel.
201181 Well lit and cozy, with a small
lounge and bar. Peruvian food, pasta,
wood-fired pizza, and some Thai-influenced
dishes. VO. Lunch and dinner. Well
reviewed.

Kaia Shenai, Mariscal Castilla 563, tel.
991-769196 Simple meals, daily menu,
vegetarian options. Casual atmosphere.

El Edén, Av. Mariscal Castilla 960, tel.
201605 Cafe with light meals: pasta,
empanadas, chocolates, juices and coffee.
Huge selection of bottled jams and juices.
Gluten-free and vegetarian options.

Héroes, Mariscal Castilla 501, tel. 215004
Notable for the relaxed atmosphere,
American-style food and weekend brunch
specials.

Cielito Lindo, Av. 9 de Noviembre s/n (pink
door), tel. 788148 Mexican desserts and
drinks in a colorfully lit setting.

Quinta Los Geranios, Cabo Conchatupa
s/n, on south side of main highway, one
block east of Mariscal Castilla, tel. 201093
Good, inexpensive local-style food in garden
setting. Great homemade ice cream.

Shopping.
 Pablo Seminario, Av. Berriozabal 405,
tel. 201086, www.ceramicaseminario.com/
en An locally and internationally renowned
ceramic artist whose work is inspired and
informed by pre-Columbian designs and
techniques. Creates both unique art pieces
and utilitarian ware.

Begonies' Botanicals, Arica 682, tel. 984-
751791, tinyurl.com/yaatkhj6 Handmade

organic cosmetics using local ingredients.
No petroleum, preservatives, perfumes,
colors or animal testing. Soap, shampoo,
moisturizers, DEET-free repellent, massage
oil, toothpaste, etc.

Mon Repos, Cabo Conchatupac s/n,
on main highway opposite El Maizal
restaurant, tel. 201174 Alpaca clothing
and handcraft store.

Yanahuara

Inkallpa Lodge and Spa, Paradero Posta,
tel. 984-769168, www.inkallpa.com
Environmentally minded, employs mostly
locals. Spa treatments available. Can
arrange various activities.

Casa Andina, Quinto Paradero, Yanahuara,
tel. 984-765501, www.casa-andina.com 92
rooms and 4 cottages available. Gym, sauna
and spa, plus a planetarium. Excellent
views.

El Descanso, on eastern outskirts, south
side of main highway. A traditional *chichería*
run by local personality Doña Mercedes
where you get the rundown on how to
brew *chicha* corn beer.

Pachar

Natura Vive, (*see Ziplining, p. 45*)
Transparent sleeping capsules bolted onto
the side of a cliff high above the Urubamba
Valley.

Sacred Valley Brewing Company,
(*Cerveceria del Valle Sagrado*), at the
Pachar Bridge, tel. 984-553892, www.
sacredvalleybrewingcompany.com Four
standard beers and various seasonals.
Food available, party last Saturday of every
month. SPS.

Ollantaytambo (a.k.a. Ollanta)

Hotels.

Pakaritampu, Av. Ferrocarril 852, tel. 204020, www.pakaritampu.com Comfortable, well decorated hotel just minutes walking from the railroad station. Suite available. Organizes various tours.

El Albergue, entrance on railroad station platform. tel. 204014, www.elalbergue.com Delightful views, location, atmosphere. Sauna. Restaurant. Organic farm. Owned by longtime local residents and artists, the Randall-Weeks clan. Books and crafts for sale. Try Mama Wendy's *Matacuy*, or *Caña Alta* quality cane-botanical liquors from the adjacent *Destilería Andina*.

Apu Lodge, Laricalle s/n, tel. 436816, www.apulodge.com At the upper end of Laricalle, down a cobblestone street. Quiet area. All rooms have great views of ruins and town.

Picaflor Tambo Guest House, Laricalle 444, tel. 436758, www.picaflortambo.com Small, cozy, light-filled hotel on a small Inca street.

Las Orquídeas, Av. Ferrocarril 406, tel. 204032, tinyurl.com/ya2tyvcq Just outside the center on the way to the railroad station, Small, simple, pleasant.

Hostal Andean Moon, Calle del Medio s/n, tel. 204080, www.andeanmoonhostal.com Has a garden and beautiful rooftop views. Equipped with a jacuzzi. Sometimes noisy.

Full Moon Lodge, Esquina Cruz s/n, tel. 989-362031, http://fullmoonlodgeperu. com On the edge of town, access through a garden-tunnel. Garden with hammocks and fire pit. Inexpensive camping spots on Av. Estudiantil.

Casa de Wow, Patacalle 840, tel. 204010, www.casadewow.com Small B&B, great for groups and backpackers. View of ruins from some rooms. Shared kitchen. Organizes walking and cultural tours as well as *san pedro* excursions.

Hostal Andenes, Ventiderio s/n, tel. 436712, http://hostalandenes.com Large, centrally located hostal with reasonable prices.

Hostal Tambo, Calle Horno 409 (just off main square), tel. 984-489094, http:// hostaleltambo.com Pleasant low-end spot with bougainvillea-filled patio.

Restaurants.

Café Mayu, inside El Albergue Hotel *(see above)* Modern, european twist on Peruvian foods, using produce from their own organic garden. Reasonably priced. Try the brownies. Make a reservation. Excellent station platform coffee shop for visitors awaiting the Machu Picchu train.

Hearts Cafe, Av. Ventiderio s/n, tel. 436730 Casual café with vegan and vegetarian options. VO. SPS.

Piccolo Forno, Calle del Medio 120, tel. 984-736385 Friendly owner Mino serves good Italian food and a variety of pastries, sandwiches and energy bars. Craft beer.

La Esquina Cafe-Bakery, east side of Pl. de Armas, tel. 204078 Wide selection of dishes. Salad bowls, soups, burritos, sandwiches. Great pastries.

Coffee Tree, west side of Pl. de Armas, tel. 436734 Good for coffee but does a variety of food styles as well. Open breakfast to dinner. VO.

Doña Eva, Calle Ollantay, facing the market near the *colectivo* stop there. Inexpensive nosh, fixed menu and a la carte. Popular with locals.

Bars.

Exercise caution in local bars: drugging and sexual assaults against women have been reported. A reliable bar is:

Porfi's English Pub, east side of Pl. de Armas, tel. 950-309777 Serves English ale on tap and has drinks uncommon in Peru.

Shopping.

Awamaki, 618 Calle del Horno, tel. 436744, www.awamaki.org Local NGO works to empower women through weaving. Shop sells traditional weavings and more modern pieces. Arranges volunteer stays.

Choco Museo, a half block from the ruins, next to the artisan market, tel. 436753 All things chocolate; workshops.

Treks, Biking, Horses.

KB Tambo Tours, kbperu@hotmail.com, www.kbperu.com Horse rides, trekking and mountain biking, 1-10 day itineraries. Contact by email. (Similarly named tour agencies exist in Ollanta and Cusco – make sure you get the one you want.)

Hostal Tambo (see Hotels above) rents horses for trips to the quarries, Pumamarca and elsewhere. Reserve at least 24 hours in advance, more for large groups.

MACHU PICCHU AND SURROUNDINGS

Santa Teresa

While in town check out the Cocalmayo Hot Springs and the Cola de Mono, a six-section canyon zipline claiming to be the longest in South America (see Ziplining, p. 45).

Hotels.

EcoQuechua Lodge, tel. 630877, www.ecoquechua.com Just outside Santa Teresa. Offers various tours to Machu Picchu and other local attractions, plus massages. Good food and ambiance, friendly management.

Hostal Yacumama, Julio Tomás Rivas E7, tel. 984-274444, www.yacumamahotel.com Private baths and hot water. Restaurant. Sheltered from the noisy discotheques along the main drag.

Hospedaje El Sol, Av. Calixto Sánchez s/n, tel. 989-606591, https://hospedajesol.com Basic but clean, reliable rooms. All have private bathrooms and hot water. The ones facing the street can be a bit noisy from the bars.

Cocalmayo campgrounds, at the hot springs outside town, along the riverside dirt road heading north. Camping is included with the entrance fee to the springs. Be warned: the bugs are vicious.

Restaurants.

Mijuna Wasi, Av. Calixto Sanchez s/n Extensive offering of Peruvian and some international food for breakfast, lunch and dinner. Reliably good; friendly owners.

Aguas Calientes

A night spent at Aguas Calientes (confusingly, a.k.a Machu Picchu Pueblo) will allow you more time at Machu Picchu. The town is named for its hot springs; the pools are not that clean and the water is tepid. (There are nicer hot springs at Lares and Santa Teresa.) Open from 5am to 8pm, no nudes, swimsuits for rent all over town. Cleanest and least crowded in early morning. Another attraction is the Butterfly House, a 20-minute walk down the "Walking to the ruins" trail below, just before the campground. Displays and (Spanish only) tours of the over 100 local butterfly species. Visit in the morning, when the butterflies tend to be more active.

Buses to the Machu Picchu. Buses depart from *Av. Hermanos Ayar.* The ride lasts around half an hour. First bus leaves at 5:30am (expect a long line) and departures continue until early afternoon; last bus down leaves from Machu Picchu at 5:30pm. Tickets available next to the main bus stop. Buy in advance as things are hectic there during peak times. Tickets also available in Cusco from Consettur: **www.consettur.com**

Walking to Machu Picchu. Fit hikers can walk for the workout (about 1.5 hours) and to save money. Follow the road to Machu Picchu for roughly half an hour, cross the bridge, turn right down the lane leading to the Machu Picchu museum. Pick up the trailhead, marked by an obvious sign, shortly after the museum. A long flight of stone steps ascends the right side of the bus road, taking about an hour.

Hotels.

There are hundreds of hotels and cheap hostels to choose from, but that wasn't always the case. See the Exploring Cusco Museum **www.peterfrost.org** for the transformation since 1979.

Inkaterra Machu Picchu Pueblo Hotel, www.inkaterra.com *The* fancy hotel: bungalow accommodations, lovely grounds, superb birdwatching and orchid garden, but slightly isolated at one end of the town.

Inkaterra El MaPi, Av. Pachacutec 109, www.inkaterra.com A more affordable yet still luxurious alternative to the above. Made from recycled and restored materials.

Tierra Viva Machu Picchu Hotel, Av. Hermanos Ayar 401, tel. 211201, www.tierravivahoteles.com Located in a quiet area but still close to the plaza. Elevator beautifully decorated with Andean scenes.

Hostal Presidente, Av. Imperio de los Incas 127, at the old railroad station, tel. 211034 www.hostalpresidente.com A small, comfortable place with private bathrooms.

Gringo Bill's, Colla Raymi 104, tel. 211046, www.gringobills.com Up town a little, the locally renowned, homey, 28-room place. Good restaurant.

Rupa Wasi, Huanacaure 105, tel. 211101, www.rupawasi.net Five beautiful, clean wooden rooms. CV. Affiliated with the Tree House restaurant.

Supertramp, Chaskatika 203, tel. 435830, www.supertramphostel.com Dorms, bar, restaurant. Wild murals cover the walls. Great for budget backpackers.

Jardines de Mandor, Railway Km. 114, tel. 634429, www.jardinesdemandor.com Located 3.5km (2.2mi) outside of town near the eponymous waterfall. Inexpensive campsites plus a cottage. SPS.

Municipal campsite, 20-minute walk downhill from the center, near the butterfly house. Good for one night's stay; bugs can be vicious.

Restaurants.

El Indio Felíz, Lloque Yupanqui 103, tel. 211090 Tastelessly named, but otherwise tasty. Peruvian/French owner/chef; *trés bon.* The second floor is a good place to wait for your train.

The Tree House, Huanacaure 105, tel. 435849 Attached to Rupa Wasi hotel. Fusion of Asian, Italian and Peruvian flavors.

Chullpi, Av. Imperio de los Incas 140, tel. 211350 Peruvian fusion food in a comfortable atmosphere.

Ayasqa, Av. Hermanos Ayar 401, tel. 984-022706 Good Peruvian food in a nice setting

Disco/Bar: Wasicha Pub, tel. 984-754621

Machu Picchu Ruins

Machu Picchu Sanctuary Lodge, tel. 984-816956 , www.sanctuarylodgehotel. com Located right beside the ruins, and the only place to stay at Machu Picchu itself. Comfortable and convenient, with expensive and often hard-to-get rooms. Reservation essential. The hotel operates the public cafeteria adjacent to the ruins, serving a good, but expensive buffet lunch.

THE HIGH PLATEAU NORTHWEST OF CUSCO

Chinchero
Hotels.

La Casa de Barro, Miraflores 147, tel. 306031, www.lacasadebarro.com Best hotel in town. Family-run, built of adobe. Rooms are airy and beautifully decorated, all with private bathrooms. Campsites. Restaurant. Arranges adventure and *ayahuasca/san pedro* tours.

Hostal Mi Piuray, Jr. Garcilazo 187, tel. 306029 Colonial-style house built around a beautiful central courtyard. Rooms are small with low ceilings but clean. Hot water, wifi, breakfast included. Calm, quiet location.

Shopping.

The handcraft market is in the plaza in front of the church near the ruins. There are many textile centers on *Av. Garcilazo*, plus:

Centre for Traditional Textiles, *Manzanares s/n* (just south of the large produce market), tel. 306014, www. textilescusco.org A weaving association and small museum, daily 8:30am-4pm. Weaving demonstrations, courses, and textiles for sale. The museum is a replica of a mid-century rural house and shows how the residents of Chinchero lived then.

Cerámicas Callañaupa, Av. Garcilazo 150, tel. 954-667885 Beautiful bowls, plates, traditional *keros* mugs, paintings and rooftop bulls (*see p.96*) for sale.

Maras / Moray

There are basic hostels and restaurants in Maras, but nothing in Moray.

Limatambo

Andean Spirit Lodge, tel. 984-763109, www.andeanspiritlodge.com A secluded retreat center offering yoga retreats, vegetarian food from their garden, and local day trips, including the condor viewing point at Chonta. SPS.

VALLEY ROAD SOUTHEAST

Southern Cusco

Restaurant El Vallecito, road between San Jerónimo and Paruro, Km 2.5, tel. 984-667575 Traditional *Cusqueño* food. Quite meaty. Open weekends and holidays. Lunch only.

Saylla

La Hacienda del Tio Juan, Cconopata, Saylla, tel. 974-791145, tinyurl.com/ycw3ha5x Traditional *Cusqueño* food with a few fish-based northern Peruvian dishes. Turn right after Saylla police station, just before Primax gas station, then look for a sign to your right. Open weekends and holidays, lunch only.

Lucre

Quinta Lucre, Lucre, 27 de Noviembre s/n, tel. 957-639353, www.quintalucre.com Traditional *Cusqueño* food in a garden. Open for lunch weekends and holidays.

Andahuaylillas and Huaro

The map in the main plaza in Andahuaylillas shows the locations of all the following recommendations, except the ones in Huaro. The restaurants **Chiri Q'oncha**, **Sumaq'Cha** and **La Guille** serve traditional food and all have been suggested.

Casa Campo, Cusco 911 (turnoff immediately after bridge into town, marked by a sign), tel. 984-115620, www.casacampoandahuaylillas.com A combined hotel/restaurant with an ecological concept: the food, toiletries and construction materials come as much as possible from local materials. Run by the lovely and attentive Solaligue family. Reservation only.

El Nogal, Pl. de Armas s/n, tel. 977-222727 Small rooms but clean and cozy. One faces the plaza and has a balcony. Attached restaurant.

Aventura Andina, 1km (0.6mi) south of Andahuaylillas, tel. 984-162510, www.aventurandina.com Hotel/restaurant

combination, with 23 beds and rooms from 2-4 people. Arranges tours of local churches and archaeological sites, plus mountain bike excursions.

Casa Retiro, in Huaro, Bolevar 172, tel. 984-942576 A meditation retreat with 70 beds, a central garden with inspirational mantras, and a guest kitchen. Offers plant medicine and energy work. Reservation only.

El Huerto del Ukumari, in Huaro, San Martin s/n, immediately after the bridge into town, tel. 984-990264 Traditional Peruvian and regional food and homemade ice cream. VO. Produce comes mostly from their own gardens. Open weekends for lunch.

Sicuani

Many basic hostels and restaurants are clustered in the center on the noisy *Av. Arequipa*. For something more pleasant, try:

Hotel Wilkamayu, Av. Confederación 420, tel. 312151, www.wilkamayuhotel.com An attractive colonial family home and centered around a small garden, with a restaurant and 23 rooms ranging from one to five people. Decorated with old phones, typewriters, gramophones and local artifacts. Arranges tours to the nearby sites of Q'eswachaka, Raqchi and Machu Pitumarca.

VILCABAMBA REGION

Quillabamba

Hotel Quillabamba, Av. Prolongación Miguel Grau 590, tel. 282887, www.hotelquillabamba.com

Zeus Hotel, crnr of Dos de Mayo and Espinar, tel. 281720, www.quillabambazeushotel.com

Huancacalle

Hospedaje Sixpac Manco, tel. 971-823855, Sponsored by explorer Vincent Lee and friends and run by the Cobos family. Clean, inexpensive, friendly, and warm showers.

Cachora

Casa de Salcantay, tel. 984-281171, www.salcantay.com Beds for up to 25 in well-maintained rooms. Dutch/Peruvian owners can help organize treks.

Casa Nostra, tel. 958-349949, www.choquequiraotrekk.com Organizes treks to Choquequirao and northwards. Premises are sustainably constructed with adobe and eucalyptus.

Huanipaca

Villa los Loros, 17km (10.6mi) out of town, tel. 244552, www.choquequiraolodge.com Rustic, cozy lodge with a restaurant and beds for up to 20 people. Can arrange treks to Choquequirao and further afield. Picks up clients from Cusco or Abancay.

SOUTHERN PERUVIAN AMAZON

In southeastern Peru, the rich volcanic soils of the region plus the extreme altitude gradient of the eastern slope of the Andes have created an extraordinary variety of rainforest habitats within a relatively small area, harboring unparalleled biodiversity. Two main areas can be visited from Cusco: Manu and Tambopata. The area is confusing and good maps can be hard to find; check **www.peterfrost.org** for maps and further recommendations.

Manu

The Manu Biosphere Reserve is one of the major conservation units of South America, encompassing the complete drainage of the Manu River. Manu is isolated and difficult to get to and consequently is not the most economical rainforest destination; it is, however, one of the best, and although Amazonian wildlife is difficult to observe, Manu provides your best opportunity. It is home to much wildlife that has been exterminated or is extremely difficult to see in other parts of the Amazon, including 14 species of primate (the highest count for any one locality in the Americas), and all four of the top Amazon predators: the jaguar, the giant otter, the harpy eagle and the black caiman.

Tambopata

This region lies upstream from Puerto Maldonado, where the Tambopata River joins the Madre de Dios. Biodiversity is tremendous and it is more accessible than Manu (though human impact has been greater here), with daily scheduled jet flights and buses from the TT from Cusco to Puerto Maldonado, and a shorter river journey once you are there. Various tourist lodges are located along the river. Generally, the further these are from Pto. Maldonado, the less human presence and the better the wildlife viewing.

CHAPTER ONE

THE CITY OF CUSCO
Where Four Quarters Met

CUSCO BEFORE THE CONQUEST

According to an Inca myth current at the time of the conquest, the founding Incas, Manco Capac and Mama Ocllo emerged from Lake Titicaca at the islands of the Sun and the Moon, sent to earth by the solar and lunar deities to bring culture to a barbarous world. From there they began a lengthy quest (about 500km/312mi if they took the shortest route over the La Raya Pass) which ended in a valley far to the north, at the spot where Manco probed with his golden staff, and the earth promptly swallowed it. Obeying this omen, they founded their civilization and the Inca city of Cusco here.

An alternative and somewhat contradictory myth of the Inca origins, also current at the time of the conquest, concerns a more complicated family – Manco Capac, the three Ayar brothers, and their wives. They emerged from three caves known as Tamputoco, at the mythical origin place of Pacarictambo (Lodging-house of the Dawn), south of Cusco (see *Maukallacta, p.293*). One of the brothers, Ayar Cachi, was so violent and wild that he destroyed entire mountains with his sling-shots. For safety's sake the rest of the family lured him back into his cave and entombed him there. There he remains to this day, causing occasional earthquakes with his struggles. God forbid he should ever get loose. (Some would argue that he *has* got loose, but that's another story.) His wife, Mama Waco, an early feminist, remained free and later more or less single-handedly conquered a town in the Cusco Valley, terrifying its inhabitants by ripping the lungs out of one warrior's body and blowing them up like balloons. Of the remaining brothers, one grew wings and flew off into the sun, another turned into a stone on the mountain of Wanacauri, which became one of the most sacred Inca wacas, and the last, Manco Capac, inherited all the wives and reached Cusco to found the Inca empire.

Modern archaeology suggests that the Titicaca myth may be closer in spirit to the truth, since the evidence suggests that the Incas established their hegemony in the region by peaceful means (*see next page*). Cusco began to dominate its neighbors as early as 1100 AD, and these proto-Incas eventually established political influence and a pattern of peaceful regional exchange.

The Inca claim to have replaced barbarism with civilization is often dismissed as mere imperial propaganda, but the archaeological record in this part of the Andes suggests more than a grain of truth to it. The rise of the Incas in the Cusco Valley spared this area the centuries of brutal rivalry, tribalist fragmentation and constant warfare that enveloped the rest of the region in a sort of Andean Dark Age after the collapse of the Tiwanaku and Wari civilizations, around 1000 A.D. (During the following centuries, for example, some areas north of Cusco show evidence of something like 50% of all deaths resulting from violence.) Under such circumstances the Cusco option – exchanging fully autonomous misery for Inca rule with peace and security – may well have been an offer many peoples didn't even want to refuse. However, when Inca expansion began to reach more distant regions where stable and sophisticated societies such as the Nazca and Chimu had endured, the local rulers doubtless took exception to that excuse for an Inca takeover of their territory. In some cases the locals were able to negotiate semi-autonomous political arrangements with Cusco, in others it meant war.

CUSCO BEFORE THE EMPIRE
Archaeology Rebuts a Legend

Accounts distilled from the oral histories of the Spanish conquest tell us that the Inca expansion began suddenly in 1438, as if from nowhere, when the man later known as Pachacuti rallied the divided ethnic groups of the region against a common enemy, the Chancas, who were invading in force from the northwest. Before this, Cusco was just one more Andean village at war with its neighbors during an extended period of regional conflict which began after the fall of the Wari and Tiwanaku civilizations, c. A.D. 1000.

According to the legend, Pachacuti defeated the Chancas, reorganized the Cusco region, built a new imperial capital, and went on to unite a vast area under Inca hegemony, a task continued by his son Topa Inca. Thus *Tawantinsuyu* – the empire of the Four Quarters – was born.

This version of events suggests that Tawantinsuyu was less than one hundred years old when it was overthrown by the Spaniards, in 1532. When we contemplate the enormous complex of roads, agricultural terraces and monumental structures in the Cusco region alone, and calculate the time and manpower required to build it, this chronology seems to require a mind-bending suspension of disbelief.

Fortunately, recent archaeological work has shattered this traditional view, revealing, for example, that people living as far as 60km (38mi) away from Cusco were under the control of the Incas for several centuries. Furthermore, these groups were incorporated into the early Inca state through peaceful means rather than military conquest. Archaeological survey work conducted across the greater Cusco region indicates that incipient state formation began as early as 1100 AD – more than three hundred years before the Chanca War! From this early period onwards there was a gradual consolidation and centralization of social and economic power in Cusco. Archaeological work indicates that the period of early state development in the Cusco region (AD 1100-1400) was characterized by widespread regional exchange, rather than being a time of regional conflict. Recent research has also revealed that the Incas, rather than competing with other ethnic groups, already dominated the local social and political organizations during this early time period, and that Cusco was already the center of economic influence in the region.

Some event indeed took place around 1438 to launch the Incas under Pachacuti on their career of Imperial expansion, but it was preceded by centuries of regional consolidation over a much wider area, and involving many more ethnic groups, than was previously believed. It is clear that our understanding of Inca history, and the growth of their empire, is still in its infancy.

— Brian Bauer

The peaceful era of Cusco's dominion came to an abrupt end around 1438, after Cusco was attacked from the north by a group of tribes called the Chancas. Rallied from near-defeat by a son of the reigning Inca king Wiracocha, the militarily unprepared inhabitants of Cusco triumphed. The very stones of the mountainsides were said to have sprung to life and fought on the Inca side. This son seized power from his father and took the title Pachacuti, meaning "Shaker (or Transformer) of the Earth" (*see p. 69*). Thereafter, Pachacuti is credited with an astonishing series of accomplishments: the complete rebuilding of Cusco in the distinct and impressive masonry style whose remains are so admired today; the building of Sacsaywaman, Ollantaytambo, Machu Picchu, Pisac and other sites; the form of worship; the system of government and land tenure.

Pachacuti may also have been the proponent of a new official Titicaca origin myth of the Incas, deploying it to legitimize Inca control in the Titicaca region, which was an early target of Inca expansion and an extremely important pilgrimage center. The myth also established an extraordinary relationship between the Inca and his people: he was divinely descended from the Sun; the Coya, his queen (who was also his sister), was in turn the daughter of the Moon. Thus the Inca's power was as absolute and unchallengeable as that of any ruler in history. To rebel was to defy a god. This paradigm was the foundation of Inca political legitimacy, and similar politico-religious strategies were evidently also at work in some earlier Andean dynasties and civilizations.

Pachacuti's son Topa Inca carried on his father's work, pushing the frontiers of the empire into modern Ecuador, Bolivia, Argentina and Chile. A combination of techniques sustained this expansion. Military conquest played a part, but so did skillful diplomacy – some of the most important territories were allied chiefdoms with considerable autonomy, rather than being totally subordinate domains. Chincha, for example, a coastal state which virtually monopolized maritime trade, was treated with great caution and respect.

The empire's lifeblood was *ayni*, the practice of reciprocity: ritual generosity and favors to local rulers on a huge scale, in exchange for loyalty, labor and military levies, wives and concubines for the Inca nobility, specialized regional products, and so on. The emperor maintained fabulous stores of sumptuary goods – the "art" for which the Andean region is justly famous – to meet his ritual obligations and create new alliances.

By the time Topa's son Wayna Capac came to power the empire had perhaps already overreached itself with military campaigns on the frontiers of modern Ecuador and Colombia, and at Wayna Capac's death during an epidemic it was beginning to fragment. A disastrous civil war broke out between factions of the north and south headed by two of Wayna Capac's sons, Atawallpa and Wascar. After years of strife, the northern faction under Atawallpa prevailed. Given a few more years, Atawallpa, a strong if rather ferocious leader, would probably have succeeded in re-unifying the empire. But by then the barbarians were at the gates.

Suspect Sources

The dynastic story of Pachacuti and his sons is the widely accepted version of Inca history. But unfortunately, certain details only hold up if we ignore numerous contradictory and puzzling references in the Spanish chronicles of the conquest. In truth, we have no clear cut Inca history, and there are various reasons for this. First and foremost, the Andean peoples had no written language or codices; history and most other cultural information was transmitted orally. Thus, when the Spanish chroniclers collected information from the vanquished Incas, they conducted interviews. Most of these Spaniards spoke Quechua poorly, if at all, and their information was often distorted by the poor quality and the personal agendas of native interpreters. Moreover, their informants were often desperate, for reasons of survival, to ingratiate themselves with their interrogators. And, since the Spanish arrived at the end of a fratricidal civil war, they would inevitably hear many conflicting versions of the Inca rulers.

Finally, we have to consider that the Spanish chroniclers were viewing the affairs of a culture vastly different from their own through the narrow optic of crusading medieval Christians, who had recently driven the last of the heathen Moors out of the Iberian peninsula and were inclined to view the native Peruvians simply as more of the same.

Modern structuralist ethnohistorians, exemplified by the late R.T. Zuidema of the University of Illinois, propose an interpretation of the chronicles which replaces the Inca dynastic succession with a sort of mythic saga of the royal *panacas* (lineages) of Inca Cusco. In this view Pachacuti himself may or may not have been a historical individual, but in any case he was primarily an archetype, embodying the deeds, attributes, functions and achievements of his *panaca*. These ethnohistorians are saying, in effect, that nothing is truly known about Inca history prior to 1532.

With uncertainties as profound as these prevailing among the experts, the story of the Incas told to visitors is often highly impressionistic and adorned with the biases and personal obsessions of the teller. Your local tour guide can get away with murder, and often does.

So be aware: the account you are reading is *The Only True One!*

Just kidding.

PACHACUTI

Pachacuti (sometimes spelled "Pachacutec") was the warrior-king who launched the Inca expansion around 1438. He was not initially chosen to be the supreme Inca, but when the Cusco region was threatened with invasion by the Chancas from the north, he wrested power from his brother, Inca Urcon, and his father, Inca Wiracocha – who were preparing to flee rather than fight – and rallied the Incas against their enemies. In two legendary battles he smashed the Chanca threat and began the expansion that transformed the Incas from a regional power into an empire.

This is, of course, "mytho-history", passed on to 16th-century Spanish chroniclers who wrote it down by the victorious *panaca* in this power struggle, but there is no doubt that Pachacuti was a towering figure in the story of the Incas. His name was in fact a title, meaning "Transformer of the Earth," or "He Who Overturns Space and Time." His impact on the Andean world was such that he fully earned this sobriquet. He has been compared to Alexander the Great and Charlemagne as one of the great conquering statesmen of history.

He was more than simply a warrior: he is credited with founding the basic systems of government and administration by which the Inca empire was ruled. All of the famous monuments of the Incas were built, or at least started, during his reign: Sacsaywaman, Pisac, Ollantaytambo, and the rebuilding of the Inca city of Cusco itself. Machu Picchu and the Inca Trail, too, seem to have been a personal project of his. Pachacuti is also credited with establishing sun-worship as a pan-Andean religion within a framework of cultural and religious diversity that allowed considerable local autonomy.

During the controversial time of the 500th anniversary of Columbus's landing in America, the mayor and municipal authorities of Cusco responded to Spain's sanitized "Meeting-of-Two-Cultures" narrative of the Spanish Conquest by building a monument to Pachacuti, which today towers over the lower end of the city, about halfway between the center and the airport.

The Pachacuti tower, with its huge bronze statue, is open to the public (entry by BTC). Its faux-Inca stonework – a medley of incompatible styles – raises purist eyebrows, but the panorama of the city and its surroundings from the tower is excellent.

– P. F.

CUSCO AND THE CONQUEST

The first Spaniards to see Cusco were three ruffians sent from Cajamarca by Pizarro early in 1533 to speed up the collection of treasure for Atawallpa's ransom. They came and went, leaving posterity no word of their reactions. Not long afterwards, literate Spaniards arrived and were hugely impressed by the great structures of Cusco. "We can assure your Majesty that it is so beautiful and has such fine buildings that it would be remarkable even in Spain," wrote an early chronicler. The Spaniards arrived as allies to the Cusco-based faction of the Inca civil war, and for a while they had the run of the city. They passed the time looting, extorting treasure and abusing the natives, leaving most of Cusco's buildings undisturbed for more than two years after Francisco Pizarro's triumphant entry on November 8, 1533. But then a much abused native, Pizarro's puppet Inca, Manco II, escaped and returned – puppet no more – leading a massive army of between 100,000 and 200,000 Indians against the Spanish.

Thus began the six-month siege of Cusco – and thus also began the destruction of the Inca city. On May 6, 1536, Manco launched his main attack on the trapped Spaniards. The Indians used slingshots to rain red-hot stones on the city. "They set fire to the whole of Cusco simultaneously and it all burned in one day, for the roofs were thatch," wrote the chronicler Cristobal de Molina. The Spaniards – bottled up in the Inca armory of Suntur Wasi where the chapel of El Triunfo now stands – survived to break out and put down the rebellion (see p.114). But the glorious Imperial City was left a smoking ruin.

Manco withdrew to Ollantaytambo. Hernando Pizarro and his forces attacked him there, but the subsequent battle ended badly for the Spanish (*see p.171*). Nevertheless, they kept up the pressure, and the Inca decided to abandon this stronghold for the remote mountains of Vilcabamba, where he and later his sons survived as a rebel state for nearly 35 years before their final defeat in 1572 (*see p.295*).

One of the puzzles of the Conquest is how a ragtag vanguard of 168 Spaniards managed to overthrow a highly organized empire of many millions. Granted, the Spaniards were battle-hardened veterans of European wars, wielding military technologies vastly superior to anything the natives had, but victory against such odds requires some explaining.

The Spaniards arrived in Peru with such exquisite timing that their priests saw the hand of God at work in it. Some five years previously the Incas had been weakened by an epidemic that took many thousands of lives, including that of the emperor Wayna Capac and his chosen heir. This emperor had established his court at a new northern capital in what is now the city of Cuenca in Ecuador, setting the scene for the rivalry that erupted upon his death between the northern Incas of Tomebamba and the southern faction of Cusco, each with their respective candidates for the Inca rulership: Atawallpa and Wascar. The resulting war of succession was long, bitter and bloody, and left the Incas weakened and divided after it ended with the victory of the northern Inca, Atawallpa. His victory was so recent that, though his troops had taken Cusco, the victorious new emperor was still on his way there, pausing for a fast and ceremonies at the hot springs of Cajamarca in northern Peru. This was the moment when strange news reached the highlands: weirdly-dressed, hairy men accompanied by outlandish beasts had landed on the shores of the empire...

The numerical insignificance of the Spaniards may even have worked to their advantage. Atawallpa had an army of tens of thousands with him at the northern Peruvian highland city of Cajamarca, and it must have been simply inconceivable to him that this tiny handful of men could pose a threat. So he let them march into the Andes, where they subsequently tricked him, ambushed him, captured him, held him hostage for a fantastic ransom (duly paid), and finally killed him. It's a famous story, admirably told, as is so much else, in John Hemming's *The Conquest of the Incas (see Bibliography)*. After the killing of Atawallpa the Conquest played out in several chapters, but the Incas never recovered. The Spaniards always kept them off balance by exploiting the bitter enmities of the civil war, playing different factions against each other such that the Incas could never form a united front to defeat them, though Manco Inca's rebellion initially came close. Divide-and-conquer was the vital ingredient of Spanish victory.

After the Conquest, the Spanish began to rework Cusco to their liking. Despite the enthusiasm of some chroniclers and conquistadors for Inca architecture – some even built their mansions in the Inca masonry style – the buildings and streets did not generally suit Spanish taste. Moreover, evidence that the Inca civilization was highly advanced provoked discomfort among the Spaniards and complicated the task of justifying its destruction. And so the dismantling of Inca Cusco began soon after Manco's rebellion. Inca cut stones were re-used higgledy-piggledy in new construction, while the buildings of Sacsaywaman served as a public stone quarry.

For a few decades after the Conquest, Cusco remained the main city of Peru. It became the focus of conflict during the civil wars between Pizarro's men and a faction led by Diego de Almagro, as the conquerors fought among themselves over the spoils of victory. It was also the headquarters of the Spanish campaign against the last desperate resistance of the Inca Manco and his successors, in their mountain-ringed refuge of Vilcabamba northwest of Cusco.

But in 1535 Pizarro founded a new capital at Lima on the coast. Other new cities rose: Trujillo, Arequipa. The focus of power shifted to Lima, and the focus of wealth moved to the fabulous silver deposits which had been discovered at Potosí, hundreds of miles to the south in modern Bolivia. There was no more loot to be had in Cusco; even the silver route from Potosí had passed it by. Gradually the city faded into relative obscurity.

Events, natural and political, shook Cusco out of its torpor occasionally during the long centuries of eclipse. In 1650 a violent earthquake transformed many of the fine colonial buildings into heaps of rubble. The Inca walls and foundations stood firm. In 1780 the Cusco region came to the shocked attention of the Spanish crown as the scene of an Indian uprising led by the mestizo rebel Tupac Amaru II. The insurrection came closer to succeeding than any indigenous movement since Manco Inca's rebellion, but it was ultimately crushed. Tupac Amaru II himself was put horribly to death in the main square of Cusco, as commemorated by the two plaques there (*see p.89*). Three decades later there were a couple of premature, abortive creole uprisings against the Spanish, two tremors among the early rumblings of Independence from Spain that were being felt across the continent. But those great political convulsions of the 1820s largely passed Cusco by. Another violent earthquake shook the city in May of 1950. Once again many post-Inca buildings came tumbling down; once again the Inca structures held fast.

Now Cusco was beginning to emerge from the long years of provincial obscurity. In 1948, Hiram Bingham, scientific discoverer of Machu Picchu, had inaugurated a new road built from the Urubamba River up to the dizzying ridge where the ruins of the Incas' lost city are perched. Overseas visitors began to arrive in Cusco, drawn by the mysterious ruins and intriguing customs of the Incas and their modern descendants – creating a momentum which has continued to build ever since.

Cusco itself has become one of the symbols of a new nationalism and a recovered pride in the greatness of Peru's pre-Hispanic heritage. The Peruvian government has channeled millions of dollars into conservation and restoration of archaeological and colonial monuments, better roads and transport services, and new hotels. This has been part of a plan sponsored by UNESCO, which has declared Cusco a World Heritage site.

THE INCA LEGACY

The Incas built an empire comparable in size to the western Roman empire, stretching from southern Colombia to the Rio Maule in southern Chile; bounded in the east by the Amazon forests, in the west by the Pacific Ocean. Like the Romans, they built their empire largely on the achievements of earlier civilizations. They inherited the accumulated culture and knowledge of more than four thousand years of continuous civilization in Peru, which started around 3000 B.C., with the early pre-ceramic textile-making and pyramid-building cultures of the coast, such as Waca Prieta and Caral, whose ruins survive on the Chicama and Supe rivers. Every major technical development of the Andes had already occurred before the rise of the Incas: cultivation of potatoes and high-altitude maize, domestication of animals, metallurgy, irrigation, stoneworking, and so on. The Incas took these achievements and refined them – creating better bronze alloys and improving the *quipu* record keeping system, for example – and added their uniquely effective style of statecraft, which included an extraordinary ability to mobilize and rule millions of people over an enormous area of land. They created a powerful cultural synthesis within a strong centralized state, building a pan-Andean, Quechua-speaking culture, whose roots live on tenaciously to this day, though stem and branch have long since been hacked down.

It is worth reminding ourselves that the Incas, and the millenia of Andean culture that preceded them, represent a significant event in human history. If left alone, they perhaps would have developed into a unique society, as distinct from Europe as China. Yet their civilization was brought to an abrupt end, and little of what they created has entered the mainstream of human culture because they were overwhelmed by a race that was blind to all but the material aspects of their world. But much of what sustained Andean civilization was not material, and the spirit of that ancient way lives on in the hearts and customs of the millions of native inhabitants of the Andes. In this sense it is possible after all that we have not heard the last of the Incas.

CUSCO: THE LAY OF THE LAND

The Inca empire was called *Tawantinsuyu* – the "Four Quarters of the Earth." Cusco was the heart of it, and its exact center was considered to be the main square of the city. To the north lay the *Chinchaysuyu* – northern Peru and modern Ecuador, plus Pasto in southern Colombia; west lay the *Contisuyu* –

the south-central coast regions; south lay the *Collasuyu* – the altiplano of southern Peru, half of Chile, the Bolivian highlands and northwest Argentina; and east the *Antisuyu* – the unconquered Amazon jungle. From the name of the inhabitants of this region – "Antis" – we get the Spanish word Andes.

Most of Cusco's Inca settlement was clustered on the ridge between the Tullumayo and Saphi rivers. Its tightly-thatched and steeply-pitched roofs gave the buildings an almost spired look. The streets were narrow stone alleys between high walls enclosing courtyards the size of city blocks, where few doorways broke through the long stretches of impeccably-laid stone. Springs and reservoirs in the hills fed water channels which flowed everywhere, bursting to the surface in countless sparkling fountains. The austerity of the stone compounds was softened by crops and flowers growing on scores of watered cultivation terraces which penetrated the heart of the city.

Two huge squares straddled the Saphi River, encompassing the colonial Plaza de Armas, Plaza Regocijo, and a stretch of land that today is covered by buildings. These were the *Wacaypata* (a.k.a. *Aucaypata - see Walking Tour site 1 below*), now the main square, and the *Cusipata*. This latter stood west of the Saphi River, which was where the Inca state held its most spectacularly drunken festivities, and where there was also a barter market at certain times. Plaza Regocijo currently occupies part of the old Cusipata and even takes its name from it: both mean "Joyful Square" in Spanish and Quechua, respectively.

According to one Spanish source, Pachacuti's redesign of Cusco laid the city out in the form of a puma. This interpretation finds further support in some of the original street and district names, such as *Pumac Chupan*

75

(Puma's Tail), which are in the appropriate location for the mighty puma's body parts. The outlines of the scheme can, in fact, still be seen in the layout of the city center (see p. 79).The puma may have been Pachacuti's personal totem, but in any case it was certainly a symbol of warrior power.

Cusco was the most exalted public pilgrimage center of the Andes (Machu Picchu was much more private and exclusive), and so every ranking citizen of *Tawantinsuyu* tried to visit Cusco once in his lifetime.

Despite its importance, Cusco was not the largest city in the Inca empire. The Chimu capital of Chan Chan, near modern Trujillo, was bigger, as was the Inca northern administrative center of Huánuco Pampa, now an abandoned ruin on a desolate plateau in the central highlands. But access to Cusco was restricted and, perhaps to emphasize this point, all non-Incas had to leave the city once a year, in early September, while the Inca nobility performed the *sitwa*, a ritual cleansing ceremony.

Withal, it was a colorful and cosmopolitan place because thousands from regional nobilities with their families and retainers from all over the empire also lived there. Quechua was the *lingua franca*, but many other languages were spoken in the courtyards, and many varieties of clothing and headdress were worn in the streets.

Remembering that the Incas conceived their city in the shape of a puma, the best place for a good general view of the Cusco Valley is the animal's head: the cross at Sacsaywaman, *Cruz Moqo* (see p.118 for how to arrive). (*Cristo Blanco* gives most of this view if you don't have a BTC – see p.121 for the walk there.) As you face out over the city from this point, northeast is to your left. There stands Cristo Blanco, the statue of Christ the Redeemer.

The highest of the jagged peaks beyond Cristo Blanco is Pachatusan, which means Fulcrum, or Crossbeam, of the Universe. It is probably so named because it was considered a critical point on the horizon; viewed from the supremely important location of the Qoricancha, the Sun Temple, the sun rises directly behind this peak on the day of the winter solstice. To the right of the statue lies the broad valley of the Huatanay River, flowing toward its junction with the larger Vilcanota. This is the route to southern Peru and Bolivia – one of the Four Quarters of the Inca Empire known as the *Collasuyu*. There, too, lie the modern suburbs of Cusco, and the airport. The huge snowcapped peak visible beyond the valley on clear days is Ausangate (6,384m/20,945ft) in the Cordillera Vilcanota, about 100km (62mi) distant.

The cryptic "B.I.9" inscribed beneath *Viva el Peru* on the hill opposite stands for Infantry Battalion 9, the local army unit. The adjacent hill to the right bears the Peruvian national shield. These inscriptions can be considered as recent examples of an ancient Peruvian hill-writing tradition dating back to the Lines of Nazca on the Peruvian coast. However, in recent years the practice has gotten utterly out of hand. We now have political parties, schools, government ministries, police stations, and every Tomás, Ricardo or Enrique who feels like it, scratching the slogan of his choice over the Andean landscape. Once it was art, now it's an institutional ego-trip.

A little farther to the right (SSW) lies the Huancaro Valley, marked by a swathe of eucalyptus trees, that was once the route of the royal Inca highway to the *Contisuyu*, the western quarter of the empire. The route to the northern quarter – the *Chinchaysuyu* – ran up the hillside to the right, about due west across the defile of the river Saphi. This is now the route to Abancay and Ayacucho. The highest peak to be seen in the ranges lying in that direction is called Mama Simona. Directly behind you lie the ranges that separate Cusco from the Sacred Valley of the Incas. Pisac lies to the NE, in the direction of the old highway to the eastern quarter, the *Antisuyu*.

CUSCO CITY WALKING TOUR

Each entry in this section has a number referring to its location on the city map. For museum and church hours plus ticket information, see Museums, p. 49 and Churches, p. 50. It's about 4km (2.5mi) to the recommended halfway point (#18) and 6km (3.8mi) in total.

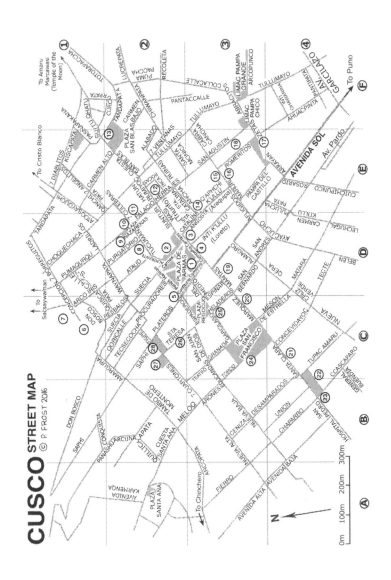

CUSCO STREET MAP

© P. FROST 2016

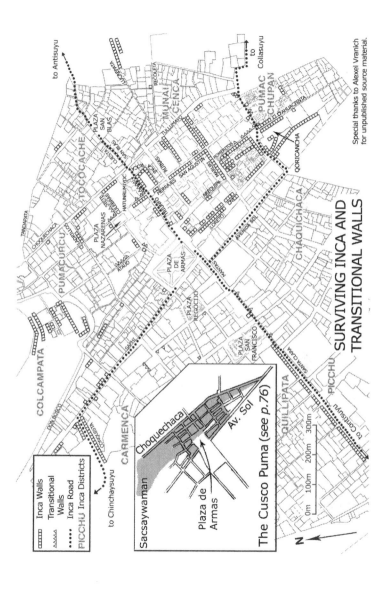

SURVIVING INCA AND TRANSITIONAL WALLS

Special thanks to Alexei Vranich for unpublished source material.

Inca Walls
Transitional Walls
Inca Road
PICCHU Inca Districts

The Cusco Puma (see p.76)

0m   100m   200m   300m

N

SPANISH WALLS BY INCA MASONS

According to the late archaeologist J.H. Rowe of U.C. Berkeley, much of what is normally taken to be Inca stonework in the city of Cusco is not so at all: it is transitional stonework done after the Conquest by native craftsmen in the service of Spanish masters. The Spanish thought well enough of Inca architecture to imitate aspects of the style in their own buildings.

Examples of this abound throughout the city center: the House of Serpents (10), the House of Valleumbroso (20), the House of Pumas (26), the north wall of *Hatunrumiyoc* street (E2), the east wall of *Romeritos* street (E3), and many others *(numbers refer to the city map, p. 78)*.

How do we distinguish Inca from transitional construction? Well, with rare exceptions, it is not Inca if: the wall is not battered (inclined inwards); there are different grades and colors of stone mixed in the same wall; a vertical joint is located directly above another (sloppy construction); or the height of the stone courses is irregular instead of diminishing progressively from bottom to top. And it very likely isn't Inca if the wall has motifs such as snakes and pumas carved in relief onto the stones.

Very few genuine Inca doorways, and none of the principal ones, have survived in Cusco. The best surviving Inca interior doorway is in the Qoricancha between the temple buildings on the west side of the interior courtyard. The best exterior doorway is a half block away at *Romeritos 402*. There is another at *Choquechaca 339*. The most important surviving Inca walls in the city center are at the Qoricancha, and on the streets of *Ahuacpinta* (F4), *Herrajes* (E2), *Hatunrumiyoc/Inca Roca* (E2), *Q'aphchik'ijllu (a.k.a. Pasaje Arequipa)* (E3), *Maruri* (E3), *San Agustin* (E3), *Santa Catalina Angosta* (D3) and inside Incanto restaurant there, and *Intik'ijllu (a.k.a Loreto)* (D3).

— P. F.

(1) The Main Square / Plaza de Armas

This square was originally more than twice its present size. It was divided in two parts by the river Saphi (which becomes the Huatanay), which now flows beneath the buildings on the west side of the square, opposite the Cathedral. Today's *Plaza de Armas* is the part that was once called the *Wacaypata*, the Weeping Square, so-called because of the mourning that supposedly took place there when a ruling Inca had died. It was flanked by the palaces of the Inca emperors, one of whom was alive, while the others were mummies, who nevertheless continued to preside over their family lineage and were consulted through mediums.

In Inca times this square featured a stone, covered with sheets of gold, known as the Stone of War, where offerings and ceremonies were made at the start of military adventures. This stone gave the square its other Inca name: *Aucaypata*, the Square of War, a kind of pun on its other name. There was also an *usnu*, an Inca tiered-platform used during ceremonies, topped by a rounded stone, shaped like a woman's breast and encrusted with gold and jewels. A channel carved around its base carried sacred libations away to the Huatanay River. From here, astronomers observed the position of the sunset in relation to stone towers on the western horizon.

This was the great civic square of the Incas, the site of solemn parades and great assemblies. Each territory conquered by the Incas had some of its soil taken to Cusco to be mingled symbolically with the soil of the *Wacaypata*, as a token of its incorporation into the empire. The square was reported to have been surfaced with white sand from the coast, mingled with numerous tiny ritual objects of gold, silver, coral, shells – an observation apparently confirmed by excavations under the main square conducted in 1996, which uncovered a set of four tiny llamas made of gold and shell. When the Spaniards began building their cathedral here in the late 1500s, the wily royal official and chronicler Polo de Ondegardo appropriated the sacredness of this sand to the new colonial order by having it mixed into the mortar of the cathedral masonry.

Later, converted into the Plaza de Armas in colonial times, the square witnessed many executions, including those of Tupac Amaru I, the last ruling Inca; the rebel conquistador Diego de Almagro the Younger; and Tupac Amaru II, the 18th-century Indian leader, along with his family.

(2) Chapel of Sagrada Familia, The Cathedral, and Chapel of El Triunfo

The NE side of the square is dominated by the complex of the *Sagrada Familia* (Holy Family) chapel, *The Cathedral*, and chapel of *El Triunfo* (The Triumph). All three of these sites are accessed through the ticket office located in the former. Audio tours are available with your entrance ticket (CRA), and guides can be hired. The *Sagrada Familia* is the newest of the three, built between 1723 and 1735, and is a fine example of the French-influenced neo-classical architecture that appeared in the Americas when Bourbons replaced Hapsburgs on the Spanish throne. The first altar on your right is classical baroque style, while the one to the left is the more playful rococo. Two altars further on are covered in mirrors, a decoration which to Andeans didn't represent vanity but rather brightness and a reflection of one's behavior. The huge baroque altar at the back is cedar and alder covered in pure gold leaf, not paint. In the painting left of this main altar the Virgin's robes form the shape of a mountain, a typical native linkage of Christian image and mountain-worshipping sensibilities of the Andes.

The *Cathedral* is the largest and most impressive of the three churches at 4,000m^2 (43,000ft^2) with five naves, 11 chapels and seven altars. It is built on the site of *Quiswarcancha*, generally thought to have been the Inca Wiracocha's palace, although J.H. Rowe suggested that this building was a huge *kallanka* assembly hall. Construction began in 1559 and was not completed until nearly 100 years later. The builders heedlessly filled in the subterranean Inca drainage channels, leading to major flooding problems during construction. The building was barely finished when the massive earthquake of 1650 severely damaged it, forcing 14 years of remodeling and reconstruction. The Cathedral contains nearly 400 colonial paintings, including many from the Cusco school, which flourished in the 17th century. During that period, Cusco painters supplied religious art to the whole of Spanish America. Throughout the Cathedral, there are plenty of local idiosyncrasies and smuggled Andean symbolism to look for from the Cusco school; the following tour points out the best known ones.

The Cathedral walking tour starts at the entrance from the Sagrada Familia and goes counterclockwise around the perimeter; imagine that your starting point is six o'clock and that the entrance to El Triunfo across the main nave is 12 o'clock. After passing through the great door between the Sagrada Familia and the Cathedral, look back at the paintings around the doorway. These are scenes from the life of the Virgin by Marcos Zapata, one of the most famous of the Cusco school painters, known for his fondness for blue-and-red dominated color schemes. In the *Capilla de la Virgen Inmaculada,* the first chapel on your right, a painting on the left side of its altar depicts a noticeably pregnant Virgin Mary, a detail unheard of in European religious art. The Virgin of Almudena is seen in her painting (outer wall of the choir, directly across from the *Capilla de San Jose* at about 5 o'clock) showering wheat from her dress down on the Christians of Madrid, under siege by the Moors. She is brazenly draped with a golden serpent, hardly a benign motif in Christianity, but a symbol of wisdom and femininity to indigenous Andeans.

In the *Capilla de Santiago de Compostela* (third from the entrance), on the right wall is a historically interesting painting of the Cusco earthquake of 1650, which severely damaged most of the colonial (but not Inca) construction in the city. The colonial Cusco that we see today was largely built after that date, and its artistic sponsor and inspiration was Manuel Mollinedo y Angulo, archbishop of Cusco from 1673-1699. This cleric was a wealthy art lover and patron from Madrid, who donated much of his fortune to the rebuilding of Cusco and sponsored the famous local artists, Diego Quispe Titu, and Tomás Tuirutupa. He was fond of Cusco's Corpus Christi festival and helped to make it famous. He features in several Cusco paintings, one in the Cathedral and two in the Museum of Religious Art (*see p.93*).

The painting on the back wall of this chapel portrays Saint James, patron of the Spanish armies, as a mounted warrior slaying Inca foot soldiers — probably a reference to the Spanish defeat of Manco Inca's rebellion. On the left here we see an Andean Crucifixion scene with Christ wearing a long skirt, a reflexive resort to sumptuous textiles from a people whose millennial weaving traditions insist that a god, no matter what the circumstances, be adequately draped.

An unassuming egg-shaped stone about 60cm (2ft) high sits to the right of the main Cathedral entrance doors (three o'clock on your imaginary clock face). This carved stone is said to represent the Inca creator god Wiracocha, who was sometimes depicted in the form of an egg, and is considered by some locals to be one of the holiest surviving Inca relics in the city. The stone has a checkered recent history, having been sequestered for a time by church authorities, who noticed that it was being surreptitiously venerated under cover of devotion to an adjacent Virgin. It then reappeared in its current, less prominent position, at first alone and unadorned; later quarantined in a glass case; most recently open again, but behind a rope. Despite these attempts made to isolate and desanctify it, the stone always seems to be surrounded by offerings of flowers or coca leaves.

On the highest wall arches perpendicular to the main doors are two paintings by Marcos Zapata showing the victory of heavenly hosts over demons. The one on the right shows an elephant trampling a medieval dragon, neither of which (one suspects) the painter ever saw; in the one opposite, across the main nave, a Narcissus-like figure vainly gazing at his reflection in a pool is believed to represent the painter himself — a sort of self-mocking artist's signature from a time when paintings were rarely signed.

Around the corner, at about 2 o'clock, is the painting of the Virgin of Belen on the outer wall of the choir. This painting tells the story of the eponymous statue, which fishermen discovered floating in a box off the coast of Peru with a note saying it was destined for Cusco. The statue ended up in the Church of Our Lady of Belen, on the western edge of Cusco, and is credited with many miracles. Bishop Mollinedo y Angulo features prominently (left foreground, kneeling) in the painting.

One of the Cathedral's great treasures is the *Señor de los Temblores* (Lord of the Earthquakes – in the chapel right of the entrance to El Triunfo) – whose statue supposedly calmed the aftershocks of the 1650 earthquake. The image's black color is not original: it comes from the long-term buildup of soot from candles and oil lamps, plus the pollen from the flowers cast upon it during its annual procession. He is set upon an altar of 26kg (57lb) of solid gold, plus silver and plaster, and emerges once a year *(see Calendar p. 51)* to be paraded around the historic center under a rain of red wildflowers representing the blood of his sacrifice. His multi-level silver bier is in the *Sala de la Platería* (Silver Room), just left of the Triunfo doorway. This room also contains the bier for the monstrance, an ornate gold and jewel-encrusted vessel containing the host during the Corpus Christi procession. Notice the pelican pecking a bloody hole in its own breast to feed its young, a symbol of Christ's sacrifice.

Behind you at nine o'clock is the Main Altar, a single piece covered in sheets of beaten silver weighing in at 1,250kg (2,750lb) and aptly described by the historian Luis E. Valcarcel as "baroque at its very worst." However, the carved wooden choir facing it is particularly fine, featuring carvings of the 83 martyrs of the early Christian church, women above and men below.

The sacristy (left of the Silver Room) contains an exceptional Crucifixion, variously attributed to Van Dyck, Alonso del Cano, and an anonymous Cusco artist. The painting is curiously androgynous, with a male upper body and a seemingly female lower one; legend has it that it was the work of a native painter who, in splendid Andean holistic tradition, couldn't make sense of the idea of a supreme god who was only male. The sacristy also has portraits of all the bishops of Cusco, including Fray Vicente Valverde, who accompanied Pizarro during the Conquest and granted absolution for the capture of Atawallpa and slaughter of his retinue in Cajamarca. Directly across from the sacristy, beneath the main altar, is a crypt with the remains of various bishops of Cusco.

On the wall left of the sacristy, a famous painting of The Last Supper by Marcos Zapata shows Christ and the Apostles about to dine on New World items such as guinea-pig (the main course at sacred feasts in Inca times) and papaya. Judas (front right, with his bag of silver, and much swarthier than the others) stares out at us with a look of complicity, unlike the other disciples who are gazing at Christ; Cusco folklore claims the face of Judas was intended as a portrait of Francisco Pizarro. We can also observe the phenomenon, at Christ's side, of Saint John, beardless, youthful and androgynous, which might even lure us into an Andean fantasy version of *The Da Vinci Code*, if we felt so inclined.

Just left of and below this painting, an alabaster slab has been removed from the floor to reveal the *Unu Punku* (Water Gate), the remains of an Inca spring and water channel.

In one of the Cathedral towers lives María Angola, a huge bell cast in 1659 whose deep knell is said to be audible 40km (25mi) away. This bell, the largest in South America, is supposedly named for a black woman who tossed 11kg (25lb) of gold into the crucible, thus ensuring success after two previous castings had failed. There is a local legend that an Inca prince was walled up in one of the towers when it was built, and that when the tower falls the Inca will emerge to claim his birthright and free his people. After the earthquake of 1950 thousands of believers waited hopefully for the towers to collapse, but despite severe damage they remained standing and were later repaired. In April 1986, Cusco suffered another strong earthquake, which again damaged many of the city's colonial buildings, including the cathedral.

The Chapel of *El Triunfo* (The Triumph) is built on the site of *Suntur Wasi* (The Roundhouse), the main Inca armory where the Spanish were trapped during Manco Inca's siege in 1536. When the Incas burned the city the thatched roof of Suntur Wasi caught fire, but then mysteriously went out – an event which came to be seen as a miracle. Titu Cusi, son of Manco, witnessed the siege and later stated that the Spanish had black slaves stationed on the roof to put out the flames. But long before his account was written, the event had inflated into the miracle of the "Virgin of the Descent," a vision of the Virgin Mary descending to extinguish the flames, accompanied by Saint James (Santiago) on horseback, spreading terror among the Indian hordes. Miracles acquire an irresistible momentum, and this one has passed into legend. The Spanish subsequently broke out and recaptured Sacsaywaman, ending the siege (*see p.114*).

El Triunfo was the first Christian church in Cusco, built in 1538 to commemorate the Spanish victory over Manco and the miracle of 1536. It was completely leveled in the 1650 earthquake and subsequently rebuilt; nothing of the Suntur Wasi or the original church remains except for some stones in the main altar. A mural below an arch high on the left side of the church depicts the miracle, mentioning the Virgin's descent from heaven to "this sacred place of Sundorguaci (Suntur Wasi)." On the outside of the church, on either side of the main exit door, two large alcoves feature weathered but partially legible Spanish inscriptions, characterizing the miracle as a joint effort, with Mary putting out the flames and Saint James scattering the hostile barbarians.

The simple cross in an alcove above the main altar is supposed to be the original Cross of the Conquest, carried by the Greek conquistador Pedro de Candía. A small crypt beneath the church contains some of the ashes of the famous chronicler Garcilaso de la Vega in a silver chest with the crests of Peru and de la Vega's family (left and right, respectively). These were returned to Cusco from Spain by King Juan Carlos in 1978.

(3) Acllawasi / Santa Catalina Convent

To the right of the cathedral on the SE side of the square stands a colonial arcade, *Portal de Carrizos*, behind which you can see a long Inca facade, interrupted by modern doorways. This was the *Acllawasi*, the House of the Chosen Women. Its western wall is the longest surviving Inca wall in Cusco, leading away from the square for the entire length of *Intik'ijllu (a.k.a. Calle Loreto)*, a pedestrian-only street. Here lived the fabled "Virgins of the Sun" (as the Spanish misnamed them), and the Inca's concubines. They were dedicated to religious service, and wove exquisite garments of vicuña and alpaca for the Inca (which were worn once and then burned), brewed his *chicha*, and made other objects for his personal use. Certain among them were chosen to bear his children.

Tradition says that at the time of the Conquest a mighty condor fell dying into the patio of the Acllawasi after being attacked by a hawk. This ominous sign was later interpreted as a prediction of the death of *Tawantinsuyu* at the hands of the Spanish. Fittingly, after the Conquest part of the Acllawasi became the *Convent of Santa Catalina*, home of a cloistered order of nuns; a small and dwindling group of them occupies it to this day. The entrance to the Santa Catalina Museum is on *Santa Catalina Angosta*. A joint ticket for this site and the Qoricancha (#17) can be purchased here at a discount.

At the corner of *Santa Catalina Ancha* and *Triunfo* is a superb remnant of Inca wall, once part of a great compound known as *Hatun Cancha*. Some chroniclers described this, or part of it, as Pachacuti's palace. The Spanish chronicles are especially confusing and inconsistent on the matter of Inca palace ownership in Cusco, so in most cases a grain of salt is required.

A few steps further down the street, another remnant juts out into the sidewalk, and continues into the adjacent building, which is now the Incanto restaurant.

(4) La Compañía

The great church to the right of the Acllawasi is that of *La Compañía*. This building stands on the ruins of *Amarucancha* (the Serpent Courtyard), thought to have been the palace of Huascar, a son of emperor Wayna Capac whose short rule was ended by his half-brother Atawallpa. Its walls run parallel to Acllawasi along the west side of *Loreto*, and they contain a fine, walled-in colonial entranceway bearing the two carved serpents which give the building its present-day name. There are also fine niches inside the school courtyard and inside the Hostal Loreto.

La Compañía (the Company) is named for its builders, the Company of Jesus, the Jesuits. Its construction became the subject of a terrible wrangle between the Jesuits and local ecclesiastics, because its sheer size and grandeur, not to mention its location, seemed a direct challenge to the primacy of the cathedral. The controversy went on for years and its reverberations reached Madrid and Rome. Although the first structure was destroyed before completion by the earthquake of 1650, work was begun afresh, and the final arbitration of Pope Paul III against the Jesuits, came too late – the building was almost complete. All the local clergy could do was to have the side entrances kept back from the square and embargo the casting of a great bell designed to rival María Angola.

The church's altarpiece is a vast tableau of gilded woodwork punctuated with saints and angels, a classic of its kind that, when lit, fills one's entire field of vision with a mighty panel of shimmering gold that could provoke the unwary to swoons or religious visions. Notable works of art in the church are the scene from the life of St. Ignatius Loyola, attributed to the Cusco artist Marcos Zapata; the "Cristo de Burgos," a Crucifixion effigy of agonized realism located by the main altar; and the documentary scenes evoked in two paintings, one on either side of the main door. These show the marriages of Doña Lorenza Idiaquez of Cusco to Beltrán García de Loyola (right), and of Martín de Loyola to Doña Beatriz Ñusta, granddaughter of Manco Inca (left). Martín de Loyola was the man who pursued and captured Manco Inca's son, the last rebel Inca, Tupac Amaru I. These paintings are of great historical interest for their depiction of contemporary detail. Both the bridegrooms, incidentally, were closely related to St. Ignatius Loyola, founder of the Jesuits and hero of the Counter Reformation, which may have something to do with why the paintings are there in the first place. Also interesting is a painting (inside left, by the door) of St. Ignatius scourging heretics labeled Luther, Calvin, etc. Both the bell towers can be climbed for excellent views over the Plaza and up the ravine of the Saphi River.

Outside La Compañia, to the right of the entrance, is a metal plaque from 1950 commemorating the executions of Tupac Amaru II (a.k.a. Jose Gabriel Condorcanqui) and others after the 1780 indigenous uprising, an event so important that the city commemorated it again in 1981 – 200 years after the executions – with another plaque in the square across from La Compañia.

The buildings and arcades on the fourth (SW) side of the square are all colonial era constructions occupying land that formerly opened onto the Incas' *Cusipata*, the Square of Festivals, and are built on top of the Saphi River.

(5) Casana / Palace of Wayna Capac

On the west corner of the square along the *Portal de Panes* stood the Casana, which most chroniclers agree was the city *Palace of Wayna Capac*. Francisco Pizarro occupied the building after his troops entered Cusco in 1533. Little remains today except one corner, now occupied by a jewelry store. To the right stood the great hall of *Cora Cora*, which became part of Gonzalo Pizarro's share of the conqueror's loot. After Gonzalo's failed rebellion against the Spanish crown in 1548, the building was demolished and its land was salted.

Towards Colcampata (Place of Storehouses).

Uphill, parallel to *Procuradores*, runs *Suecia* (D2). The buildings on the left conceal the remains of the great hall of *Cora Cora*, which was was captured by Manco Inca during the great rebellion. From this salient, Manco's troops directed a withering hail of slingshot fire and arrows upon the Spanish in *Suntur Wasi*.

Sites #6 and #7 require a steep climb up *Resbalosa* (C2). If you are still acclimatizing or have simply had enough, you can visit these sites later or take a taxi. If you skip these for now, #8 can be accessed by walking up *Cuesta del Almirante* (D2).

(6) Church of San Cristobal

Parallel to Suecia, yet farther uphill, runs *Resbalosa* (Slippery Street) (C2). Walking up this steep street past *Quiscapata* (Spiky Place), you arrive at *Don Bosco* (C1), the main road to Sacsaywaman, directly in front of the steps leading to the *Church of San Cristobal*. The puppet Inca, Cristobal Paullu Inca, became — outwardly, at least — a devout Christian, and dedicated this church to his patron Saint. The entrance ticket to San Cristobal (CRA) includes a climb to the top of the bell tower, which has excellent views of the city. The church itself is unexceptional, though it has some oddities such as a bloodied Jesus in a glass coffin and various curious votive offerings, including toy airplanes, Hot Wheels and

Transformers, next to saint statues. The church pales next to the great retaining wall of Colcampata, which flanks the adjacent square.

(7) Colcampata

According to folklore, *Colcampata* was the palace of Manco Capac, the founding Inca. The lower retaining wall has eleven great niches the size of doorways. The remains of Colcampata itself are located above this wall and considerably farther back into the hillside. You can reach this ruin by following the main road uphill from San Cristobal church and turning through the gateway marked "Qolqanpata..." on the left just past the left hand curve in the highway. On the right, about 50m (160ft) along the driveway, stands an ancient doorway, the remains of the palace where Paullu Inca and Carlos Inca held court after the Conquest. The foundations of the building are still visible among the eucalyptus trees. Just behind the one standing entranceway is an enigmatic stone, about 1.20m (4ft) high, which appears to be carved in the shape of a frog or toad. In Inca times the ruling Inca would plant the first corn of the empire's new season at this spot in September of each year. The harvest from this ritual planting would later be used to make sacred *chicha* for the highest rituals.

Towards Pumacurcu (Puma's Spine).

(8) The Admiral's Palace / Inka Museum

The Admiral's Palace stands on the corner of *Ataud* (Coffin) and *Tucumán*. How an Admiral of the Waves came to have his home 11,000 feet above sea level is not on record. The house dates from the early 17th century and originally belonged to Admiral Francisco Aldrete Maldonado. The coat-of-arms over the doorway is that of the second owner, the Count of Laguna. The first, according to the story, was a man so arrogant and self-important that he would begin his prayers, "Holy Mary Mother of God, our relative..." He is said to have been found hanged mysteriously in this very courtyard after roughing up a priest who came to complain of an injustice.

The building was badly damaged in the 1950 earthquake but was restored with a modern annex added. It is now the Inka Museum, belonging to Cusco's main university. The museum contains abundant displays of Inca and pre-Inca culture, numerous scale models of Inca ruins (Machu Picchu and Choquequirao are particularly impressive), and Inca weaponry and mummies. It's really too much to take in at once. The place is a veritable palace, with an enormous courtyard surrounded by miniature profiles of Francisco Pizarro next to that of Queen Isabel of Spain. One of the stairways is guarded by ferocious creatures sculpted in stone: a three-toed lion (his head was knocked off by the quake, but later repaired), and a hideous, cloven-hoofed...something. The corner window on the second floor overlooking the street has a central column which, seen from outside, is carved in the shape of a woman's head and naked torso. Seen from inside, however, the figure is that of a bearded man.

(9) House of Jerónimo de Cabrera / Museum of Pre-Columbian Art

Continue walking up *Tucumán* (D2), past Purgatorio (Purgatory). Just beyond this stands the Plaza de las Nazarenas. To the left as you face the Plaza coming from this direction stands the *House of Jerónimo de Cabrera*, founder of the Peruvian coastal city of Ica and later the city of Córdoba in Argentina. Jerónimo's house is now occupied by the *Museum of pre-Columbian Art*, well worth a visit for those interested in the art of ancient Peru, via a collection of superb artifacts that are presented simply as art, rather than as references for the chronology or context of Andean civilization.

(10) House of Serpents

Across the Plaza is the *House of the Serpents* (now the Hotel Palacio Nazarenas), named after the numerous snakes carved in relief onto its masonry. This is a typical "transitional" structure, built by Inca masons working for Spanish conquistadors. The house is said to have belonged to Mancio Sierra de Leguízamo, who claimed to have looted the Punchao, the famous golden image of the sun from the Qoricancha (*see #17 below*), and then lost it the same night at dice. This must have been empty grandstanding, since Francisco Pizarro ensured that all the captured Inca treasure was melted down into bullion before distributing it. In any case, the boastful conquistador's story caught on and gave rise to a Spanish expression in use to this day: "to gamble away the sun before it rises."

The house is also noteworthy for the massive and bizarre coat-of-arms carved in stone above the main entrance, which sports a pair of mythical beasts with serpent tails.

Running down the righthand side of the House of the Serpents is a narrow alley, named *Siete Culebras* (Seven Snakes) after the high relief snakes carved upon the walls which give the building its name. The wall is mostly transitional, but the foundation is pre-colonial Inca. A tunneled arch runs across the alley connecting the building to the chapel of the old Seminary of San Antonio Abad.

(11) Seminario of San Antonio de Abad

This was an early colonial seminary for catholic priests (now the Hotel Monasterio), built in 1595. The chapel was added after the 1650 earthquake and is decorated in the indigenous Baroque style with gilded-framed paintings showing the life of San Antonio de Abad. The heart of the former seminary is a colonial courtyard, replete with a fountain, gardens and 300-year-old cedar tree. The two crests that flank the door are the Royal Crest of Spain and that of the bishop Monsignor Antonio de la Raya who founded the seminary in 1598.

Towards Tococache (Salt Cave – the Incas probably mined salt here at one time)

(12) Museum of Religious Art

The colonial building erected on these walls once belonged to the Marquis of Buenavista and later became the Archbishop's Palace. Subsequently the church dedicated part of the building as an art museum. Bishop Mollinedo y Angulo, Cusco's patron of the arts and fervent promoter of Corpus Christi (*see p.51*), features in two of the works in the room dedicated to paintings of the festival.

The museum is located in a historic building, which according to folklore was the palace of Inca Roca, the sixth Inca. Current historical (as opposed to folkloric) opinion holds that this structure was actually an usnu platform, used to conduct ceremonies; the Spanish adapted it by hollowing out the core, keeping some of the walls, and converting it into a mansion. The massive Inca wall of the palace runs, almost intact, the length of *Hatunrumiyoc* (Street of the Great Stone), and is also well preserved along the rear and the south side of the building. *Hatunrumiyoc* is named for the famous 12-angled stone which features prominently about halfway along the megalithic wall – and on every bottle of Cusqueña beer. A colorful "Inca" stands here, guarding the stone and collecting tips for photos. The stone is renowned for its size and for the perfection with which its twelve corner-angles fit the neighboring blocks of masonry. Some writers have speculated on a symbolism in the number of angles – one for each month of the year, for example – but despite the stone's current fame there is no evidence for any special significance. The stone and wall were in fact covered by another wall during the Inca period; this was demolished in modern times. Also, twelve angles in one plane is by no means a record for Inca masonry. The local historian Dr. Victor Angles (no relation) mentions a stone with no fewer than 44 angles in one plane at the ruins of Torontoy near Machu Picchu.

High up on the wall of *Hatunrumiyoc*, at the eastern end, is a section of what looks like Inca masonry, built in regular courses of dark grey andesite, which contrasts sharply with the greenish dioritic porphyry and the polygonal style below. This upper course is actually a classic example of transitional masonry, built shortly after the Spanish conquest.

(13) Church of San Blas

Following the direction of *Hatunrumiyoc* downhill to Choquechaca then straight up the *Cuesta de San Blas*, you come to the *Church of San Blas*. A project currently underway will transform the entire church into a museum with a separate entrance, though masses will continue to be held at certain hours. Founded in 1562, this small adobe building is believed to stand on the spot where the Incas had a temple to lightning and thunder. It is unremarkable today except for its extraordinary carved pulpit. This pulpit, dating from the late 17th century, is unsurpassed in the Americas, and is sometimes claimed to be the finest piece of wood-carving in the world. Starting at the base of this elaborate cedarwood work, carved from a single massive tree trunk, we find eight agonized heretics groaning under the weight of the pulpit (or do they represent the people who had to haul this massive piece of wood up from the rainforest?). Above them are seven ghastly chimera, looking like masks from Greek theater. Winged angels and baroque columns support the cornice of the pulpit, below which are five figures: the four evangelists and the Virgin Mary. The backdrop is dominated by the figure of St. Thomas. The canopy is alive with figures: the nine doctors of the church, numerous seraphim bearing the implements of the Crucifixion, and at the very top the figure of St. Paul. Under St. Paul's feet sits a human skull, which is thought to be that of the woodcarver who created this remarkable work. There is some dispute as to this man's identity; most often the carving is attributed to one Juan Tomás Tuirutupa, an Indian leper who was a protegé of the art patron, Bishop Mollinedo y Angulo.

Plaza San Blas, where the church is located, was remodelled during the administration of Daniel Estrada, a very popular local mayor who became renowned for his propensity to build fountains everywhere. Here stands one of the largest of his fountains. On Saturdays there is a handcrafts market in the square.

The streets around San Blas have some repute locally as an artists' district. There are many small workshops, studios, and galleries in the area (see Shopping, p. 33). Local folklore has it that this area was an artists' district even during Inca times, when the area was filled with gold- and silversmiths from Chimor, and potters, painters, armorers and carvers from throughout the empire. The streets preserve much of Cusco's colonial charm, and most of them are pedestrian only. Some of the street names are wildly colorful: Atoqsayk'uchi (Where the fox got tired); Siete Angelitos (Seven Little Angels); Siete Diablitos (Seven Little Devils);

Saqracalle (Demon Street); *Pantaqcalle* (Confusion Street); *P'aqlachapata* (Bald Men's Place); *Pasñapakana* (Young Girls' Hiding Place); *Miracalcetas* (See Stockings). Much has been done to make San Blas more attractive for tourists, and it is a very pleasant place to stroll around. Be careful at night though, especially on the streets leading up NE from *Tandapata*, since there are still thieves (*see Robbery, p. 17*).

The San Blas lookout affords an excellent and accessible view of the city. Ascend *Pasñapakana* (E1) all the way and you'll find a small plaza with excellent views of the city and lots of explanatory signage in Spanish.

THE ROOFTOP HERDS OF CUSCO

Gaze out at the buildings of Cusco from on high and you'll see a veritable herd of ceramic bulls inhabiting the rooftops. These always come in pairs, are usually modestly painted, and have other images around them such as crosses, ladders, suns and moons. The bulls are likely an adaptation of an Inca sacred object called *illa* or the closely related *conopa*. These are ceramic or stone carvings of llamas and alpacas, often containing a hollow which is filled with alpaca fat and buried in the fields or otherwise used in ceremonies, even nowadays, to protect the herds and ensure fertility. When the Spanish conquistadors introduced bulls to Peru, the villagers of Pucará, just beyond the La Raya pass on the way to Puno, were reputedly impressed by their strength and turned them into a rooftop version of the illa that we see today. The town gives the bulls their name, *Toritos de Pucara* (Little Bulls of Pucara), and is still one of their main centers of production. At

some point the Christian cross was added between the bulls, but pagan suns and moons are often still present in the design.

Despite their illa origins, the bulls aren't for herd fertility; their purpose is to protect and bring prosperity and happiness to the human inhabitants of the house. They are always a housewarming gift from friends or family, and they go facing in the same direction as the house on the highest part of the roof, where they are placed during a party celebrating completion of the roof before the people move in. These bulls are sold in all sizes as souvenirs and can easily be found at the suggested bazaars (*see p. 34*), often with wild, technicolor paint and details.

– Leo Duncan

Towards Munai Cenca (Pretty Nose). Backtrack down *Cuesta San Blas* and halfway along *Hatunrumiyoc*, then head left down the stairs to walk around the back of the Palace of Inca Roca. Turn left down *Herrajes*, and go right on *Santa Catalina Ancha*.

(14) Palace of Topa Yupanqui / Casa Concha Machu Picchu Museum

At the end of the street, where it turns the corner, you see the walls of the colonial mansion of José de Santiago Concha. Stout royalists, the Conchas occupied the house throughout the colonial era, and Martín Pio Concha was the last colonial governor of Cusco before Independence. The House of Concha is especially noted for its fine balconies. Most notably today, it serves as the *Casa Concha Machu Picchu Museum*, home to the artifacts returned to Peru by Yale University in 2011-2012 (see p. 214). The exhibit seen here originally toured the U.S. in the early 2000s, and was then repatriated to Cusco and installed in this building, belonging to the UNSAAC. The exhibits are housed in a series of rooms, and include memorabilia from Hiram Bingham's expedition, along with some of his photos and a substantial selection of the artifacts found at Machu Picchu in 1912.

Casa Concha and Pucamarca (*below*) were both part of the same complex during Inca times, which Garcilazo states was formerly the Palace of Topa Inca Yupanqui.

(15) Pucamarca / Site Museum

The rear of what may have been Topa Inca's palace, running along *Maruri*, is largely intact, though punctuated by post-Inca doorways which open onto colonial patios and shops. The Inca name for this building was *Pucamarca* (Red Settlement). *Maruri* 314-315 is now home to the Cusco headquarters of Scotiabank and the *Puca Marka Site Museum*. Scotiabank opened this small site museum in 2006. It's worth seeing for the excellent Inca walls and niches and the rotating exhibit to the right of the entrance. The second floor has an exhibition (SST) of the work of famous Peruvian photographer Martin Chambi, one of the first (and still the greatest of) major indigenous Latin American photographers.

(16) Cusicancha

Opposite the Scotiabank on *Maruri* stands this huge space, now belonging to the Ministry of Culture where a series of Inca courtyards once stood. The place is an oasis of spacious calm amidst the tumult of modern Cusco. The site has a checkered history, having belonged to a series of high ranking Cusco families and then become a military barracks for most of the 20th century. Entrance is free, and you can wander among the restored foundations of Inca buildings (of interest to *aficionados* of Inca architecture) where, according to Spanish chroniclers, the emperors Pachacuti and Topa Inca were born. Some local archaeologists claim these buildings housed the mummies of the royal Incas, though how they determined this is unclear.

Towards Pumac Chupan (Puma's Tail – the area corresponding to this part of the city, according to the puma configuration conceived by the Incas).

THE CITY OF CUSCO

(17) Qoricancha / Monastery of Santo Domingo

Following the pedestrian-only *Romeritos* street, you arrive at the *Monastery of Santo Domingo*. This church is built upon the remains of the fabled *Qoricancha*, the Court of Gold (some local guides I have spoken with suggested that the name may actually have been *Qorik'ancha*, meaning Resplendent Gold), the most famous temple of the Americas. Juan Pizarro, one of the four Pizarro brothers, was given this site by his brother Francisco as part of his share of the loot from the conquest. During the 1536 battle for Sacsaywaman, Juan was struck a mortal blow to the head, and as he lay dying he willed the site to the Dominicans. They have taken over the administration of this site and there is a separate entrance fee.

Only three Spaniards ever saw the Qoricancha in its full glory. These men were sent by Pizarro from Cajamarca, where the Inca Atawallpa was being held prisoner, to speed up the collection of the royal ransom. They were among the roughest of Pizarro's unlettered soldiery, and their appreciation of this wonder of the world was confined to awe at the sheer quantities of gold they found there. With their own hands (the horrified Indians refused to help) they prised 700 gold sheets weighing 2kg (4.5 lbs) each from the walls. They reported an altar weighing 86kg (190 lbs) and a ritual font lined with 55kg (120 lbs) of gold. Aside from these financial details they left no account of the Qoricancha.

The first looters took only the largest and most accessible pieces. Members of Pizarro's main party later recalled a plethora of precious objects: a field of maize made with silver stems and leaves, and ears of gold; golden llamas, figurines, jars and pitchers. All these exquisite treasures ended up in the crucible; nothing survived.

The first three conquistadors did not remove the holiest religious symbol of the empire, the sun image known as the Punchao, though they reported its existence. This all-gold image was a young boy surrounded by reflective golden discs with a central cavity containing a dough made from the hearts of dead Inca emperors. Subsequently it seems to have vanished – taken, presumably, before the main party of Spaniards arrived. In 1553 Cristobal de Molina wrote, "The Indians hid this sun so well that it could never be found to the present day." However, when the Spanish invaded Vilcabamba in 1572 they brought back an object which they claimed was this golden sun disc, minus the figure in its center. Viceroy Toledo sent it to the king of Spain, along with a letter suggesting that it would make an excellent gift for the Pope. That is the last known historical reference to it; perhaps the Vatican has it stuffed in a closet somewhere.

In *The Conquest of Peru*, William Prescott tells us that the Punchao discs were positioned to catch the morning sun and throw its rays into the gold-lined temple, filling it with radiant light. There was a silver disc of the moon as well, in keeping with the Incas' parallel worship, and we may infer that this was set to cast moonlight into a silver-lined temple of the moon. Aside from these two principal temples there were shrines to Thunder and Lightning; to the Pleiades and other stars; to Venus; and to the Rainbow. There were also chambers to house the *wacas*, or sacred objects, of conquered tribes.

The splendor of the Qoricancha is beyond imagining today. It housed 4,000 priests and attendants. Religious observance was constant. Offerings to the gods and the Inca's ancestors were made each day. The original temple enclosure stretched hundreds of meters, all the way down to the confluence of the Tullumayo and Saphi rivers, now the intersection of *Av. el Sol* and *Tullumayo*. At this spot the accumulated ashes from a whole year's sacrifices were cast into the waters each January.

One vital aspect of the Qoricancha, however, has since been largely forgotten: it was the Incas' principal astronomical observatory. The Inca caste of *Amautas* (learned priests) included a sect of *Tarpuntaes* — effectively, the royal astronomers. Their task was to study the celestial bodies, note the advance and retreat of the sun, fix solstice and equinox dates, predict eclipses, and so on. This function was vital to everything from sacred rituals to the planting of crops. From various sites around the Qoricancha, the Tarpuntaes could have observed a great number of important astronomical events, such as the June and December solstice sunrises, the heliacal rise of the Pleiades, and the December solstice sunset behind the mountain called Killke. Also, early chroniclers tell us there were once great monoliths called *sucancas* standing on the mountainous horizons of the Cusco Valley at strategic points visible from the Qoricancha, marking the azimuths of the winter and summer solstices.

The system was yet more complex. The Qoricancha was the hub of a kind of conceptual wheel – called the *ceque* system. Each *waca* on the system had its day of the year and was cared for by a specific Cusco *ayllu*, or clan. So the ceques were an integral part of daily life in Cusco, and the movements of the heavens were an integral part of ordinary consciousness. Familiarity with the Quechua zodiac is common among Peruvian *campesinos* to this day.

THE CEQUE LINES OF CUSCO

Inca Cusco encompassed one of the most extensive and complex ritual systems history has seen. Known as the *ceque* system, its center was the Qoricancha, the hub from which 42 lines, or ceques, radiated like the spokes of a wheel. Stretched along these lines lay at least 328 *wacas*, the shrines of Cusco's sacred landscape. Some were natural features of the land, such as springs, rock outcrops, caves and lakes; others were constructed sites such as houses, walls and channels which were associated with events in Inca mythology.

Most of our information on the ceques comes from a Jesuit priest, Bernabé Cobo, writing in 1654, more than one hundred years after the conquest. The record is incomplete, and it is difficult today to understand the full scope of the ceque system and what it meant to the Incas. But, in typical Inca fashion, it seems to have functioned simultaneously on multiple levels, ranging from mundane matters such as marking boundaries between local kin groups (*ayllus*) to marking a few important days on the Inca calendar.

For example, several of the shrines marked locations on the horizon where the sun would rise or set on the June and December solstices.

How the ceque lines looked on the ground – or even if they were visible at all – is impossible to tell today. Some may have been simply conceptual, with only the *wacas* along them appearing as features of the landscape. But others would have been visible on the ground, because they were ritual pathways which people walked along on certain days.

Historical references suggest that other ceque systems existed outside of the Cusco region. The Cusco lines were certainly the largest system, but colonial documents suggest that many other Andean communities had similar shrine and line systems. Indeed, "ritual radiality" seems to have represented a core concept in pre-Hispanic Andean religion. Traces of other *ceque* systems exist today, and as recently as the 1970s indigenous people were still walking the ritual lines and venerating shrines located on them in remote parts of the *altiplano* of Bolivia and Chile.

One very important *ceque* line ran far beyond Cusco, 150 air km (94 air mi) south-east, ending at the pass of La Raya, the divide between the Urubamba and Lake Titicaca watersheds. Each year at the time of the winter solstice the Inca priests walked this entire line, making offerings to the *wacas* along it.

On certain rare occasions, such as the investiture of a new Inca, or when Tawantisuyu was beset by natural calamities, a vast ceremony called the *Capac Cocha* was held. Priests set off from the *Aucaypata* (Cusco's main plaza) with offerings to all the major wacas of the empire – a process that must have taken months to complete. This was one of the few times when the Incas practiced human sacrifice at certain designated *wacas*.

One question that remains open is whether *ceque* systems existed in Andean culture before the rise of the Inca empire. The famous Nazca lines, dating from more than one thousand years before the Incas, bear certain similarities, but they radiate from many different centers, not just one, as did Cusco's.

– **Brian Bauer**

The monastery of Santo Domingo, which was built over the ruins of the Qoricancha, obscured most of this archaeological jewel until 1950, when the earthquake fortuitously felled much of the Spanish building and laid bare the inner Inca walls which you can see today. Some questionable restoration has been carried out here (close inspection will reveal what is original and what is recent; newly-cut stones, for example, display chisel marks at the edges). Nonetheless, the surviving walls of the Qoricancha represent the finest Inca stonework in existence. The stone font in the central courtyard is the same one whose gold lining so excited the first conquistadors, but it has been substantially reworked to Spanish design. To your left as you enter here stand two lesser shrines against the wall that runs along *Ahuacpinta* street. These possibly housed the hostage idols from around the empire. No explanation exists for the three holes bored through the wall at floor level between these rooms, but speculation has it that they were used for channeling away ritual *chicha* or the blood of sacrificial animals; they may even have been simply for water drainage from the courtyard.

The two rooms to the right of the main courtyard are believed to have been the temples of the Moon and of Lightning, although, as is so often the case, this is folklore, not historical fact. The Sun Temple itself has entirely disappeared, but the surviving outer wall is one of the most famous Inca structures in existence, an ovoid, tapering construction whose perfection of line has amazed architects and laymen alike ever since the Conquest. This structure is actually best seen from outside the building, from the street of *Arrayan*.

Between the terraces of the Qoricancha and *Av. el Sol* stands a park which was built in the early nineteen-nineties. A small subterranean museum, whose entrance is on *Av. el Sol*, houses some of the artifacts that were unearthed there during the attendant archaeological excavations.

(18) House of Four Busts

After having your fill of the Qoricancha, continue down *Zetas* and hang left onto *San Agustin*. At *San Agustin 400* stands the *House of the Four Busts* (the back of what is now the Hotel Palacio del Inca). It is named after the four Spanish nobles carved in relief over the doorway. Traditionally these are held to be the four Pizarro brothers, though there is no historical evidence to support this. There is an excellent line of Inca walls along the upper block of San Agustin, which once formed the east wall of *Pucamarca (#15 above)*. Returning to the Plaza de Armas via *San Agustin*, you will come to the corner of *Santa Catalina Ancha* and *Ruinas*. The ruins that Ruinas is named after are of more recent vintage than the Inca ones on this walk. During the 1836 Peruvian civil war, Mariscal Agustin Gamarra's troops bombarded and destroyed the Augustinian convent there for the monks' failure to support the nascent republic, resulting in the eponymous ruins. This is a good point to end the tour if you plan to do part of it another day. The walk to here is about 4km.

A QUIET WALK THROUGH CUSCO

The city's barely-regulated growth has left many of Cusco's streets intolerably noisy, crowded and polluted with diesel fumes. However, the San Blas and San Cristobal neighborhoods are still pleasant to stroll through. For a downhill walk (*see City Map, p.78*) that takes you through the center of Cusco entirely on pedestrian-only streets (except at *Maruri*), start on *Saphi* (C2). Climb partway up the steep steps of *Amargura* then turn right onto *Qoricalle*. At the end turn down *Procuradores*, cross the Plaza de Armas and continue on down *Intik'ijllu (a.k.a. Loreto)*, turn left on *Maruri* then right on *Romeritos*, cross *Zetas* with Santo Domingo on your right, and continue down *Ahuacpinta* all the way to the end. Descend the steps to the right, and you will arrive at the main post office on the corner of *Av. Sol* and *Av. Garcilazo*.

– P. F.

Part Two of the Cusco city walking tour takes you towards Picchu (Hilltop).

(19) Monastery of La Merced

Start from the Plaza de Armas, walking west along *Mantas*. On the north side of the street, in front of *Mantas 118*, is a metal plaque in the ground with arrows pointing in the directions of the four *suyos*, or quarters, of the Inca Empire (*Tawantinsuyu – see p. 74*). A little further on stands the church, convent and museum of La Merced. The church's facade is pockmarked with bullet holes, whose origins are variously traced to a failed independence uprising in 1814, Mariscal Gamarra's violent suppression of the Augustinians in 1836, or more recent disturbances in 1950...or maybe bullets from all three occasions?

The entranceway of the monastery and museum (to the left of the church - SST) contains two intriguing paintings from colonial times. The painting on the left portrays the brutal ethos of the Conquest in all its gory actuality. Mounted and armored Spaniards battle the fierce Araucanian Indians of Chile; among the horsemen, a white-cloaked Mercedarian friar wields his lance, which is tipped with a deadly steel-pointed crucifix. Overhead, celestial warriors led by the bloodthirsty St. James (a.k.a. Santiago, patron of Spanish warriors against the Moors, and virtually the god of war in the medieval Christian pantheon), are busy performing miracles on behalf of the Spanish; the arrows fired by the Araucanians have all turned in flight and are falling on the Indians themselves. The painting to the right shows the first missionaries of the Mercedarian order being clubbed and roasted to death by those same heathens, while a more successful group makes converts in the foreground. In the second lobby, another interesting painting depicts a damned soul in hell being devoured by zoomorphic demons. At the bottom is a list of his complaints about life in hell.

The cloister is a fine piece of Spanish architecture, surrounded by a large mural depicting the life of San Pedro de Nolasco, founder of the Mercedarians. Spread throughout the building, you find one of the finest collections of old paintings in Cusco, among them a Rubens scene of the holy family. There is a rich variety of opulent religious vestments, including an unusual item—a tunic bearing four skulls, three of them wearing the crowns of a King, a Pope and a Bishop, and the fourth apparently a commoner's hat; reminders that we're all the same mortals in the end.

A room on the west side of the patio holds the monastery's collection of valuable gold, silver and precious-stone items, including the famous monstrance (a vessel used for displaying the communion Host), a solid gold extravaganza four feet high, encrusted with diamonds and pearls. Note the huge pair of pearls in the center, uniquely matched to form the body of a mermaid. The signage claims this as the world's second largest pearl, but Google tells a different story.

Several plaques commemorate the conquistador Diego de Almagro, the first conqueror of Chile – later executed by the Pizarro brothers – whose bones lie in the vaults below. His mortal enemy Gonzalo Pizarro – also later executed – lies somewhere below you too. Scattered through the cloister on the first and second floors one finds some bizarre or macabre examples of religious art: a decapitated San Laureano, spouting blood, holding his own head and being helped out of his difficulties by two rather lovely archangels; an ancient sage being carried bodily along by angels while profoundly lost in a good book; an Andean Jesus dying in the arms of a traditionally dressed indigenous woman; men using a wheel to remove the intestines of a crucified saint. At the back of the church itself (open evenings only) are two paintings of cherubs, apparently dusting off and then crowning the Sacred Heart of Jesus; and near the opposite wall in a glass case, an effigy of the child Jesus known as the *Niño Doctorcito* (Little Doctor Child) and surrounded by votive offerings such as toy planes, motorbikes and racing cars. (This last figure is also known as the "Naughty Child" because, according to legend, he escapes at night to play with his friend and fellow effigy *El Niño Melchor de Marcacocha* in the Ollantaytambo church.)

You can visit the underground cells that were once home to one Father Salamanca, decorated with the colorful biblical murals this monk painted throughout his lifetime.

(20) House of Valleumbroso

Follow *Mantas* away from the main square, to Marqués, and you come to the *House of the Marquis of Valleumbroso* on the left side. The grandiose portal of the old Cusco mansion is a magnificent example of Spanish construction in the Inca style. The columns and the upper lintel are obviously Spanish, but the inner doorway itself is very Inca-influenced masonry. But notice that the sides are vertical, not trapezoidal, and that the double-jamb is recessed on the inside, not the outside; these features identify the door as a Spanish construction. The building is now the Cusco School of Fine Arts.

Several inscriptions in the walls along this street denote historic buildings and residences, such as the *Casa de Alonso de Toro*, mansion of one of the earliest and most feared conquistadors, now home to the "Rock & Rollos Pizza Cafe" and other precarious enterprises; the courtyard of this building is in serious disrepair. At *Marqués 230-234* the *Taller de Martin Chambi Jimenez* was where that renowned mid-20th-century photographer kept his studio.

(21) Church and Convent of Santa Clara

Continue in this direction along the south side of Plaza San Francisco and pass under the *Arch of Santa Clara*, with its four condors and statue of Liberty on the summit. It was built in 1835-36 to mark the founding of the Peru-Bolivia Confederation and originally featured the coat-of-arms of that short-lived political enterprise. Modifications made in 1852-1876 replaced it with the Peruvian coat-of-arms and shifted the symbolic focus to Peruvian independence (1821), since by then the Peru-Bolivia Confederation was but a memory.

The *Church and Convent of Santa Clara* will shortly come up on your left. This is a cloistered nunnery – the oldest in Peru – which is chiefly noted for an altar set with thousands of mirrors. The entrance is on Santa Clara, shortly before San Pedro market. As you walk down Santa Clara, you are walking down the *Andén de Chaqnapata* along the former Inca highway leading to the SW quarter of the empire known as the *Contisuyu*, which encompassed a swath of Peru's modern-day south coast region.

(22) San Pedro Market

The main market of Cusco is a place not to be missed by the visitor. The market has been made much safer for tourists than it used to be, but be on the lookout for pickpockets. Standard advice applies (*see Robbery, p. 17*). Due to this mild gentrification effort tourist handcraft stalls are now scattered throughout the market, but these are the least of it as far as local life is concerned. The main food market is a great tin-roofed hall with hundreds of stallholders – mainly women – selling every imaginable item of food: spices, fruits, meat, vegetables, plus coffee and tea from Cusco's northern jungle. Here you see the prolific variety of produce grown in the multiple climatic regions of Peru, which range from rainforest through desert and temperate climes to frozen wasteland. The market is also a social world of its own: the vendors' children play hide-and-seek among the stalls; women arrive from distant villages to barter grain or potatoes for items ranging from salt to sewing needles. There are stalls for hot meals, others for fruit juices (neither section recommended for unconditioned stomachs, however); inhabitants of the market never need to leave it by day. The surrounding streets are cluttered with more stalls: an area for pots and pans here, one for Primus stove repairs there.

There is an order in all this chaos. Inevitably it invites comparison with the well-oiled, stainless-steel world of a Euro-American supermarket, where the only person you speak to is the cashier.

(23) Church of San Pedro

One more block brings you to the *Church of San Pedro*, located directly opposite the San Pedro Market. The church was built with stones taken from an Inca structure which was situated just up the hill. The main entranceway bears the coat-of-arms of the Spanish crown. The side entrance is on *San Pedro*. Tours of the site are not available, but it is possible to attend mass.

Towards Quillipata (Place of the Kestrel).

(24) Plaza and Monastery of San Francisco

Trace your steps back through the Santa Clara archway and find yourself in the wide open spaces of *Plaza San Francisco*.

Outside, the Plaza also provides the interested visitor with a nice crash course in basic Andean botany. The square has been planted with native Andean shrubs, trees, flowers cacti and crops, many of them labeled with both local and scientific names. Also notice the bust of Mariscal Gamarra in the centre of the Plaza, the very same general responsible for blasting Cusco's Augustinian monastery to rubble. Evidently the city hasn't held it against him.

At the NW corner stands the *Church and Monastery of San Francisco*. The magnificent collection of colonial paintings, surviving in excellent condition, includes a Last Judgement (with scenes surpassing Hieronymus Bosch for baroque cruelty) by the famous Cusco painter Diego Quispe Tito, and Flemish renaissance-influenced works by Marcos Zapata. The cloister of the monastery is a superb example of colonial architecture, with paintings of incidents from the life of St. Francis of Assisi around its courtyard. Many of the ceilings are decorated with elaborate and colorful frescoes. At the head of one stairway is an enormous painting, nine meters by twelve, of the Franciscan family, crowned with saints, coats-of-arms and rubrics, representing a total of 683 people.

Off the courtyard are two sepulchres containing macabre arrangements of bones and skulls, some pinned to the walls to form the lettering of morbid homilies ("What you are, I once was; what I am, you will be"). Via the stairs you reach the choir, which is interesting for its carved wooden panels (featuring cohorts of slaughtered saints), and the fascicule, a huge cylindrical device of wood inlaid with ivory, for displaying religious texts and hymns to groups of seated monks. There is also a 17th-century German organ, in reasonably good working order. All-in-all, one of Cusco's finest religious buildings.

(25) House of Garcilaso de la Vega / Regional Historical Museum

Follow *Garcilaso* until it opens onto Plaza Regocijo. There, on the corner with *Heladeros* (Ice Cream Makers), stand the graceful colonial arches of the House of Garcilaso de la Vega, the mestizo chronicler. This elegant building was severely damaged in the April 1986 earthquake but has been restored and is now the home of the *Regional Historical Museum* (entrance by BTC). The museum has a small glyptodon shell, similar to the one at Pikillacta (*see p.278*) and a collection of archaeological material and colonial paintings.

(26) House of Pumas

At *Santa Teresa 385* you find the House of Pumas, an Inca-style transitional-period doorway with six animals, probably pumas, carved in relief upon the lintel.

(27) House of Diego de Silva

Opposite this house, set back from the street in a small treed plaza, stands the Inca-walled House of Diego de Silva. The Viceroy Francisco de Toledo watched discreetly from these windows as his victorious troops returned from Vilcabamba in 1572, dragging with them the captive (and soon to be executed) last Inca, Tupac Amaru I. The soldiers attempted to force him to remove his royal fringe as a sign of respect for Toledo, but he refused, instead touching the fringe and bowing in Toledo's general direction, thereby earning a beating from his captors.

(28) Convent of Santa Teresa

Next to this house stands the Church and Monastery of Santa Teresa, also built on Inca foundations. The balcony high up on the corner with Saphi was once used by the colonial authorities for making civic announcements and hearing public complaints. This church is not open to the public on any regular basis, but if the door is open, take a look. The interior is one of the prettiest in Cusco.

CHAPTER TWO

OUTSIDE THE CITY
Walks and Tours Close to Cusco

GETTING THERE. The most interesting and accessible area for walks and taxi-tours close to the city lies roughly in the arc between northwest and northeast of Cusco. Here squats the massive ruined complex of Sacsaywaman, along with other well-known ruins and shrines close to the paved highway to Pisac. The nearby hills are criss-crossed with pathways. Most are gentle enough for the average weekend hiker, yet there are tremendous views, and the entire countryside is dotted with fascinating places to discover and explore: Inca dams, roadways, shrines, carvings, walls and terraces; abandoned colonial brick kilns; grottoes, caves and waterfalls.

One can visit all four of the major ruins (Sacsaywaman, Qenqo, Puca Pucara, Tambomachay) plus the other sites listed below (Cristo Blanco, Lanlakuyok, and Amaru Marcawasi, a.k.a. The Temple of the Moon) by a few different options. In descending order of cost:

1) A taxi can take you directly to any of the individual sites except Amaru Marcawasi, which has limited road access. (*See Walk I, p. 136*)
2) The eastbound public bus *Señor del Huerto* leaves from Mercado Rosaspata in Cusco (*see p. 21*), passes Cristo Blanco (get off here for Sacsaywaman), Qenqo, Lanlakuyok, and Puca Pucara before stopping at Tambomachay and returning to the city.
3) To walk from the Plaza de Armas (8km/5mi, 4-5 hours), ascend Don Bosco street north to Sacsaywaman (*see City Map C1, p. 78*), follow

the paved road east from there to Qenqo, follow Walk Ia on p. 136, then continue past the ruins of Chuspiyoq to the last two ruins. Alternatively, cut out Sacsaywaman and Qenqo and take Walk Ib from San Blas. You can also walk directly up to Cristo Blanco (*see p. 121*).

You can mix and match these methods to visit only some of the sites. Entrance to the four major ruins is by BTC.

SACSAYWAMAN

This site stands on a hill looming over the city to the north. The limestone blocks in the three tiers of outer walls which form the perimeter of this awe-inspiring ruin are the vastest of any Inca site – yet even these enormous stones are fitted with that extraordinary Inca perfection. Every visitor should see this. The name has been variously translated as "Speckled Falcon" and "Royal Eagle," and also (taking the name to be a corruption of the Quechua words *Saqsa Uma*) as "Speckled Head." This last interpretation refers to the idea that the city of Cusco was laid out in the form of a puma, whose speckled or tawny head was the hill of *Saqsa Uma*.

History

The origins of Sacsaywaman are uncertain. It is commonly attributed to the period of the Inca Pachacuti, the man essentially credited with founding Tawantinsuyu, and seems to have been under construction throughout the period of empire. Prescott, in *The Conquest of Peru*, states that 20,000 men were employed in its construction over a period of fifty years. But these figures have been supplied, like so much of Inca history, by the imagination of Garcilaso de la Vega, a chronicler justly honored for his literary talent, but suspect on many points of historical detail.

Sacsaywaman is usually described as a fortress, chiefly because a great battle was fought there between Spanish and Incas in 1536. The defensive aspect certainly seems to have been considered by the architects, but it was more than simply a military structure. The Incas did not divide their world into different functions as we do. Such a large center as Sacsaywaman clearly had various functions. It was an important religious site; some have suggested that the zig-zag configuration of the outer walls represents a lightning bolt, and this was a temple to the important lightning deity. Others assert that the zig-zags represented the teeth of the conceptual puma whose body was the city of Cusco and whose head was the hill of Sacsaywaman. Of course, since things could have many different meanings simultaneously in the Inca mind, these two ideas are not mutually exclusive. The huge complex of buildings on the hill, now almost entirely gone, probably also served as an administrative center, with its adjacent storehouses. (The chronicler Cieza de León refers to Sacsaywaman as a "Storehouse of the Sun," where all manner of goods were stored, and Garcilaso recalls playing in the ruins of these buildings as a child.)

In *The Conquest of the Incas*, Hemming tells us that the largest stone block in the mighty outer walls of Sacsaywaman stands 8.5m (28ft) high and weighs 361 tons. The three parallel zig-zag ramparts that clad the north side of the hill stretch for more than a thousand feet, in 22 salients, perhaps designed to make an attacker expose his flank. For structural strength, the most massive stones are set at the apexes of the salients. This is one of the most astounding megalithic structures of the ancient world.

The early Spanish noted a veritable labyrinth of buildings on the summit, with room enough for the estimated five thousand troops who garrisoned it during Manco Inca's rebellion. The hilltop was crowned with three great towers, whose foundations can still be seen, named Muyucmarca, Sayacmarca and Paucarmarca.

One outstanding aspect of Sacsaywaman is that, unlike most famous Inca sites, it appears to have belonged to the Inca state in general, rather than a specific Inca emperor. Its location, looming above the capital city, its enormous esplanade, its singular architecture, its three tall towers, its massive outer walls – in this author's view these details suggest Sacsaywaman as a mighty multi-function complex emblematic of Inca strength and identity, just as certain famous buildings symbolize specific nations today. No doubt on suitable occasions subject tribes of the empire got to parade on the esplanade, while taking note of what they were up against if they resisted the Incas.

For hundreds of years after the conquest, until the 1930s, Sacsaywaman served as a kind of pre-cut stone quarry for the city of Cusco, so it is not surprising that the site has been denuded of the smaller stones that once covered the hilltop. Only the mighty outer walls were too massive to be looted. With all the buildings gone it will never be possible to settle archaeologically the question of Sacsaywaman and what purpose it served.

All of the structure survived the first years of the Conquest. Pizarro's party entered Cusco unopposed in 1533 and lived there securely for more than two years. They were caught totally unprepared by the rebellion of Manco Inca which exploded in 1536. Sacsaywaman was lightly-garrisoned and fell quickly to Manco's troops, and thereafter they used it as a base from which to launch sorties against the beleaguered Spaniards. The bitter struggle for these heights became the decisive military action of the Conquest. Manco's failure to hold Sacsaywaman cost him the war, and the empire.

It was in May 1536, after weeks of siege and fighting in the streets, that the Spanish cavalry under Juan Pizarro broke out of the city and charged NW into the hills beyond the Saphi River, whose valley lies to your right as you face the city from Sacsaywaman. Reaching the tablelands above the city, they wheeled east and doubled back through the hills to capture the rocky knoll opposite the fortress, known today as the *Rodadero*.

From this knoll the Spanish made repeated attacks across the level plaza against the walls of the fort throughout a full day. Late in the afternoon Juan Pizarro, half-brother of Francisco, was mortally wounded by a slingshot stone to the head. "They buried him by night so that the Indians should not know he was dead, for he was a very brave man, and the Indians were very frightened of him," recalled the conquistador Francisco de Pancorvo in later years.

THE PIZARRO BROTHERS

The conquistadors were violent, lawless men – often too much so to live comfortably in their own country. Their greed and ambition frequently led them to disaster, and the Pizarro brothers were prime examples of this. Each of these four bastard half-brothers from Estremedura, a hardscrabble region of Spain, came to a relatively sticky end. Of the conquering Pizarros, Juan was the first to die. After being struck on the head at the battle of Saqsaywaman, he survived long enough to dictate a will leaving the Qoricancha, part of his loot from the Conquest, to the Dominican Order. (Hence, the Dominican monastery standing there today - *see p. 99.*) Juan was as heartless in death as he was in life: he left nothing to the indigenous woman "from whom I have received services" and took a moment to disown his daughter by that same woman. He left his entire fortune of 200,000 ducats to his younger brother Gonzalo.

Hernando Pizarro was incarcerated at the instigation of political rivals furious at his execution of Diego de Almagro in 1538, and who accused him of provoking Manco's rebellion. He spent twenty years rotting in a Spanish jail between 1541 and 1561, albeit in a gilded cage: he lived like an imprisoned drug lord on his spoils from the Conquest. To further swell his coffers he married his niece Francisca, heiress to Francisco Pizarro's fortune. She moved into his cell with him and bore him five children over nine years. He died in 1578, old and embittered over the insult to his distinguished career.

The egregious Gonzalo, Manco's chief tormentor and provocateur, rebelled against the Spanish crown in 1546, killing the first Viceroy of Peru and briefly taking control of the territory. Captured and executed in 1548 for high treason, Gonzalo's riches were seized by the crown, and his residence in the Plaza de Armas, Topa Inca's former palace, was razed and the ground sown with salt. A sign placed there read, "Here dwelled the rebel and traitor Gonzalo Pizarro."

Francisco Pizarro himself, the leader and chief strategist of the Conquest, also met a sticky end. In 1541, vengeful rivals from the Almagrist faction, which had been defeated by the Pizarros, broke into his undefended palace in Lima. Most of his followers fled, but the old conquistador donned a breastplate and managed to kill one of his attackers before succumbing to his wounds. (Seven of Pizarro's assassins escaped and were given refuge in Vilcabamba by the rebel Manco Inca, whose reward was also to be murdered by them.) Francisco Pizarro left behind a string of illegitimate children but left his fortune to the legitimate Francisca, whom Hernando would later marry.

Only a younger cousin, Pedro Pizarro, died respectably in bed, after writing his memoirs of the Conquest.

— P. F. / Leo Duncan

The day after Juan's death was a critical one for the entire Spanish occupation of Peru. The whole country was in open insurrection against the invaders. All settlements except for Lima and Cusco had been overrun or abandoned. All three Spanish columns dispatched from Lima to relieve the highland city had been massacred to the last man. Everything now hinged on this action at Sacsaywaman. If the Spanish failed to take this stronghold they were doomed; most of their slender forces were concentrated on this exposed hilltop, and there could be no easy escape to the city.

As the attacks continued throughout the day, 5,000 fresh Inca troops arrived to reinforce their comrades. Meanwhile, "in the city the Indians mounted such a fierce attack that the Spaniards thought themselves lost a thousand times." But that evening the Spanish assaulted Sacsaywaman with scaling ladders, seizing the outer walls and driving the defenders into the fortified complex dominated by the three towers. After two more days and nights of close and bitter fighting, the conquistadors finally overwhelmed the native garrison. Both Incas and Spanish had fought with desperate bravery. Several chroniclers recall an Inca noble commanding the fort who "strode about like a lion from side to side of the tower on its topmost level. He repulsed any Spaniards who tried to mount with scaling ladders. And he killed any Indians who tried to surrender." Gonzalo Pizarro was anxious to capture this Inca noble alive (for what grim purposes we may well imagine), but when the tower was taken the commander leaped to his death from the ramparts rather than surrender.

The Spanish reports of the battle made much of their own heroism (as always, giving no credit whatsoever to their native allies), and of the suicidal perils of scaling the walls. But J.P. Protzen notes that at their western end, Sacsaywaman's walls were unfinished and quite low – thus, vulnerable to attack. Most likely it was here that the conquistadors broke the defences.

The slaughter in the battle was appalling. "They put all those inside to the sword, there were 1,500 of them," wrote a Spaniard. Thousands more had died defending the citadel. In the grim dawn following the battle, flocks of condors descended to feast on the corpses. The coat of arms granted to the city of Cusco in 1540 bears a tower and a circle of eight condors commemorating the Battle of Sacsaywaman and its grisly aftermath. This melancholy symbol survived until the early 1990's, when "indigenist" sentiments in the mayor's office led to its replacement with the "Disc of Echenique," a fierce pre-Hispanic (not Inca) feline motif, named after the Peruvian president who once owned it. Despite popular folklore, this disc has nothing to do with the Punchao, the Disc of the Sun (see p.99) Somehow it ultimately wound up in the Museum of the American Indian in Washington.

Coat of arms granted Cusco by the King of Spain (left), and Cusco's official Municipal crest since 1992, the Disc of Echenique

In 1982, rains caused a section of the outer walls to subside, revealing the hastily-buried remains of eleven high-ranking Inca warriors who must have died in this battle.

The destruction of Sacsaywaman began after the defeat of Manco's rebellion. The outer walls remain – too massive, perhaps, for the Spanish to destroy. But the complex of towers and buildings was razed to the ground. There was nothing to be seen of them until Luis Valcárcel exposed the foundations in 1935 during excavations to commemorate the 400th anniversary of the Conquest.

Access

This ruin can be taken in as part of a popular tour that includes three other ruins close to Cusco (*see below*), or visited very easily on its own. It lies about half an hour's walk or ten minutes by taxi from the Plaza de Armas. The walk uphill along Don Bosco passes Colcampata (*city map #8*); follow the main road until you come to a ticket kiosk and signboard announcing the ruins. A footpath (steep but not drastic) leads you up to the east flank of the ruins, along the valley of the Tullumayo River.

In the Ruins. Read the history above to get the most out of this tour. Most organized tours start from the Main Entrance at the SW edge of the site. This tour assumes that you are going independently and starting at the pedestrian entrance to the SE. From here, walk up the steep-ish path along the edge of the Tullumayo River ravine until you pass the second ticket booth on your right. Turn left and follow the signage to the *Cruz Moqo* cross. From here, there are excellent views of the city and surrounding mountains without the crush of tourists and vendors often at Cristo Blanco. Continue NW up the trail through the eucalyptus trees, eventually turning right and going up a flight of stairs. You will pass by a small open field with two cordoned-off 10-niche buildings, one directly above the other. Continue up the wooden stairs on the right and then go left up the stone steps, bringing you to the top of a hill dominated by three large towers in Inca times. Today only the foundations are left.

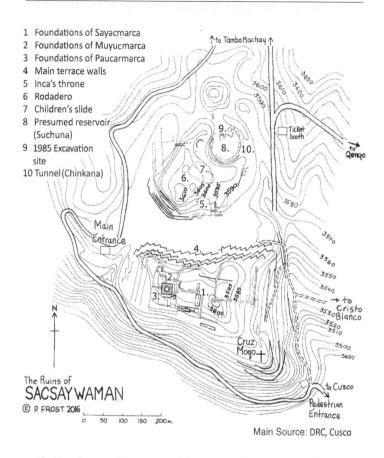

1 Foundations of Sayacmarca
2 Foundations of Muyucmarca
3 Foundations of Paucarmarca
4 Main terrace walls
5 Inca's throne
6 Rodadero
7 Children's slide
8 Presumed reservoir (Suchuna)
9 1985 Excavation site
10 Tunnel (Chinkana)

The Ruins of
SACSAYWAMAN
© P. FROST 2016
0   50   100   150   200 m.

Main Source: DRC, Cusco

The *Foundations of Sayacmarca (1)*, a rectangular tower, are identifiable by two large altar-like bases in the center, which were probably great stone supporting-columns. Continue to the left, skirting around Sayacmarca, then through a grassy plaza. Go up the steps for a view of the *Foundations of Muyucmarca (2)*, a tiered, cone-shaped tower (Muyu = circular shape in Quechua) which once had a great cistern and a system of conduits to feed water to the Inca garrison, the remains of which are clearly visible. The *Foundations of Paucarmarca (3)* are just visible behind and to the left of this. Beneath the towers ran a warren of tunnels connecting the fort to the outer walls. To this day, many fantastic legends are told about Sacsaywaman concerning labyrinthine tunnels of enormous length into which people descend, to be lost forever or to emerge, gibbering mad, clutching a corn cob made of gold.

From Muyucmarca, continue down a small flight of wooden and then stone steps to see the *Main Terrace Walls (4)* and "parade ground" or esplanade. The signage represents the terraces as *Andenes Illapa*, or "Lightning Terraces," but there is nothing other than conjecture and good storytelling to show that they represented lightning worship. Follow the cordoned pathway to the left, angling west and downwards towards the main entrance. There is a good, labeled aerial photo of the area north of Cusco and a map of Sacsaywaman here. Head east over the grass, parallel to the three tiers of massive zig-zag walls, and take the opportunity to marvel at the size of the stones in the terraces. Cross to the north side of the esplanade and continue up the steps marked "Suchana Chincana." Following the trail to the left, you'll pass by a cordoned-off stepped dais with finely carved, flat surfaces overlooking the esplanade, which is known informally as the *Inca's Throne (5)*; it would seem a good place from which to review parading troops, except that it does not directly face the esplanade: it is angled toward the southeast. In fact its closest approximate alignment, if there was anything in particular, was towards the sacred peak of Huanacauri in the mountains beyond the Cusco valley.

Follow the trail to the top to reach the *Rodadero Summit (6)*. This rocky knoll which the Spanish first captured was covered with carved and stone-clad surfaces. Walk west over the Rodadero and follow the cordoned trail down to the right. You'll quickly come to the *Children's Slide (7)* on your right — natural grooves in the glacier-scoured rock, worn smooth by generations of children, and more than a few grown-ups. (This is incorrectly signed as "Suchuna".) This puzzling geological formation is apparently a "slickenside," the result of two rock strata grinding against each other with such pressure that the rock melts, leaving smooth grooves where the surfaces have been left exposed.

Just NE of the slide is a huge ovoid construction called *Suchuna (8)*. This was uncovered by the local DRC beginning in 1985. The structure is believed to be the remains of a reservoir that supplied water to Cusco. Suchuna must have been an important religious site because, according to the chronicle of Pedro Pizarro, the Spanish went to the trouble of destroying and burying it. Walk along the western edge of Suchuna, checking out the elaborate, carved niches, platforms and the semicircle of ashlars and niches encircling a rock garden. A major burial site was found in the terraces just west of Suchuna, consisting of over 90 burials arranged in rows. The majority of these were interred in clay capsules, and all faced towards the sacred mountains of Ausangate or Huanacauri.

Continue around Suchuna to its northern end to see the *1985 Excavation site (9)*. These are the remains of Suchuna's associated ritual baths and shrines. Remains of ritual offerings were found here during excavations, particularly quartz crystal and pink spondylus shell from the coast of present-day Ecuador. This type of offering is commonly associated with the veneration of water in Inca religion. Continue to the eastern edge of Suchuna to the *Chincana (10)*, an apparently natural tunnel through limestone bedrock. Thrill-seeking visitors may shuffle their way through its pitch-dark confines, occasionally screaming in terror while confident of emerging safely at the far end. To the north and NE of Suchuna lies a maze of carved rock outcrops, caves, and tunnels, all typically puzzling pieces of Inca work, in which bare rock has been sculpted into endless variations. The tunnel exit is about 20m (65ft) NE within these rocky passageways.

CRISTO BLANCO

The *White Christ* embracing the city of Cusco in his open arms is a scaled down replica of the one in Rio de Janeiro (8m/26ft versus 30m/100ft).

The funds to construct it were donated by grateful Palestinian refugees relocated to Cusco in 1944, and it was built in San Blas by local sculptor Ernesto Olazo Allende. The statue resides on top of Pukamoqo hill, which, according to legend, was a sacred Inca site holding soil from all four corners of the Inca empire. The site makes for a panoramic view of the city, if you can handle the crowds.

Cristo Blanco can be reached either from Sacsaywaman by those who have a BTC (*see map, p. 119*), or by the ticketless but fit by climbing steeply up from the corner of *Atoqsayquchi* and *Tandapata* in San Blas (*see City Map E1, p.78*). The ascent is a leg- and lung-busting flight of stairs on Atoqsaycuchi up 100 vertical meters (330ft) over 0.75km (0.5mi). Pass a basketball court on your right, then 100m (330ft) later the stairs split; take the left fork up. At the main road, a short walk to the left brings you to the statue.

QENQO (Zig-Zag)

From Sacsaywaman, follow the road leading NE for about 2km (1.25mi), or head north from Cristo Blanco until you hit the road junction, then turn right. You come to the ruins of *Qenqo*, lying below the road embankment to the right. *Note: Walk la below (see p. 136) starts from Qenqo.*

These are not precisely ruins, for Qenqo is one of the finest examples of that Inca hallmark—the great rock carved *in situ*. It is an eroded limestone outcrop, riddled with fissures, all artfully carved to utilize the rock's natural shape.

Qenqo was a *waca*, a shrine. Inside its caves we find large niches and what looks like an altar. The early Spaniards mentioned caves around the city where they found and looted the mummies of lesser royalty, which were kept in niches along with gold and precious objects. This was almost certainly such a place; one Spanish chronicler reported that Pachacuti's mummy was kept here. Excavations here in the 1930's unearthed ten sets of human remains.

The upper, north sector here features an amphitheater with 19 large niches built around the base – all that remains of a high, curved wall focused on a standing rock. This was perhaps a phallic symbol or a sitting puma – its original form was obliterated by the conquerors – and was evidently a focus of some religious cult. It is easy to imagine mummies placed in these niches as part of an Inca ceremony at this rock.

The upper face of the outcrop is now off limits to visitors, but in the hope that the DRC will find a way to reopen it in future, this is what you can see there: stone steps lead to the top of the rock, where there are more enigmatic carvings: the zig-zag channels *(paq'chas)* that give the place its name, which served to course chicha, or perhaps sacrificial blood, for purposes of divination, and a pair of thick studs, reminiscent of the bollards used to tie up a ship – purpose unknown. June solstice observations show that the tops of these "bollards" are illuminated at sunrise, leaving an approximate puma-head shape in the shadow around them, with the sunlit bollards representing its eyes, leading to speculations of a special solstice meaning here. To the left (west) of here, on the edge of the outcrop, look for the carved figures of a puma and a now-headless bird, perhaps a condor. Towards the eastern edge of the rock stands a foot-high carving of a gable-ended house.

Qenqo Chico, the outcrop just downhill from Qenqo, is also features intricate and intriguing bedrock carving on its summit and is surrounded by a fine polygonal-style retaining wall with a zig-zag section on its southern side. Unlike the main site, the rock carvings here are still accessible.

KUSILLUCHAYOQ AND AMARU MARCAWASI (TEMPLE OF THE MOON)
These are described later in this chapter, along with the walking routes to reach them *(see Walk I, p.136)*.

LANLAKUYOK ("X ZONE")
1km (0.6mi) along the paved highway north from Qenqo lies the *X Zone (see map, p. 138)*, so called because of the X-like intersection of the modern roads here. The site is properly called *Lanlakuyok*, and it lies

on the border of *Chinchaysuyu* and *Antisuyu*. At this writing the site is closed due to restoration work but will hopefully be open again in the future. This area is a limestone dome partially ringed by an Inca wall on its southern edge and riddled with caves and Inca carvings, especially niches. Some of the caves extend far into the earth, yet no matter how deep you go there always seem to be coca leaves and burnt offerings brought by locals. Ian Farrington suggests that the site held the mummy Topa Inca Yupanqui's brother, Amaru Tupac Inca, who governed the city in the emperor's absence. There are many legends concerning the site: that one of the caves extends beneath the city of Cusco and comes out in the Qoricancha, or that Punchao, the golden Inca sun image, is hidden in its bowels. If you decide to plumb its depths, take a headlamp and a caving buddy and let someone know where you're going. The site is now ringed by a barbed wire fence and monitored by DRC employees but has seen some robberies and rapes, so go in a group, not alone.

PUCA PUCARA (Red Fort)

This small site stands to the right of the highway about 4km (2.5mi) beyond Qenqo. It is misnamed – it was not a fort. More likely it was a *tambo*, a kind of post-house where travelers were lodged and goods, animals, etc., were housed temporarily. Nevertheless, the stonework is of the highest quality, and a water channel, ritual bath and viewing platform once connected it with Tambomachay *(see below)*. The Spanish chronicler Bernabé Cobo states that the latter was the hunting lodge of the Inca Pachacuti, but since there are no signs of dwellings at that site perhaps he was referring to this place, which is close by. The last ruins in this circuit stand just a few hundred meters up the road.

TAMBOMACHAY (Cavern Lodge)

The site is named after the cave located high above the site to the north. Popularly called the *Baño del Inca* (the Inca's Bath), this is a rather finely preserved example of a site for ritual bathing and perhaps a water cult. We know that the Incas revered water as one of the principal elements of life, and they frequently practiced devotional ablutions. Here, where a spring emerges from the hillside, the Incas built a series of three waterfalls, painstakingly channeling them through fine stone channels. Note an element of mystery in the location of the spring itself. The slope behind it is simply not high enough or large enough to provide so much water; one assumes that it comes underground from the mountain opposite, via a U-shaped natural conduit.

To see the site's eponymous cave, walk out of the site's western end and follow the trail north; you'll quickly see the cave above you.

INCA STONEWORK

People have always marveled at Inca stone masonry – the famous "Inca fit," so snug that one often cannot slip a razor blade into the joints between stones that often weigh many tons. No civilization of the Old World took so much trouble with stone, and consequently none matched the accomplishments of the Andean masons.

Many bizarre and fantastic theories have attempted to explain how these wonders were performed. Colonel Fawcett, the eccentric early-20th-century explorer, published a tall tale that has been on the lips of tour guides ever since. In his book *Exploration Fawcett* he claimed the Incas possessed an Amazonian herb capable of dissolving stone. Awestruck early Spanish chroniclers claimed that the natives had enlisted the aid of demons. Nowadays, this identical psychology operates in reverse: it was not evil demons but godlike extraterrestrials who built the things. Either way, according to this thinking, those primitive Incas couldn't have done it themselves.

Yet there is a rich body of scientific work showing that they not only could, they did...

Who Worked the Stones?

Although the Incas did not have the hard steel tools necessary for rapid chiseling, nor the engines and draft animals that Old Worlders would have used for shifting 100-ton rocks, they did have a vast mass of

125

surplus labor due to the legendary efficiency of their agriculture. They also had a labor conscription system (*mit'a*) capable of channeling these energies into great public works projects. Communities from throughout the empire sent labor contingents to work temporarily for the state. Workers were fed and housed, rewarded with cloth, and even allowed their share of drunken parties. Many of them worked in weaving workshops, potteries, and mines, some served in the army, others built roads, quarried stone and raised the massive structures whose remains we marvel at today. The Incas understood the use of the inclined plane, the stone roller, and almost certainly the lever (*see below*). With these techniques and so much manpower they could cut huge stones and move them over long distances.

How They Cut Them

The Incas typically started their stonework at the quarry itself. To quarry stones the masons made a starting cut along a natural weakness in the rock, probably using hard stone such as hematite as a tool. Then, wedges were used to widen the fissure until the rock broke away from the main

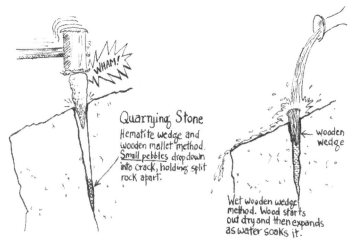

WHAM!

Quarrying Stone
Hematite wedge and
wooden mallet method.
Small pebbles drop down
into crack, holding split
rock apart.

← Wooden
wedge

Wet wooden wedge
method. Wood starts
out dry and then expands
as water soaks it.

126

mass. The wedges were made either of another, harder stone, which they drove in by pounding, or wood, which split the rock by expanding when soaked in water. One of the "tired stones" (blocks in transit from the quarries that never reached the construction site) near Ollantaytambo (see p.178) sits to the right of and slightly above the modern road to Quillabamba. It shows clear evidence of how the masons were shaping it and also re-cutting it because of an accidental fracture.

An interesting discovery has been reported at the Rumicolca quarries, 35km (22mi) from Cusco (see p.280) A modern quarryman says he found small round pebbles at the bottom of a crack in a half-split rock that was in the process of being quarried. These pebbles would have had a ratchet effect, dropping down and preventing the crack from closing again after it had been fractionally opened by a blow on the wedges at the top.

The Inca masons dressed stones into the smooth, perfect shapes required for building by simply pounding on the stones repeatedly with another, harder stone, chipping and flaking away the worked surface. This method is not as laborious as one might think because a reasonably skilled worker can get a rhythm going, allowing a rapid, relaxed drop-and-catch technique such that the hammerstone will bounce back at each blow, eating away the face of the worked stone at a surprising rate. Using this technique, J.P. Protzen, a leading researcher into Inca stoneworking, turned a shapeless lump of andesite into a smooth cube about 25cm (10in) along the edge in only an hour and a half.

Dressing Stone : the striking tool will bounce, making a rapid hammering motion.

Evidence that the Incas used such a technique is visible everywhere. Even the finest of their masonry is covered with tiny pockmarks made by this pounding process. This technique, incidentally, helps to account for the deeply recessed, or beveled, edges of the blocks in Inca walls. It is hard to get a sharp, right-angled edge using stone hammers because the corners tend to break off.

The intermediate stage between splitting rock and fine dressing may have called for a rough-cutting process whose nature has not been determined. However, a partially-cut block examined by the author at Phuyupatamarca on the Inca Trail was apparently being cut by the same pounding process used for fine dressing, and Protzen references other stones showing the same process under way.

How They Moved Them

Once the stone was cut, how did they transport multi-ton colossi such as those at Sacsaywaman and Ollantaytambo? The assumption about ancient stone-moving techniques has generally been that the stones were placed on sleds, which were then hauled over log rollers by large teams of people pulling on ropes. We know that the Inca understood the principle of rollers because examples still exist, including one by the Temple of Three Windows at Machu Picchu (see p.240). There a large block rests on a small cylindrical stone, which evidently served as a roller to facilitate maneuvering of the larger stone. However, this technique was only being used for wiggling stones into position, not for transportation over long distances. In practice, bigger rollers tend to swing out of alignment easily and are difficult to work with in field conditions.

With enough people almost anything can simply be dragged across open country. Excavations near Ollantaytambo beneath an 80-ton "tired stone" revealed that over long distances the Incas dragged the stones over friction-reducing cobblestone roadbeds by brute force, without rollers. The stones being transported were rounded on the underside to prevent them from digging into the ground.

Things change when working on steep slopes and in tight spots: the amount of space available for the hauling crew is drastically reduced, and the problem then becomes how to apply force to the object to be moved. Dragging or roller methods could not, for example, have worked on a steep ramp like the one at Ollantaytambo, which ended in a sheer 16m (52ft) drop-off (*see p.178*); there would have been nowhere for the hauling team to stand. Rollers on a slope also pose the problem of friction – not enough of it. Crews could easily lose control of the stone on a steep ramp, leading to a catastrophic accident with fatalities and the stone shattered or irretrievable far below. The Incas must have had an Archimedes somewhere in their history, because they appear to have understood that the way to do this was with levers.

While working for a television documentary on Easter Island, intrepid architect and ancient mystery cracker Vincent R. Lee came up with some new ideas as to how pre-industrial engineers moved huge stones into tight places. To test his theories, he built a 17m (56ft) long, scaled-down replica of the ramp at Ollantaytambo, and then tried moving a thirteen-ton stone up it, rotating it 90 degrees at the top of the ramp. Using a combination of a sled, a ladder-type roadbed, and

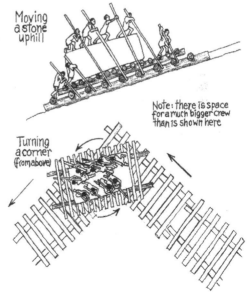

Moving a stone uphill

Note: there is space for a much bigger crew than is shown here

Turning a corner (from above)

levers, he accomplished this feat successfully in two hours with a crew of only 26 people.

Vincent Lee and friends placed their trial stone on a sled and levered it forward along a kind of ladder, greased with lard and laid flat on the ground as a roadbed. Sections of ladder were "leapfrogged" to make the roadbed continuous, and the "rungs" were used as points of leverage by people standing on the sled or on top of the stone. The sled could be rotated simply by levering forward on one side and/or pulling back on the other. If the stone started to slide back downhill it could easily be stopped using the levers as brakes.

The gain in mechanical advantage (ratio of exerted to applied force) was immense: Lee calculated about 1:3 for a man standing on the ground; 1:5 if he rides the sled; and 1:7, 1:8 or more if he stands on the stone. The added weight of people on the stone or sled was more than offset by the increased leverage.

One detail that led Lee to suspect that the Incas used such a method was the configuration of the Ollantaytambo ramp itself. Right at the top, where there is no room for a hauling crew, one would expect the builders to have made a gentler gradient, to allow for the added difficulty of raising the stone. Instead its gradient increases to a daunting 25%. Lee reasons that, having necessarily dispensed with any hauling crew and shifted exclusively to the lever method at that point, the Inca engineers chose to get their stones up the last section in the shortest possible distance.

Lee's crew was able to move its 13-ton stone (plus about 2.5 tons of sled and people) up a 25% incline, moving an average of 450kg (990lb) per person! The largest stone at Ollantaytambo weighs 52 tons; following those calculations, it would have taken 101 people to move that stone up the ramp – a number which the dimensions of the ramp and the top of the stone would easily have permitted.

Lee has shown that it is both possible and efficient to move very large stones as described. Of course, this does not prove that the Incas *did* move them this way. However, there is evidence that ancient Egyptians did use a very similar technique. It is not much of a stretch to imagine ancient Peruvians arriving independently at the same method. This seems by far the most satisfying theory to date – and the only one to cover all the bases of the Inca stone-moving riddle. (*See Vincent R. Lee's* Ancient Moonshots, *Bibliography.*)

THE STONES OF SARAGURO

An astonishing story of long-distance stone transportation comes to us from the Spanish priest Martín de Murúa. Writing in 1605, he reported that emperor Wayna Capac ordered two palaces built in Cusco, then dismantled and transported north to his new capital at Tomebamba, now Cuenca in modern Ecuador. At the town of Saraguro, near their final destination, a lightning strike shattered one of the main lintel stones. Wayna Capac took this as an ill omen and abandoned the project. (Murúa does not report the stone-moving crew's reaction to this news.)

Saraguro is well over 1,600km (1,000mi) away, across spectacularly rugged mountain terrain, so Murúa's uncorroborated tale was always taken as legend. Then in 2004, archaeologist Dennis Ogburn examined numerous well-cut andesite stones scattered near Saraguro and applied modern geochemical sourcing techniques to demonstrate that they really *were* from the Rumicolca quarries near Cusco. He found more than 450 of them, the largest weighing more than 700kg (1,600lb). Ogburn speculates that the task of dragging these stones was a punishment assigned to some miscreant tribe, though it also seems possible the stones were passed from hand to hand, being moved by successive communities as they traveled north. Whichever is true, the stones likely represent the longest known distance over which such heavy objects were transported in the pre-European Americas, over daunting terrain without the wheel or draft animals.

– Leo Duncan

How They Fit Them

The foregoing explains how the Inca cut individual stones and the methods probably used to transport and shift them into place. But how did they achieve the legendary "Inca fit," so perfect that, as generations of awed commentators have noted, one cannot insert even the thinnest steel blade between them? First, bear in mind that the Incas faced a huge technical challenge of their own making by never cutting right angles and flat surfaces, which would have made it vastly simpler to cut and join stones neatly and precisely to their neighbors. (Why they didn't is a matter for speculation, but the unique aesthetic appeal of Inca walls is undeniable, and one practical advantage was the highly anti-seismic characteristics of their construction style.)

Once again, practical theorist Vincent R. Lee proposes an ingenious answer to the stone-fitting question. The idea is based on a method still used in cabinet-making and the fitting of corners on log cabins, known as "scribing and coping."

The modern "scribe" is an instrument like a draftsman's compass, used to mark the upper of two corner logs with the exact profile of the lower one. It uses a bubble level to maintain a constant spatial relationship between two surfaces. Lee shows that the bubble level can be replaced with a plumb-line to create a similar artifact within the technical capabilities of the Incas.

Scribe is used to measure, as lower surface is cut

Hypothetical Inca "scribe"

these points measure space between upper and lower stone

string passes through hole in horizontal bar

plumb bob

scribe

cope (cut surface)

Surface to be cut

The "cope" is the term used by log cabin builders for the cut which is made in the upper log. In an inversion of this technique, Lee proposes, the Incas cut the upper stone first and then used a scribe to trace a perfect replica of the upper profile on the lower stones, pounding away (or "coping") the excess with hammer-stones. The basic principle involved is the same as that used for duplicating door keys.

This operation requires (a) that the cut stone be fixed immovably in place directly above the one to be cut; (b) that the cut upper face is free of obstructions; and (c) that there is enough space in between the stones for the masons to use the scribe while cutting the lower stone. Considering the mass of some of these stones, all this would seem the hardest part of the operation. In a recent refinement of his theory Lee resolves some of the difficulty, suggesting that the cut upper stone was moved up a ramp onto a temporary construction terrace built above and behind uncut lower stones. (*See illustrations*)

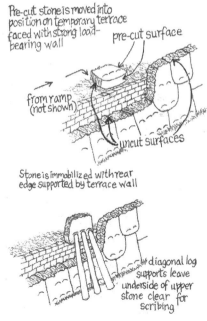

Pre-cut stone is moved into position on temporary terrace faced with strong load-bearing wall

pre-cut surface

from ramp (not shown)

uncut surfaces

Stone is immobilized with rear edge supported by terrace wall

diagonal log supports leave underside of upper stone clear for scribing

The front of this temporary terrace was a very solid wall that supported the back edge of this upper stone when it was tilted forward into position above the lower stones. The upper stone was supported from the front by logs dropped into precut sockets in its outer face, leaving its underside clear. (These sockets were intended to be carved away later, but many examples can still be seen on the unfinished walls of Sacsaywaman.) With a few additional braces the upper stone was solidly supported such that its underside could be traced with a scribe as masons replicated its profile on the uncut stones below.

This theory also helps to make practical sense of the deeply recessed joints and beveled edges in virtually all Inca stonework: the rigid scribe bridged the entire space between the upper and lower stone, and beveled edges would have allowed it to transition into the gap as the masons opened up the correct measurement between faces. A right-angled edge would have blocked it if the lower stone had been even slightly too thick.

The "scribing and coping" technique represents a vast improvement over any "trial and error" method of lowering stones into place and lifting them again to perfect the joint, since the stones could be cut and fitted perfectly in one operation. It also beats the idea of templates, which, though appealing in theory, are unworkable in practice due to stubborn problems of weight, strength and rigidity at this scale in any material available to the Incas.

Some sceptics (J.P. Protzen among them) regard this theory as too hypothetical, no specimen of its principal artifact – the Inca "scribe" – ever having been found by archaeologists. But it was a simple and perishable instrument which would not necessarily have survived over the centuries. Other theories are hypothetical too, and this one has been shown to work well in practice.

(A detailed account of the scribing and coping theory appears in Vincent R. Lee's paper *Sacsaywaman: An Inca Masterwork. See Bibliography.*)

But What About the Aliens?

The grandiosity and precision of some Inca stonework has convinced many that these feats were supernatural. Of course the techniques described above were a staggering challenge when working with huge stones, but even if the proposed theories are mistaken in their particulars, the genius of Inca stoneworking does not require supernatural explanations. Innumerable clues left by the builders tell us that they were made by humans using methods we can understand and replicate: stone hammers, peckmarks on stones, bronze crowbars, sockets, ramps, the mundane chaos of construction interrupted 500 years ago, all point to human organization and ingenuity. One characteristic of existing Inca walls, for example, is that the load-bearing (i.e. horizontal) joints of the stones are always made to fit perfectly over their entire surface, whereas the vertical joins are often joined perfectly only to a depth of a few centimeters from the outer surface, with mud and rubble used to fill internal gaps. This is elementary physics and practical engineering. If the Incas had possessed stone-melting lasers and liquids, anti-gravity fields and the like for moving and cutting stone, why would they have resorted to time-honored construction shortcuts?

Another simple fact suggesting that their techniques were neither mysterious nor extraterrestrial is that the Spanish saw them in action, albeit on a much smaller scale. Much of the "Inca" masonry in the city of Cusco was actually done after the Spanish Conquest (see box, p. 80). The Inca masons were working for Spanish masters to a different design and with declining quality, but the style of workmanship is still unmistakably theirs.

The Spanish themselves did not lack the technology to perform such work, and nor do we today. What we lack are other Inca traits: endless patience and a profound spiritual reverence for their working material, the stone itself. Here is the subtler explanation for how the Incas were able to perform amazing exploits with huge stones: their society was mostly unified and well fed, and their workforce was not coerced, since their mightiest structures were dedicated to the deities which everyone worshipped. Thus, an undivided focus of human energies achieved what seem like superhuman feats to we individualistic moderns.

(The author is greatly indebted to Dr. Jean-Pierre Protzen and Vincent R. Lee for much of the above information.)

TWO HALF-DAY WALKS NEAR CUSCO
See map p. 138

You can wander at will in the hills north of Cusco without getting lost. The country is open, and major landmarks are always in sight. Here are two suggestions for walks that make a convenient round trip, easily done in half a day, allowing plenty of time for looking around, and well laced with interesting places to explore and scenes to photograph. Each starts from a point on the highway which can be reached by taxi. The walks take a bit longer if you embark from Cusco itself. Be sure to carry a compass on the hikes mentioned below. A note on safety: the areas described are pretty safe, but women shouldn't hike alone, and Amaru Marcawasi and Lanlakuyok should be avoided around and after dark. Rapes and assaults have been reported there in the past. See p. 41 for more general notes on safety.

Walk I: Wacas, Ceques and Solstices

This walk can be started either from the ruins of Qenqo (Walk Ia) or Pl. San Blas (Walk Ib). These paths meet at Amaru Marcawasi (*a.k.a.* Temple of the Moon *a.k.a.* Lajo *a.k.a.* Salumpunku)

Walk Ia. 1km (0.6mi), elevation +30m (100ft), 15min. Start at Qenqo. Get your bearings (*see Lay of the Land, p. 74*). There is a turnoff to the right just above Qenqo at the large *Parque Arqueológico Sacsaywaman* sign. Take it and continue for about 100m (330ft) as you pass the houses on your right. You are heading roughly east with your back to Cusco. Head through the opening in the barbed wire fence, past the sign prohibiting biking and horseback riding, and emerge onto open pasture. Head for a large rock outcrop in front of you, slightly to the right. This outcrop is the *waca* known as *Amaru Marcawasi* (also Lajo, or the Temple of the Moon). From its summit, look south back towards Cusco. On your left, you will see a few trees and a low stone wall flanking a pathway angling back towards the city; this is Walk Ib below, and you can return to the San Blas neighborhood of Cusco this way by reversing the directions in the next paragraph.

Walk Ib. 1.6km (1mi), elevation +200m (650ft), 30-60min. Starting from the San Blas church, walk uphill to the left on *Suitu Qhatu* (*see F1 City Map, p. 78*). This is the old Road to the *Antisuyu*, the jungle quarter of the Inca empire (you won't be walking *quite* that far); parts of it are quite well preserved. About 300m (1,000ft) up this street, just past a small plaza and fountain, the street forks, with a paved section going off to your right. Take the left fork for another 400m (1,300ft), climbing several flights of stone steps on the way, until you reach the paved highway. Cross and continue north, taking the right-hand trail through the vegetation past the small drainage basin, not up the road on your left. The trail turns NE and after 120m (400ft) ascends a flight of stone stairs, becoming much wider and passing eucalyptus trees and houses on your left. You'll soon come across *Kusilluchayoq*, the "Monkey Temple," which has a small building complex and various worked stones and zoomorphic carvings. This site is considered to be part of the Amaru Marcawasi complex (*see below*) and, as such, was likely part of the ancestral home of the Inca Wiracocha. Excavations discovered an adult's tomb along with two fine chicha jars. The trail continues north, passing a set of ritual baths on the left, and takes you to Amaru Marcawasi.

Amaru Marcawasi and Onwards. There are two significant caves in this outcrop on the south side and an immense fissure running right through it. Sadly, the ruins of the buildings, the fissure and the caves have been roped off and are not accessible at this writing. The cave near the SE end of the rock about halfway up is the most intricately carved. The battered outlines of snakes, pumas and a condor carved in relief on the rocks are still clearly visible at the entrance. Inside the cave there are mummy-niches, and a kind of altar onto which sunlight falls through a fissure in the rock above. This altar is said to be bathed in a pool of direct moonlight at midnight on the full moon closest to the winter solstice, hence the popular name "Temple of the Moon." The other carvings on the top of this great rock, including a feline, birds and a snake, have not yet been roped off.

Whatever the site's true purpose, it almost certainly wasn't moon worship: the moon can rarely be seen from inside the cave, and it seems

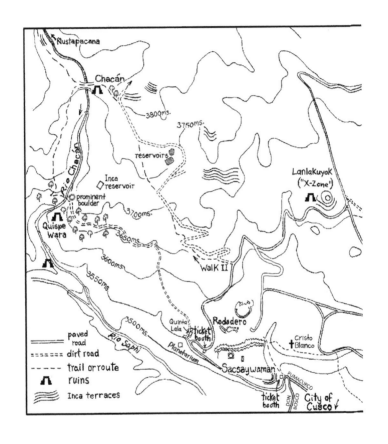

Ñustapacana

Chacán

3800ms.

3750ms.

reservoirs

Inca
reservoir

prominent
boulder

Río Chacán

3700ms.

Quispe
Wara

3650ms.

3600ms.

Lanlakuyok
("X-Zone")

Walk II

3550ms.

3500ms.

Río Saphi

Quinta
Lala

ticket
booth

Planetarium

Rodadero

Cristo
Blanco

Sacsaywaman

RUMACURCO

ticket
booth

DON BOSCO

City of
Cusco

paved
road

dirt road

trail or route

ruins

Inca terraces

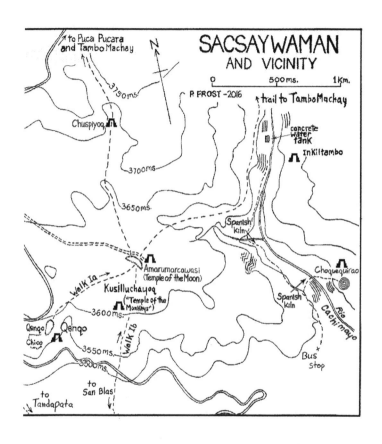

SACSAYWAMAN
AND VICINITY

0   500 ms.   1 Km.

P. FROST - 2016

to Puca Pucara
and Tambo Machay

N

3750ms.

Chuspiyoq

3700ms.

3650ms.

trail to TamboMachay

concrete
water
tank

InKiltambo

Spanish
kiln

Amarumarcawasi
(Temple of the Moon)

Choquequirao

Walk Ia

Kusilluchayoq
("Temple of the
Monkeys")

Spanish
kiln

3600ms.

Rio Cachimayo

Qenqo
Chico

Qenqo

Walk Ib

3550ms.

3500ms.

Bus
Stop

to San Blas

to
Tandapata

unlikely that the Inca would have worshipped a celestial body from underground. Farrington and Farfán (2002) suggest that this site may have been the ancestral house of the Inca Wiracocha and his *panaca*. Numerous objects were found here during excavations, including three spondylus-shell llama figurines, a gold male figurine, a gold bracelet, and *tumis*.

From Amaru Marcawasi, take the route either 1) NE to Inkiltambo; or 2) North to Chuspiyoq, Puca Pucara and Tambomachay.

1) *NE to Inkiltambo.* 1.75km (1.1mi) to Inkiltambo, 3.4km (2.1mi) to bus stop, elevation -130m (426ft), 2 hours with time at the ruins. Stand atop the *waca* with your back to where you came from. You see a small stream below, and two wide paths leading away beyond it ENE. The upper one is the original Inca road to Pisac, but this will not take you to Inkiltambo. Take the right path instead, following the signage. This winds up and around the right flank of the hill, passing some low rock outcrops on your right. The trail eventually pulls to the left and descends. Around this point, a sign marks a viewpoint with views of the Rio Cachimayo Valley and Inkiltambo. Shortly after this trail begins to descend a small but distinct trail peels off to the right, descending through the vegetation towards the Rio Cachimayo. As you reach the valley bottom, you come upon a fenced-in concrete water tank. Pass by this and cross the stream to reach Inkiltambo.

Inkiltambo ("Garden Lodge House") has several deep carved niches, which probably housed the ancestor mummies of the *ayllu* that tended this shrine. The remains of carved water channels and a ritual bath can be seen below the rock on the western and southern sides. The authorities have rebuilt a bank of 14 ventilation ducts, which they claim would have once held ceremonial offerings. On top there is a carved fissure with two deep niches set where the tunnel narrows into a crack. The sun can be seen to set dead center in this crack on the evening of the equinoxes.

Extensive restoration work has been done here recently, and admission may be charged in the future.

From Inkiltambo, turn downhill and follow the stream running down the *quebrada* (ravine) of the Cachimayo River. Pick up a trail on the righthand side of the stream. Soon you come to some old kilns, dating from colonial times, that were used to make roofing tiles. Further down the trail you pass more of these tucked under a cliff on the far side of the ravine, well below you on your left.

On the main trail, beyond the second Spanish kilns, you find a trail that leads up the righthand valley to a magnificent view across the Huatanay Valley to the town of San Jerónimo. The trail rises through a notch in a ridge to your right then passes through a park control point, and you find yourself abruptly on the outskirts of Cusco. From this point, the best way back to town is a taxi or the local bus *Inka Express*, which takes you to Limacpampa Grande (F3 city map) or the Serpost post office on *Av. el Sol* (F4), both a relatively short walk from the Plaza de Armas.

Explorer's Note: From the lower colonial kilns you can take the trail up to the ruins of Choquequirao (not to be confused with the more famous Choquequirao in Vilcabamba – *see p.307*), a circular set of terraces on a small hill. This area contains several buildings of high quality Inca stonework, a stone passageway lined with Inca masonry, a small quarry, and a large spring nearby with several pools below it. The quarry may have been a shrine to the Inca creator god Wiracocha, while the spring and terraced hills were likely important wacas in their own right.

2) *North To Chuspiyoq, Puca Pucara and Tambomachay*. 3km (1.9mi), elevation +150m (490ft). Start from the NW corner of Amaru Marcawasi. Follow a trail leading into a grassy valley which climbs northward. Continue along this trail, passing some marshy sections along the way. About 300m (1,000ft) from Amaru Marcawasi, you'll come across a large boulder with some carvings and a cave on your left. Continue north along the trail

and you'll see a wooden sign on your right indicating the ruins next to the large boulder of Chuspiyoq. Ascend the flight of stairs on the SW flank of this boulder and continue walking north along the valley bottom, following the path as it crosses to the right hand (eastern) slopes. Follow the trail for 1.5km (0.9mi) from Chuspiyoq, passing a small wetland on your left, until it reconnects with the main road. From here, the ruins of Puca Pucara and Tambomachay are an easy 200m (650ft) and 500m (0.3mi) north up the road, respectively. To return to Cusco, return via the same trail or grab any southbound bus, taxi, or *colectivo*, most of which will leave you in the vicinity of the Pisac bus stop on *Puputi* street (OM).

Walk II: Dams, Caves and Aqueducts

2.9km (1.8mi) to Chacán, elevation +180m (590ft), 6km (3.8mi) return, 3-4 hours. Start from the Sacsaywaman main entrance. A paved road runs around the northern perimeter of the ruins. Walk 850m (0.5mi) up this road past the Sacsaywaman ticket booth and you will come to a lefthand turn onto a dirt road marked with a *Parque Arqueológico Saqsaywaman* sign with a left arrow labeled "Chakan, Ñusta Pakana" and a right arrow labeled "Huchuy Qosqo." Head left and follow this road for 100m (330ft) until you reach a path off to the left. This path splits after about 100m (330ft). Ascend the right fork and follow it back to the dirt road, which you'll follow only briefly before two pedestrian trails split off left at a hairpin bend. Take the righthand trail and follow it steeply up, over several stone-lined dirt stairs. After the trail rejoins the main road, continue on for 200m (660ft) until the road takes a sharp right and a pedestrian trail continues straight ahead. Follow the trail uphill past some houses to where it rejoins the road and continue north until the road forks. Take the less traveled left fork, which passes some trees and quickly becomes a trail. Follow this, trending NNE, to the valley of the Chacán River, a place where a great natural barrier straddles the gorge. This place is also called Chacán (Bridge-place). The aqueduct runs across the top of this unusual geological formation, while the stream itself runs beneath it, some 30m (100ft) below.

Early chroniclers mention several dams on the rivers above Cusco, and this may have been one of them. Each year in our month of January, when the flood waters were peaking, the Incas would break the dams above Cusco. The ashes of the whole year's sacrifices would be thrown into the river Huatanay below the Temple of the Sun. Then, in a ritual called *Mayucati* ("following the river") young men would chase the ashes downriver all the way to Ollantaytambo, a distance of at least 100km (62.5mi).

High above the aqueduct west of Chacán stands a rock which was carved and fitted with stone walls, now mostly destroyed. This was probably another of Cusco's *wacas*. Just after crossing the natural bridge you can descend just a few meters to the right and cut back towards the cliff edge. Follow a broad fissure descending onto a natural balcony within a cave, partially carved by the Incas, which looks down into the mouth of the river-tunnel far below. Here, the Chacán River runs through a huge, tapering cave underneath Chacán. It starts out about 10m (32ft) high and narrows to about 2m (6.5ft) where the stream exits.

Explorer's Note: Those who like to indulge their inner child can walk through this tunnel, crouching as they emerge and getting their feet a bit wet. But DON'T try this if the river is running strong; check the stream's exit as you arrive from below. There is a 2m (6ft) drop to get into the cave (jump down next to the wall on your right). It is difficult to climb back up, and once inside you are fairly committed to passing through it. Afterwards, adventurers with strong ankles and a love of boulder hopping can return to Cusco by following the Chacán River down its length until the prominent boulder mentioned in the return description below.

The entire area upstream for a kilometer or so above Chacán is dotted with Inca remains, and you will pass platforms, fine terrace walls and a rock shrine by the water's edge, before reaching another ravine at the small ruins of Ñustapacana.

143

To return to Cusco, start from the aqueduct at Chacán. Look south down the Chacán ravine towards Cusco and notice the edge of a eucalyptus forest about 1km (0.6mi) away on the left (east) bank, below and to the right of a large grassy plateau. (In case the trees have been logged since this writing, you should be able to see numerous tree stumps and a dirt road currently hidden by the trees.) Walk downstream high above the righthand (west) side of the river on any convenient trail, slowly angling down towards this forest. After about 600m (0.37mi), the trail contours around a small ridge and you will notice a prominent boulder in the ravine at the forest's edge on the far bank of the river. This boulder has an Inca wall supported by wooden struts, plus a small plastic pipe running around it. A dirt road road back to Cusco begins here. To reach it, follow the trail a short distance through the forest along the right riverbank, then descend steeply to your left into the ravine. From here, it is easy to arrive at the boulder.

A small, worthwhile detour takes you about 100m (330ft) downstream from here. You will come to a great stone, carved on all sides, with remains of a walled enclosure and a water duct on the left bank of the stream. Overlooking the stream you find a stepped-pyramid shape (a common religious motif in the Andean cultures) cut into the rock, about 2.5m (8ft) high. In the center of it, notice the rounded outline that remains where some carved Inca symbol, now defaced, once overlooked the water. This *waca* is called *Quispe Wara* (Crystal Loincloth). About 180m (600ft) downstream there is another section of high quality Inca structures, walls and channels – all part of this same shrine complex.

To return to Cusco, start from the prominent boulder and follow the narrow dirt road that winds gently downhill about 2km (1.3mi). You will pass the Quinta Lala on your left. Turn left immediately beyond it, and after 100m (330ft) you reach the paved highway at the tight curve just downhill from Sacsaywaman. From here, it's an easy walk (or taxi ride) down the paved road to get to Cusco and the streets of *Pumacurco* and *Don Bosco*.

MAMA SIMONA

This is a beautiful, sloping ramp of a mountain to the SW of Cusco, visible from near the city at the high points around Amaru Marcawasi and Lanlakuyok. On a clear day, all the major peaks and mountain ranges in the region are visible from its summit. Aside from some steep sections near the top, the trail is easy and makes for a good acclimatization hike as its 4,300m (14,100ft) summit isn't too high. (4km/2.5mi to the summit, elevation +400m/1,300ft, 2-3 hours.) This hike is not within walking distance of Cusco. See **www.peterfrost.org** for hiking instructions and transportation.

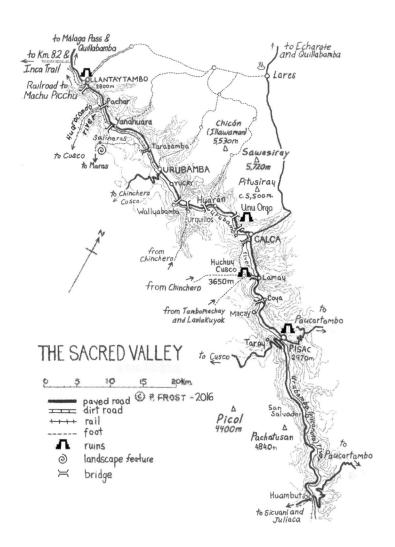

THE SACRED VALLEY

to Málaga Pass & Quillabamba

to Km. 82 & Inca Trail

Railroad to Machu Picchu

to Echarate and Quillabamba

Lares

OLLANTAYTAMBO 2800m

Pachar

Huarocondo River

Yanahuara

Salineras

to Cusco

to Maras

Tarabamba

Chicón (Illawaman) 5,530m

Sawasiray 5,720m

URUBAMBA

YUCAY

Pitusiray c. 5,500m

to Chinchero Cusco

Huarán

Unu Orqo

Wallyabamba

Urquillos

Urubamba River

CALCA

from Chinchero

from Chinchero

Huchuy Cusco 3650m

Lamay

Coya

from Tambomachay and Lanlakuyok

Macay

Taray

to Paucartambo

to Cusco

PISAC 2970m

San Salvador

Picol 4400m

Pachatusan 4840m

Urubamba (Willcamayo) River

to Paucartambo

Huambutio

to Sicuani and Juliaca

Scale

0   5   10   15   20 Km.

© P. FROST — 2016

▬▬▬	paved road
▭▭▭	dirt road
+++	rail
- - -	foot
⚲	ruins
◉	landscape feature
⋈	bridge

CHAPTER THREE

THE SACRED VALLEY
Pisac-Calca & Lares-Urubamba-Ollantaytambo

THE LAY OF THE LAND

The river which rises at the pass of La Raya, 150 air km (94mi) southeast of Cusco, runs through the very heartland of what was *Tawantinsuyu*, the Inca empire. There was an important Inca shrine at La Raya, the watershed between the Urubamba Valley and the Lake Titicaca basin. 300km (188mi) downstream, towards the eastern frontiers of the Inca realm, lay the sacred center of Machu Picchu. In between stood many of the most famous sacred or elite Inca sites, such as the Temple of Wiracocha at Raqchi, the ruins of Pisac and Huchuy Cusco, the royal palaces at Yucay and Urubamba, the imposing settlement of Ollantaytambo, and the string of ceremonial centers along what is now known as the Inca Trail.

The river which the Incas called *Willcamayu*, the Sacred River, had its celestial counterpart in the Milky Way, a key element in Inca cosmology which they also called Mayu, the River, and which was oriented along the same southeast/northwest axis as the Willcamayu during the southern summer.

So there's a reason besides marketing to call it The Sacred Valley. Today this term generally refers to the stretch between Pisac and Ollantaytambo, a broad and gently sloping river plain 500-600m (1,640-2,000ft) lower than Cusco. This valley was undoubtedly a key area of settlement to the Incas; its combination of agreeable climate and fertile plains bestow an unusual abundance for the high Andes. Here the Incas sculpted the mountain flanks with vast contour terracing and irrigation works, also channeling the main river between stone walls, some of which survives.

147

This is still a bounteous agricultural region supplying the city of Cusco with much of its table fare, particularly fruit, vegetables and corn. The white corn of the Sacred Valley, with its huge, fat kernels, is a major export crop of the region and it is said that nowhere else, in Peru or the rest of the world, does this variety of corn grow to such size and quality.

The Incas were attracted not only to agricultural wealth, but also to natural beauty, placing ceremonial sites and royal estates – such as Pisac and Machu Picchu– in the most dramatically scenic locations imaginable. The Sacred Valley is a corridor through one of the most glorious mountain landscapes in the world, its lush green floor walled in to the north by the dark granite crags and gleaming snow peaks of the Urubamba range, to the south by a more arid, rolling mosaic of russet earth and yellowed grassland, which is interrupted by verdant ravines and stretches of soaring, red cliffs towering five or six hundred meters (1,640-2,000ft) above the wandering ribbon of the Urubamba River.

(**Note:** Some confusion arises around the name of the river, owing to the Quechua custom of naming rivers by sections. In Inca times the whole river was called the *Willcamayu*. Today it is usually called the Vilcanota upstream of Pisac or Huambutío, and the Urubamba lower down, but there is no precise point where the name changes.)

The Valley, as it is simply known to locals, also was, and still is, the route to the forest regions to the east, and therefore an area with access to the fruits and plants of the tropical lowlands, which the Inca nobles were privileged to consume (most importantly the coca leaf, vital to rituals, festivals and daily pleasure). And during the formative period of the Inca state it was probably a strategic buffer region protecting Cusco from the incursions of the Antis, the fierce jungle tribes who raided the highlands from time to time.

Being at a lower altitude than Cusco, the Valley is a warmer and less physiologically stressful environment for the visitor. It is also very convenient for visiting many of the best-known attractions of the Cusco region, including Machu Picchu. Pisac is only 45 minutes from Cusco by paved highway, and Urubamba is about 1¼ hrs. With a wealth of services now available, some people now choose to spend most of their visit to the Cusco region in this area.

Pisac is usually taken as the starting point of visits to the Valley because this is where the main road from Cusco crosses the Vilcanota (downstream, the Urubamba) river. There are, however, a few points upstream worth seeing as well. To include this part of the Valley in your visit, take the road ESE from Cusco (*see Chapter Seven*) along the Huatanay Valley and turn left to double back NW down the Valley at Huambutío. This route to Pisac adds about 25km (15mi) to the journey, and for reasons of time is best left out if you are planning to visit Pisac, Ollantaytambo and points between in a single day.

The journey from Huambutío downriver takes you through an impressive gorge of red sandstone cliffs, hung with long beards of Spanish moss. The winding, paved road follows the Vilcanota River – a beautiful drive. About 20km (12.5mi) downstream you come to Huanca. High on the mountain to your left is the shrine which once a year, on Sept. 14th, becomes the scene of an enormous pilgrimage for thousands of believers in the miracle of *El Señor de Huanca* (*see Calendar, p. 51*). At Pisac the road joins the main route from Cusco and crosses the river, the valley widens, and you reach the point from which most tours begin.

See *General Information*, p. 53 for services, restaurants and hotels, and p. 21 for transport to all destinations. The distances to Pisac, Lamay, Calca and Lares are given for the NE route going over the high pass of *Abra de Corao*; the distances to Yucay, Urubamba and Ollantaytambo are given for the NW route passing through the town of Chinchero.

PISAC (33km / 21mi)

The direct route from Cusco is the road that winds over the mountains north of Cusco, past Sacsaywaman and the other three ruins described in Chapter Two (*See Transportation*, p.21). Beyond Tambomachay it crosses a pass and drops down into a broad basin, passing through the village of Corao. Beyond here, the road skirts some abrupt plunges and offers magnificent views as it winds down into the Urubamba Valley. Far below you to the left as you enter the Valley lies the village of Taray; lower down you get a superb view of the modern village of *Pisac* and the majestic ruins and terraces on the mountain spur high above it.

The Inca terracing systems were used mainly for the cultivation of maize, considered a prestige crop, sometimes grown for the preparation of the *chicha* used in ritual libations. Maize has a long growing season, which in the highlands must be shortened as much as possible by irrigation to protect the crop from frosts. Other Inca staples – potatoes and quinoa – were grown successfully without irrigation and at higher elevations.

QUINOA
The Little Grain that Could

Quinoa (*Chenopodium quinoa*, pronounced KEEN-wa) is a species of pigweed which grows in the high Andes, resisting drought and frost, requiring little attention. Of the three staples (maize, potato and quinoa) that sustained Andean civilization it's the least consumed yet by far the most nutritious. Today it's hailed as the "miracle grain" and "the sacred food of the Incas," and people consume it far from its Andean origins. It contains about twice the protein of the usual grains, with an amino acid balance similar to that of milk – with none of the cholesterol. It is also high in unsaturated oils, calcium, iron, phosphorous, vitamin E and several B vitamins.

Until recently quinoa was a subsistence crop, grown in the highland communities of Peru, Bolivia and Ecuador, and ignored by urban consumers. It grows about 1.5m (5ft) in height, and when ripe produces tiny seed in large clusters which turn deep red, purple or gold, according to variety. Nowadays the grain is processed into different forms: into flour (*harina*), flakes (*hojuelas*), pearl (*perladas*), and puffed, all available in Cusco grocery stores. The flour and flakes are particularly useful for camping trips. Try pancakes made from quinoa flour (see **www.peterfrost.org** for a recipe), or the flakes (can be mixed with oats or wheat to give it texture) for a hearty porridge that cooks fast.

— Carol Stewart

Notice the arrow-straightness of the Urubamba River below you, in contrast to the disorderly meanders farther downstream. The Incas walled in the entire river to conserve agricultural land, and this part of the work has survived – 3.3km (2.1mi) of it, the largest pre-Columbian canal in the Americas.

Modern Pisac is a picturesque Andean village, typical except for the huge, spreading *pisonay* tree that dominates the central square. (There once were two, but one died, and in fact many of the lovely *pisonays* of the Urubamba Valley are being strangled by an overgrowth of epiphytes.) Like most towns in the Valley, this village has grown and sprawled, but it remains well known for its market (originally – and still biggest – on Sundays, but now also a daily affair), which draws flocks of tourists. In spite of its popularity the market retains some of its local character, at least on Sundays in the part where villagers from miles around gather to barter and sell their produce. The tourist section is a mixed bag of handcrafts – but with so much merchandise concentrated here you can often find interesting bargains. Pisac has a sizeable cottage ceramic industry. Pots, mugs, ashtrays and beads, etc., are quite cheap.

One of the attractive features of the Sunday market is the colorfulness of the local people: different dress from different areas, and all in Sunday best. After Mass – usually at around 11am – the mayors from the local villages leave church in procession, dressed in their best ponchos and mushroom-shaped hats, and carrying silver-embossed staffs of office. Their attendants blow prolonged blasts on conch shells to clear a way through the crowd. Worth visiting is the old bakery on Calle *Mariscal Castilla*, just off the main square, with its huge adobe oven. The bread is excellent.

The Felipe Marín Moreno Botanical Gardens at *Grau* 485 also merit a visit. This small but beautiful collection of Andean plants, including cactuses, orchids and a display showing some of the thousands of varieties of Peruvian potatoes, is a good place to relax after a stimulating tour of the market.

The Ruins' History

The ruins of Pisac cling to a mountain spur, a condor's nest of a place far above the Valley. If the name "Pisac" ever had a specific meaning it has since been lost. However *P'isaca*, the name of one sector of these ruins, refers to a kind of Andean partridge. Pisac ruins are filled with wonderful examples of Inca stonework and construction, set in a stupendous location. The complex seems to feature some example of almost everything the Incas did in terms of architecture, defense, religion, agriculture, roads and residential construction. Altogether, it is one of the most spectacular Inca sites in the Cusco region. For those who are fit and like to exert themselves, it is well worth the effort of climbing up the west flank of the mountain to reach them from Pisac village. (*See p.160 for the route.*) For softer adventurers, an equally impressive way to see them is to take a taxi from the Urubamba bridge to the parking lot, within about a kilometer of the Intiwatana temple sector. An advantage of this option is that you can hike into the ruins along a spectacular Inca pathway, through gateways and tunnels, experiencing as you walk a crescendo of stunning views of the valley and Pachatusan mountain to the south, beyond the river.

Pisac confronts archaeologists with an enigma almost as baffling as Machu Picchu. It is the largest fortress-city-temple complex of the Incas, and one of the largest of ancient America. And yet the early chroniclers mention no word of it. The Spanish knew of its existence, of course; the ruins are visible for miles around. In spite of its awe-inspiring natural defenses, the Incas made no stand here against the Spaniards. During Manco's rebellion the Inca made his headquarters at Calca, some 18km (11.3mi) down the Valley, and later retreated to the terrifying fortifications of Ollantaytambo, yet farther away from Cusco.

Historical records tell us that Pisac was a personal property of Pachacuti, the early ruler who launched the expansion of the Incas. Taken in this context, the location is significant. It dominates an important stretch of the Urubamba Valley, closest to Cusco, and also controls a vital pass leading to another important highland area, Paucartambo, then on to the eastern rainforest. This route was, in fact, the main Inca highway to the *Antisuyu*, the eastern quarter. Thus, Pisac was highly strategic, both economically and militarily. It gave access to prosperous regions where the Incas sought control and protected the approaches to Cusco.

From a ritual and sacred perspective the site sits on the flanks of the local mountain, Apu Llinlli, and gazes across the valley at Pachatusan, a mountain whose importance to the Incas can hardly be overstated. With its high-status temple architecture, elaborate visual design of the approaches and surroundings, and its ritual use of water, Pisac can easily be interpreted as essentially a ceremonial center, like Machu Picchu.

A synthesis of these two possibilities is probably closest to the truth: Pisac may have started out as a border stronghold controlling the approaches to Cusco from the eastern lowlands during the formative period of the Inca state, and later, under Pachacuti, acquired its ceremonial and administrative dimensions. Most of the Inca structures we can see there today were those built by Pachacuti during the imperial Inca period, including most of the superb ceremonial structures, which rank among the finest Inca architecture in existence.

IN THE RUINS.

By Road. Most people visit the Pisac ruins this way and hike from north to south, so site descriptions are listed in that order here.

Taxis to the ruins are easily found near the bridge at Pisac. You must either purchase or show your BTC at the ticket office on the road.

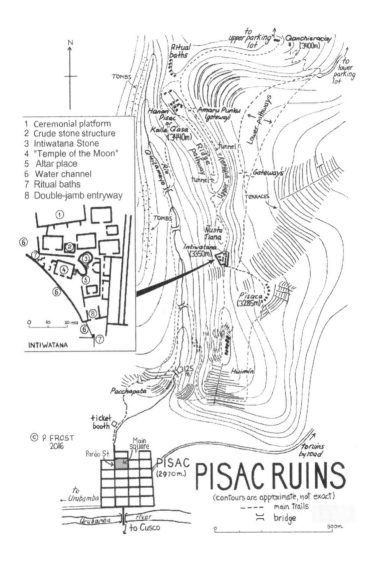

N

1 Ceremonial platform
2 Crude stone structure
3 Intiwatana Stone
4 "Temple of the Moon"
5 Altar place
6 Water channel
7 Ritual baths
8 Double-jamb entryway

INTIWATANA

0   40   80 mts

to parking lot
Qanchisracay
(3400m)

to lower parking lot

Ritual baths

TOMBS

Amaru Punku (gateway)

Hanan Pisac or Kalla Q'asa (3440m)

Río Quitamayo

Ridge pathway

tunnel

Lower pathways

Upper pathway

tunnel

Gateways

TERRACES

TOMBS

Ñusta Tiana

Intiwatana (3350m)

Pisaca (3285m)

Huimin

3125 m

Pacchapata

ticket booth

© P. FROST 2016

Pardo St.

Main square

PISAC (2970 m.)

to ruins by road

to Urubamba

Urubamba river

to Cusco

PISAC RUINS

(contours are approximate, not exact)

- - - main trails

≍ bridge

0   500m.

Three main routes lead to Intiwatana, the heart of the ruins complex: the *Ridge Pathway*, the *Upper Pathway* and the *Lower Pathways*. Take any route to hike onward to Pisac village (*see South of Intiwatana, below*). Note that any of these trails may be closed or reopened without notice in the rainy season.

Ridge Pathway. Ask to be dropped off at the upper parking lot. If returning to Pisac by road, a good option is to take this trail and circle back on one of the Lower Pathways (*see below*), sending your ride to wait for you at the lower parking lot. Alternatively, you can return from the lower pathway trailhead to the upper parking lot via a steep trail to *Qanchisracay* (this trail may also be closed seasonally).

A short walk south from this parking lot brings you to an Inca platform and a superb view onto the magnificent agricultural terraces and the Urubamba Valley ahead. Around you lie the sinuous jumble of buildings, fountains and storehouses known as *Qanchisracay* (Seven Huts) – now labeled as *Qantus Raqay*; its idiosyncratic layout is worth a short visit.

To your right a level path leads you to a low point of the mountain spur where you see several restored baths, one of Pisac's two main water sources. Their outlet channel once crossed the ridge here and fed water to the terraces below. The complex underscores the ceremonial importance of this site, and suggests a place of preparatory ritual, prior to entering Pisac itself.

The cliffs just west of here across the Quitamayo Gorge constitute the largest Inca cemetery known to archaeology. Bodies were walled up into the faulted caves of this sheer face with adobe and stone. One or two tombs were visibly grander, and doubtless held higher ranking individuals. All have been plundered, and hundreds of telltale holes pockmark the cliffs.

Ascend through *Kalla Q'asa* (Parrot Pass, perhaps named for the daily migrations of parrots from the jungle, across the ranges to the NE; they cross these passes at dawn, returning at dusk). This feverishly labyrinthine complex lies at a high point here, above and just inside

Pisac's great encircling wall. It is hard to find one's way through it, and one wonders if that was precisely the point. If the original architects had defense in mind they made a good job of it.

The Ridge Pathway to Intiwatana branches off from one of the trails on the western side of the ridge leading to the summit of Kalla Q'asa and takes you to a high point of roughly 3,400m (11,150ft). This is a steep, tortuous pathway with plenty of stairs and a narrow tunnel that may be difficult to pass through for big people. (*For easier access, see the Lower Pathways below.*) The views, however, are stupendous and allow you to see Pachatusan, the rugged mountain south of the Urubamba River that was once so sacred to the Incas, and the layout of the Intiwatana and P'isaca sectors. Partway down the descent, a walled platform along the east flank suggests a guardhouse or control point. Continue descending and you'll pass by an ascending trail to *Ñusta Tiana* (The Princess Throne), a small area of restored structures where the ancients carved a wide "throne." This appears to have been an exclusive residential compound with stunning views of the Valley and overlooked by a watchtower and a steep mountainside fitted in places with stone cladding so artful and sinuous it is hard to tell where nature ends and culture begins. The path finally emerges onto a steep crag with a fine view over the temple complex of Intiwatana.

Upper Pathway. 1.5km (0.9mi), elevation -75m (250ft). Sadly, the "Upper Pathway" connecting the Amaru Punku gateway and the Intiwatana sector was closed in early 2016 after a tourist was killed by a falling rock, and remains so at this writing. This route was the principal, scenically epic stone trail into the heart of Pisac in Inca times, designed as a series of stunning visual reveals that has few peers in the Inca heartland. Perhaps instead of simply locking it down indefinitely the authorities will someday be kind enough to make it safer and reopen it. In anticipation of that happy day, the route is as follows:

Pass through the gateway known as Amaru Punku, just east of

and below Kalla Q'asa, that once restricted access to the heart of Pisac. Observe, once again, how effectively this massive portal and its adjoining wall, extending both above and below, protected the site from unwelcome intruders.

The path beyond the gateway rises and falls along the eastern heights near the top of Pisac's mountain spur. It is a well-preserved Inca road that, in the space of a kilometer or less, gives you a full taste of what the Inca artist-engineer could accomplish: steep stone stairways, sections where the path exists only by virtue of an artful stone buttress built into a sheer rock face, and a tunnel made by enlarging a natural fissure where the cliff overhangs the vertical, and even the Incas could not extend the trail. This trail joins with the Ridge Pathway at the walled platform mentioned above.

Lower Pathways to Intiwatana. 1km (0.6mi), +20m (65ft). These require some fitness, too, but there are no drop-offs. Drive to the lower parking lot, some 100 vertical meters (330ft) below Qanchisracay, or, if you have been visiting Kalla Q'asa, retrace your steps to Qanchisracay and descend the steep, unofficial path to the trailhead (again, this trail *may* be closed).

From the trailhead where the paved area ends, two trails lead towards Intiwatana and the P'isaca sector. A suggested route: take the higher western trail to Intiwatana first, then descend through the P'isaca sector and return via the lower eastern trail. (Note that the higher trail has a very steep descending flight of stairs on it.) Both these trails pass through impressive ruined gateways set in the massive outer wall of Pisac that cuts diagonally across the mountain face, enclosing the south end of the site. Both gateways also feature the characteristic Inca double bar-and-niche arrangement at the rear of the door-jambs, which was apparently a system for securing the door-piece (separate, not attached by hinges) by means of a lateral rope or bar.

The great expanse of terracing below is a spectacular work of agricultural engineering, formerly irrigated, that once generated a huge output of maize. The careful layering, filling and drainage of these terraces, along with heat-sink stone walls and the step-profile of the slope, raised soil temperatures, shortened the growing season, and protected crops from frost. A sophisticated achievement whose remnants we find, sometimes still in use, throughout the Peruvian Andes.

Intiwatana. The upper end of *Intiwatana* (Place of Tying the Sun) features a *ceremonial platform* (1), featuring carved bedrock stone benches or altars. This spot offers the best overview of the complex. At the center of the site stands a *crude stone structure* (2), certainly an Inca style building but radically inferior to the superbly cut stonework of all the other buildings, and also different because its doorway faces north, whereas all others face south or west. Victor Angles suggested this was a shelter for servants, although it might also be interpreted as this sacred site's oldest building, perhaps preserved after the later, more imposing temple was built.

At the heart of the complex we find the *Intiwatana* itself (3), with superb stone walls artfully laid around the bedrock of a carved stone where a small pillar stands in its center. This arrangement is quite similar to a famous and better-preserved building at Machu Picchu, popularly known as the Sun Temple. Both of these structures incorporate a stone carving aligned towards the June solstice sunrise, which in the case of Machu Picchu still corresponds to a window through which the sun rose. This solar temple probably had such a window in the east wall too, but the wall was destroyed.

On a lower level to the west stands the largest building of the complex, the only one with two doorways, commonly known as the *Temple of the Moon* (4). Next to it a large natural rock, apparently an *Altar Place* (5), displays the ubiquitous but enigmatic Andean step-symbol carved in bedrock. A *Water Channel* (6) emerges from the mountain slopes to the NW, flowing into the temple complex through a series of *Ritual Baths*, or "fountains" (7), then along the western edge of this platform, culminating in a sunken bath outside the south wall of this complex (7), with descending steps, and what seem to be carved handholds for hauling oneself in and out. Perhaps a chilly cleansing plunge was *de rigeur* before entering this splendid temple complex through the fine-cut *Double-jamb Entryway* (8) that still commands access through the south wall.

To return to the Pisac road, descend from Intiwatana and take one of the Lower pathways northwards, with a short optional detour through P'isaca.

P'isaca (Tinamou, a kind of Andean partridge). As seen from above, this settlement cluster takes approximately the form of the eponymous bird, and some believe that this is the origin of Pisac's name. Another ceremonial bath heads a trail and water channel that descend from Intiwatana to this sector, and strikingly demonstrate the Inca hierarchy of water use. We see the same channel serving (a) ceremonial purposes at the temple; (b) human consumption at P'isaca; and (c) irrigation water for the farming terraces lower down the slope. The proximity of this sector to the temple area, along with its orderly layout, featuring well-made, spacious buildings and courtyards, suggests that this was the home of Pisac's ruling elites. The *P'isaca* sector has suffered some very questionable reconstruction work, which is immediately obvious to even the least practiced eye.

To descend to Pisac on foot, follow the paragraph below.

South from Intiwatana to Pisac. Two options: a trail leads over the jagged spine of the ridge, a steep but interesting route back to Pisac village (1.7km/1.1mi, -370m/1,210ft) through the district signed as *Q'ente Muyurina* (Where Hummingbirds Circle). Here you find towers for observation and/or communication, and below, a series of impossibly steep terraces, perhaps erected for defensive purposes. On the east flank of the spur here you can see a string of six identical structures that served as community storehouses, another feature of Inca city planning. Continuing south from here one can reach Pisac on foot along a steep trail through the terraces. An easier route down to Pisac from Intiwatana, which cuts out most of the steep descent through the terracing, leads through the *P'isaca* sector (2km/1.3mi, -370m/1,210ft); from there follow the trail south and then turn west and walk along a terrace until you rejoin the main trail.

On Foot from Pisac. If climbing northward on foot from Pisac village, read the site descriptions above in reverse order. (Note that the route north up the Quitamayo Ravine – *see map* – is closed at this writing.) To go one-way (3.2km/2mi, +470m/1,540ft) ascend via the Huimín terraces or P'isaca, pass through Intiwatana, and take the steep Ridge Pathway or one of the easier Lower Pathways in reverse. Once you reach the upper parking lot, pick up a ride to Pisac from one of the numerous vehicles waiting there – but arrive no later than 3pm to be sure of a ride.

Starting in Pisac, go up Pardo Street on the NW corner of the main square where the souvenir market is. Pass the ticket office where you must either show your BTC or purchase one. Keep ascending through steep terracing to approach the Quitamayo River. This path skirts the ravine, crosses a bridge, makes an initial steep ascent through a set of terraces, climbs a ridge, then encounters the precipitous south-facing terraces known as Huimín, where you climb a steep stairway to the ridgeline leading to Intiwatana. A gentler variation branches off shortly before the bridge mentioned above to follow the west bank of the river 200m (660ft) to a second bridge. A set of switchbacks climbs up to a spur at the foot of the Humín terraces; instead of climbing the stairs when you arrive here, stay level and head east for 130m (430ft) to find the gentler trail to *P'isaca*.

LAMAY (43km / 27mi)

The small town of *Lamay* is mostly just a bump in the road but is known locally for its *cuy al palo* (guinea pig on a stick, which the vendors wave around like lollipops). You'll recognize the town by the two giant, grinning statues of *cuys*, who are apparently ecstatic at the thought of being roasted on a skewer. This is a good place to try Cusco's favorite rodent. This town is also one of the trailheads for the route to the ruins of Huchuy Cusco.

HUCHUY CUSCO

Huchuy Cusco (Little Cusco) is a fascinating Inca site spread over several hectares of a small plateau commanding a magnificent view of the Urubamba Valley, about 5km upstream from Calca, and 800m (2,625ft) above the valley floor. (Entrance by SST.) It is believed to have been the royal estate formerly known as Caquia Jaquijahuana. According to myth the Inca Wiracocha built this settlement after conquering the previous inhabitants by setting fire to their town with a stone thrown from his golden sling. He later fled to this place from Cusco when the invading Chancas threatened to overrun the Inca capital, around 1438 *(see p. 66).* After the Conquest the Spaniards found the mummy said to be that of Inca Wiracocha here.

IN THE RUINS. The ruins are part stone, part adobe. There is a fine *kallanka* – the "great hall" type of building common at Inca royal and administrative settlements – some 40m (130ft) long. This building looks onto a great esplanade buttressed by terracing, which might have been used for parades and games. A building in the upper SW corner of the site has two facing walls each containing a *chacana* formation of six niches, a layout rare in Inca architecture. A fine ceremonial fountain recently uncovered in this area of the site has three carved channels leading into it and is overlooked by a small structure built to house a big niche surrounded by four lesser niches. There are signs of a post-Inca "transitional" occupation here, during which fine-dressed stones were used to build cruder houses in the Inca style. There's also a Spanish-style reservoir, partly built of fine Inca stones.

Note the use of horizontal wooden struts inside the corners of some buildings. These were previously thought to be an Inca anti-seismic construction technique, but they apparently don't serve this purpose, since the corners of Inca buildings are actually their strongest feature. The true purpose of these struts remains a mystery.

HOW TO GET THERE. Calca municipality claims that construction of a tourist cable car to the site from the nearby village of Sacllo will begin in early 2018 and should be finished by mid-2019. So get there soon to avoid the crowds. Currently, the road leading up from the vicinity of Calca has many tight switchbacks and steep dropoffs — for experienced drivers in 4-wheel-drive cars only! Before the cable car is finished, the safest way is to hike. There are three possible routes: the shortest but steepest is from Lamay; another starts from near Chinchero; the third starts from the ruins of Tambomachay. For full route descriptions and maps, see Trekking **www.peterfrost.org**

CALCA (51km / 32mi)

Calca, 18km (11.3mi) down the highway from Pisac, is a provincial capital and major town, though not from the visitor's point of view. The town's layout incorporates two main squares, a distinctly non-Spanish feature, which adheres to the town's original Inca layout. Manco Inca established his headquarters here during the great rebellion of 1536. Spanish cavalry seized the town with characteristic boldness at the beginning of the campaign, but abandoned it hastily when they learned that their rear, Cusco itself, was threatened with imminent attack. Later the town was captured again, this time by a column of Diego de Almagro's men, just back from a disastrous expedition to Chile. Manco's troops drove them out, and harassed them as they forded the Urubamba, but they joined up with their compatriots in Cusco, and subsequently pursued Manco all the way to his refuge in Vilcabamba.

Explorer's Note: About 3km (1.9mi) west of Calca a seldom-visited and fascinating Inca water shrine known as *Unu Orqo* lies off the highway to the north, with good views of the surrounding valley. Arrive directly via taxi by taking the dirt road from Calca or by getting off public transportation at the large terraces just west outside town on the main road and walking first up the stairs near their western end and then along the trail through some trees, taking the right fork near the top. A small village lies at the top of the terraces; pass north through its main square to reach the dirt road and follow it west.

The terraces, and most likely the whole site, supposedly belonged to Inca Urcon, Pachacuti's brother, who was vanquished in a deadly power struggle between these two. The complex, at the lower end of an aqueduct bringing water from the mountain of Pitusiray, features a *waca* known as *Wiracocha Orqo* with a serpentine water channel ending in a spout in the shape of either a puma or snakehead. This beautifully carved fountain is a rare specimen indeed, one of the few that escaped the attention of the Spanish. The small adjacent plaza is the site of water festival on the first Sunday in October.

About 4.6km (2.9mi) to the right of the highway west from Calca is the new *Museo Inkariy* (**www.museoinkariy.com**), marked by a huge fiberglass godmonster loosely based on Andean symbolism. This private museum features eight exhibition spaces portraying the major civilizations of Peru's prehistory in lifesize, realistic audiovisual displays along with exhibits demonstrating notable aspects of that culture, such as musical instruments, metalworking and ceramics. There is heavy emphasis on the sensational and to our eyes "alien" aspects of ancient Andean culture, but bearing that in mind it's all well done and worth a visit.

LARES (105km / 65mi)

The town of *Lares* lies in the valley of that name on the north side of the Cordillera Urubamba, putting it outside the Sacred Valley (*see Transportation, p. 21*). It's a small, sleepy town whose main draws are the nearby hot springs and the gorgeous hiking and mountain biking in the area. There are some basic, inexpensive hostels in town, plus rooms and numerous camping spots at the hot springs themselves. The springs are

1km (0.6mi) north down the main road out of town and can be reached on foot or by taxi. These baths, along with those at Pacchanta (*p. 284*) and Sicuani (*p.292*), are certainly the best within easy reach of Cusco: luxuriously hot (the hottest reaches a toasty 44 °C/111 °F) and full of minerals (so many that the waters are actually a laxative) – a welcome stop during any trek in the area.

Lares Valley Treks

The so-called Lares Trek is actually a network of different routes connecting the Lares and Urubamba valleys (*see adjacent map*). Some routes start in the Sacred Valley and head north, while others start in Lares and head SE to Ollantaytambo. All of them cross the Cordillera Urubamba, and most pass through the town of Lares at some point and the hot springs there. These treks are often combined with visits to Machu Picchu. The highlights of this trip are the hot springs, the route through remote Andean weaving communities, excellent mountain views, and the Inca ruins at Pumamarca (if your itinerary includes them - *see p.184*). Although this area is becoming more popular, there are still far fewer tourists than on the Inca Trail. No permits required. See Trekking on **www.peterfrost.org** for descriptions of four of the routes.

YUCAY (59km / 37mi)

2km (1.3mi) to the SE of Urubamba on the main valley highway lies this picturesque village – once again with two main squares, dominated by *pisonay* trees like those of Pisac. They bloom in colors of flame and scarlet in spring-time – around September/October. The squares resemble English village greens, and at Christmas time they become the scenes of a local festival that features masked dancers.

The surrounding lands were granted to the puppet Sapa Inca, Sayri Tupac (son of Manco Inca), after his emergence from Vilcabamba. The story goes that this captive Inca behaved ungraciously towards the Spaniards at the banquet marking the occasion of his land grant, pulling a thread from the tablecloth and declaring angrily that his estate in Yucay

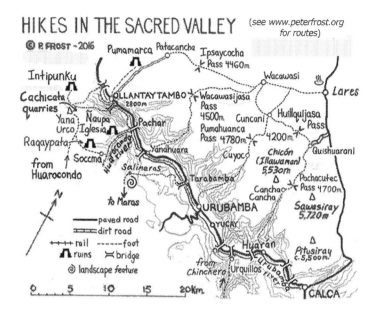

stood in proportion to the lands of his Inca forefathers as this one thread to the entire cloth.

Sayri Tupac did not survive long in Spanish-occupied Peru – dying in mysterious circumstances, probably poisoned, less than three years after leaving Vilcabamba. Historians (thinking *cui bono*), tend to finger Chilche, a Cañari chieftain allied with the Spaniards whose Yucay land claim was in conflict with Sayri's. The remains of Sayri Tupac's palace can still be seen in one of the village squares, an interesting example of post-Conquest Inca architecture.

There are also remains of fine Inca masonry on the other side of the Plaza. Before the conquest Yucay was part of the royal lands of the emperor Wayna Capac, which stretched westwards nearly all the way to Pachar. The agricultural terraces just behind the village to the north constitute one of the finest surviving Inca agricultural systems in the

Cusco region – well-preserved, and still in use. Adventurous hikers can follow trails that meander through these terraces.

URUBAMBA (57km / 35mi)

Three km (1.9mi) beyond Yucay, *Urubamba* is the sprawling and fast growing capital (whose province includes Machu Picchu) of the central valley, located at the point where the main highway from Cusco crosses the Urubamba River. It makes a good base from which to explore the area for those with time to spend a night or two in the Valley.

The center of Urubamba is pleasant to wander around in. Notice the town's coat of arms on the wall of the town hall. It bears a puma, two wriggling snakes, two *pisonay* trees, and the royal fringe of the Inca. Its only non-indigenous motif is the double-headed eagle of Spain. On the western outskirts of the town you will find a magnificent avenue lined with towering pisonays. They bloom in colors of flame and scarlet in spring-time – around September/October.

Explorer's Note. At the northern end of Mariscal Castilla street, near the entrance to the narrow Chicón Valley, lie the crumbling remains of Quispihuanca, the emperor Wayna Capac's royal estate. The modern town has severely encroached upon these ruins, and about a quarter of it is within the boundaries of the town cemetery. But it would have been remarkable in its heyday. The eastern wall held the grand entryway (still partially visible), with two 5m-tall (15ft) gatehouses flanking a long ramp leading up to a triple-recessed entrance portal 2m (6.5ft) wide. The wall was covered in plaster and held many double jamb niches, likely painted vivid reddish-orange. Those lucky enough to pass through would have encountered a wide open plaza with a *cuyusmanco*-style hall to the north and a large white boulder near the center. A channel likely directed water around this boulder, making it a center for water worship. Beside the estate, a park and artificial lake were created for the emperor's enjoyment. The ruins have not been well preserved though, and a little imagination is required to picture all of this.

About 7km (4.4mi) further up the Chicón Valley, about 600m (1,970ft) above the canyon floor, lies *Cocha Sontor* (Excellent Lake), smaller but better preserved than Quispihuanca and the likely site of Wayna Capac's hunting lodge and park. Only one building remains standing, with high adobe walls, oversized niches and narrow doorways. There was also likely an artificial lake which reflected the 5,530m (18,140ft) Chicón Mountain to the southeast.

PACHAR (72km / 45mi)

6km (3.8mi) before Ollantaytambo, you see the railway station on the south bank of the river. This is Pachar, where the rail route from Cusco joins the Urubamba Valley. Aside from the railway junction, this village is most notable for the microbrewery (*see p. 56*) and the hike to *Ñaupa Iglesia* (Ancient Church), an outstanding Inca shrine (*see map p.165*). Get off any Ollantaytambo-bound *colectivo* at the Pachar bridge, cross it to the south, turn right after the bridge, then take your second left down a dirt road along the Huarocondo River into the canyon. On your right you'll pass a well-preserved Inca bridge, still in use. Continue following the dirt road to a concrete bridge; cross the river and leave the road to follow the railroad tracks for 1km (0.6mi). You will see a trail ascending through the bush to your right. Follow this 150m (500ft) up to a large set of terraces and a flight of stairs on your right. Climb these stairs and then walk right until you reach a wide cave: this is Ñaupa Iglesia. The cave wall features a superbly cut recess and the remains of a surrounding structure with step-symbol niches. But the *pièce de resistance* at the cave entrance is an anomalous outcrop of dark andesite rock displaying superb step-symbol carvings, including what was once a ceremonial altar. Sometime during the early 20th century this stone was drilled and then blasted with dynamite, an act of vandalism that destroyed some but not all of its exquisite artistry.

You can take a pleasant and easy walk of 5.2km (3.3mi) from Pachar to Ollantaytambo by crossing the Inca bridge mentioned above and then the railroad bridge. Follow the road 0.5km (0.3mi) past some houses until it turns into a trail running along Inca terracing and hugging the base of the mountain. Continue along this trail and when it rejoins the dirt road, continue past the Inca fort of *Choqana*, which guarded the approaches to Ollantaytambo. Beyond this point the modern dirt road parallels the Inca road, which ran between stone walls close by to the south. You arrive at another Inca bridge across the Urubamba, which you cross to meet the modern paved highway.

Explorer's Note. About 8km (5mi) south of Pachar up a winding dirt road through the Huarocondo Gorge lies the village of Soccma, the starting point for the Soccma hike. This 25km (15.6mi), three-day route passes by a pristine waterfall, the Inca ruins of Raqaypata, high passes with stunning views, and (optionally) an abandoned Inca aqueduct before descending to the Cachicata quarries (*see p.183*) and Ollantaytambo. Alternative Inca Trails and KB Tambo Tours (*see p.42 & 58 respectively*) offer guided hikes of this route. See Trekking on **www.peterfrost.org** for full route details if you want to hike it yourself.

OLLANTAYTAMBO (78km / 49mi)

21km (13mi) from Urubamba, 2,800m (9,200ft) elevation. Past Pachar, both sides of the valley are increasingly lined with Inca terracing, part of the *Ollantaytambo* settlement, and there are the remains of two strategic fortifications located at narrow choke-points between mountain and riverbank on each side of the Urubamba, one named *Choqana* on the south bank of the river and another named *Incapintay* on the north. After the Spanish assault against Manco Inca's forces at Ollantaytambo in 1537, the Spanish noted that they were obliged to ford the river twice to avoid these hazards.

Ollantaytambo is said to be named for a mythical local chieftain – Ollantay. The legend comes to us from a popular 18th century drama, loosely derived from Inca sources and historical events, but heavily influenced by European romantic notions. According to the plot, Ollantay had a forbidden love for one of the daughters of his sovereign, the Inca Pachacuti. Ollantay eloped with the girl, rebelled and was defeated.

According to John Hemming in *Monuments of the Incas*, the "tambo" of the name refers not to the usual lodge or resting place, but to the tribe which inhabited this area before the Incas imposed themselves. Regardless of the name's history, non-Spanish speakers are likely to injure or embarrass themselves trying to pronounce it; phonetically, it is "Oy-Yan-Tie-Tambo," or just simply *Ollanta* ("Oy-Yanta") for short.

Historical records say that the entire Inca site of Ollantaytambo was a "royal estate" of the Inca Pachacuti, which would account for the fine stonework to be seen everywhere and the quality, abundance and scale of the ceremonial architecture.

The town stands at a strategic spot, the northwest end of the gentle Sacred Valley, where the river begins to plunge steeply toward the Amazon and the valley gradually narrows to a gorge. It is a key location, both militarily and economically. The valley is enclosed by mountains here, enabling whoever occupies this settlement to control movement in either direction along the Urubamba Valley. Besides the aforementioned forts a little way upstream, there are fortified locations downriver and also up the Patacancha side valley, which flows into the Urubamba from the north at this point. The forts downstream could have protected the town from incursions by the jungle tribes to the north and northwest and protected the critical route through Pachar, leading up the Huarocondo Ravine and across the Pampa de Anta directly to Cusco. The eastern defenses are more puzzling. J.P. Protzen, the man who has done so much to enlighten us in the matter of Inca stonework, proposes a theory in his detailed study of Inca Ollantaytambo *(see Bibliography)*. Observing that the massive defenses on the eastern outskirts of the settlement imply a major threat from the direction of Cusco, he suggests these fortifications were built during Manco Inca's occupation of the town during the Inca rebellion of 1536 but after the fall of Sacsaywaman in May of that year. More on this later.

Ollantaytambo's economic value to the Incas is clear. It lies at the junction of two major routes offering trade and control over nearby Amazon and cloud forest regions, both economically vital to the Incas.

169

Moreover, in its immediate vicinity it controls a range of altitude zones with land suitable for herding, and growing potatoes, corn and a great variety of other products. All in all it was a powerhouse wealth generator for the Inca Pachacuti and his royal family.

The Town

About 1km (0.6mi) east of Ollanta on the main road are the remains of the Inca fortress of *Incapintay* (Inca Painting) at the base of the last vertical rock face before town. The site is named for the reddish rock painting about 40m (130ft) above the road on the east-facing rock wall. According to the chronicler Guaman Poma, this painting represents the rebel Manco Inca himself, and was painted there by intrepid Inca rock climbers on his orders in 1537. Today it is badly weathered but with binoculars the outline of an Inca warrior armed with shield and weapon is still discernible. To see this, get off your transportation just before Ollanta at the remains of the Inca fort described above. To continue to Ollanta on foot, take the Inca road along the base of the cliff from here. To do this in the opposite direction, start at the Inca gate at the sharp righthand turn on the cobblestone road out of town.

Where the main road makes a sharp into town and becomes cobblestone stands an Inca bridge, now carrying a modern road. It's another awesome example of Inca engineering, built on massive foundations with two enormous boulders in the river upstream of it strategically placed here by the builders to break the current and protect the central pier during rainy season. This is the start of the Cachicata Trek (*see p.183*).

The modern town is the only Inca settlement still inhabited in Peru that has survived pretty much as the Incas laid it out hundreds of years ago, with many people still living in Inca courtyards and even buildings. Seen from above, the settlement is laid out in a form often used by the Incas, a trapezoid. The central area bordering the main square forms the wide base-line, and the streets narrow away uphill. Each block was a pair of *canchas*, self-contained enclosures housing many people, each with just one exit to the street. Some of the Inca names of the blocks survive. To get the best idea of how the town must have looked in Inca times, walk along the west wall of the town, just above the river Patacancha. This street is bounded by the walls of long canchas, with narrow parallel streets between them leading onto the central streets of the town. Functioning channels that once supplied water from the Patacancha River to the Inca settlement still flow through the town, now mainly used for irrigating fields further downstream. It was like a townhouse development, elite housing provided for the members of Pachacuti's *panaca* whose task it was to administer the great array of construction, trade and production activities taking place in Ollanta and its hinterlands in the Amazon region.

Following the main street eastward out of the principal square leads you out of the village along a road known as the "Avenue of 100 Niches," named for the niches (actually 72 by my count) along the wall. The street is a post-Conquest construction built over the former site of a huge, multi-purpose barrack-like structure of a type known as *kallanka*, whose long wall is all that remains. The road runs through what was once the building's interior.

The Ruins' History

Just across the Patacancha from the town lies a great open yard known as *Mañaraki*, beyond which a ruined gateway gives onto the towering walls and terraces of the main ruins, the impressive temple structure of Ollantaytambo. The terraces are known as *Pumatallis*, while the main complex above them is simply but misleadingly known as the Fortress. As with Sacsaywaman, this name has stuck to the place because a major battle with the Spaniards was fought in Ollantaytambo, but it was essentially a temple.

Said battle took place during Manco Inca's rebellion in 1537. The siege of Cusco had dragged on, despite the fall of Sacsaywaman, and Hernando Pizarro decided on a bold stroke to break the stalemate – to kill or capture the Inca himself, thus ending resistance as effectively as the Spanish had in seizing and executing Atawallpa four years earlier in Cajamarca. Manco was quartered with most of his army at Ollantaytambo, having abandoned the more vulnerable base of Calca. Pizarro marched "with 70 horse and 30 foot, and a large contingent of native auxiliaries." Evidently the Spanish knew nothing of the layout at Ollantaytambo, presumably never having visited it despite 2½ years of occupation at Cusco (or perhaps, as J.P. Protzen suggests, the outlying forts were newly built), for Pedro Pizarro later wrote, "we found it so well fortified that it was a thing of horror..."

The Spaniards arrived before dawn, stealing up to the main gateway below the eastern terraces in hopes of catching the garrison asleep. "But thousands of eyes were upon them, and as the Spaniards came within bow-shot a multitude of dark forms rose suddenly above the rampart, while the Inca... was seen on horseback in the enclosure directing the operations of his troops." (Prescott, *The Conquest of Peru*.)

The Spaniards were shocked by the violence of Manco's resistance. Squads of archers from the jungle wreaked havoc among the cavalry beneath the walls; boulders, javelins and slingshots added to the destruction, and the Spanish were forced to retreat. Manco had a further unpleasant surprise for Pizarro's men. Diverting the river Patacancha through prepared channels, he had inundated the plains below the walls, swamping the Spanish cavalry in mud and water up to the horses' bellies. In neutralizing the Spaniards' most terrifying and unanswerable weapon – the horse – Manco nearly succeeded in trapping and massacring this expedition, but the Spaniards fought their way to the river and forced a crossing, then battled their way back to Cusco.

It used to be thought that this battle took place below the great terraces of Pumatallis, at the main temple site often called the "fortress." But J.P. Protzen presents convincing evidence that the action was fought about a kilometer east of Mañaraki, below the terraces which face the modern visitor driving into Ollantaytambo from Urubamba. Eyewitness accounts of the battle match this area perfectly. The defenses from that direction are indeed formidable. The Spanish would first have had to take the two Inca forts which fronted the Urubamba River at places where only a narrow gap remained between the river and the cliffs – either that or ford the Urubamba to avoid them (which, according to historical accounts, is what they actually did). Then they would have had to slog under fire across the flooded plain to attack the great row of eleven terraces that still stands today, north of the Inca bridge.

Manco won this battle, but he was losing the war. When Diego de Almagro's ill-starred Chilean expedition, which had set out with 570 cavalry and foot-soldiers, returned to Cusco in 1537 the balance of arms tipped overwhelmingly against the rebel Inca. An expedition of 300 cavalry was dispatched against Ollantaytambo, and Manco, seeing that the odds against him were now hopeless, abandoned the fortress and retreated into the mountain fastness of Vilcabamba, where he, and then his sons, held out for 35 more years.

Ollantaytambo appears in the history books one last time before it vanishes into the long night of the colonial era. In 1539 Spanish troops returning from an expedition against Vilcabamba were billeted at Ollantaytambo. The campaign had been a qualified success; the Spaniards had not succeeded in capturing Manco Inca, but they had loot, and they had with them the captive Coya, Cura Ocllo, wife and sister of Manco Inca. Francisco Pizarro himself arrived on the scene, hoping to negotiate Manco's surrender. When Manco refused to negotiate Pizarro vented his anger on Cura Ocllo. She was stripped naked, flogged and then killed with arrows. So that Manco should understand fully what had happened, Pizarro had her body tied to a raft and floated down the Urubamba to be discovered by the Inca's men downstream.

IN THE RUINS.
(Entrance by BTC.) Beyond the entrance yards of *Mañaraki* (1) and *Araqhama* (2), you meet a steep climb of more than 200 steps through fortified terracing known as *Pumatallis*.

INCA TEMPLE OF OLLANTAYTAMBO

© P. FROST 2016

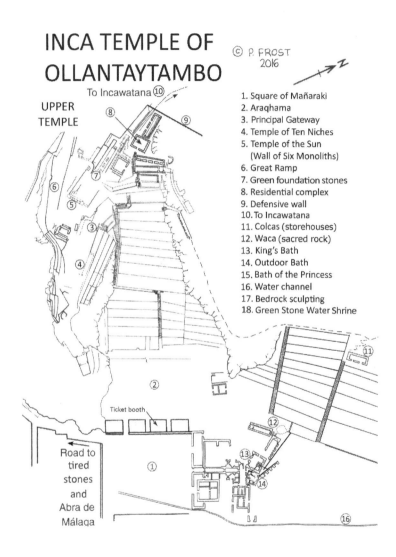

1. Square of Mañaraki
2. Araqhama
3. Principal Gateway
4. Temple of Ten Niches
5. Temple of the Sun (Wall of Six Monoliths)
6. Great Ramp
7. Green foundation stones
8. Residential complex
9. Defensive wall
10. To Incawatana
11. Colcas (storehouses)
12. Waca (sacred rock)
13. King's Bath
14. Outdoor Bath
15. Bath of the Princess
16. Water channel
17. Bedrock sculpting
18. Green Stone Water Shrine

UPPER TEMPLE

To Incawatana

Ticket booth

Road to tired stones and Abra de Málaga

At the top of these stairs is the impressive *Principal Gateway* (3), of singular and elegant design. This was apparently to have been the main entrance to the Sun Temple, but – like so much of Inca Ollantaytambo – the area behind it, with its access stairway to the temple complex, was never completed. The polygonal stonework around this gate and the terraces immediately below it display a feature unique to Ollantaytambo: small lobes on the horizontal surfaces of many stones project slightly into adjacent rising (vertical) joints, giving the walls a subtly fluid appearance, which contrasts remarkably with the massive linearity of the nearby Sun Temple. These features were clearly not structural, since they project no more than a few inches into the joint and could not have held it in position. The technique is rarely seen elsewhere, and suggests a local style of adding playful and aesthetically pleasing grace notes to the facade.

To the left of the gate stands the remains of a building known as the *Temple of Ten Niches* (4), a long structure, also of fine stonework, with the outer wall missing. This building originally was accessed only from the temple area through a single entrance, the doorway still standing at its SE end.

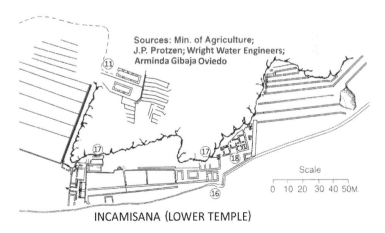

Sources: Min. of Agriculture;
J.P. Protzen; Wright Water Engineers;
Arminda Gibaja Oviedo

Scale

0   10 20   30 40 50M.

INCAMISANA (LOWER TEMPLE)

The best-known and most impressive part of the ruins is the huge unfinished structure fronted by a southeast-facing wall of six enormous monoliths of rose-colored rhyolite, above and to the left of the stairs. This structure is popularly called the *Temple of the Sun* (5). It is the best location at Ollantaytambo for observing the sun, although we can't be sure that the structure was intended for that purpose. It is unique among Inca structures in that the massive stones are straight-edged, with none of the deep beveling and polygonal jointing seen at other megalithic sites, and separated by narrow spacers made of smaller stones, fitted with the usual Inca perfection.

These huge stones were once faced with designs carved in relief. The step motif so common in Andean symbolism is clearly visible, as are the outlines of zoomorphic figures, perhaps pumas, now too defaced to be identified.

This sector is deeply puzzling to archaeologists. J.P. Protzen describes it as "...a very rough sketch of things to come. Yet the sketch is so provocative that it leaves one in suspense, trying to catch a glimpse of the splendor of the masterpiece that will never be." The six monoliths form the stunningly perfect retaining wall of a great platform. But the platform's other two sides display not stunning perfection but rough construction of recycled blocks, some of them laid on their sides instead of upright as originally intended, widely spaced and filled in with rubble – repurposed blocks that were shaped for and probably used in some other construction.

Even the famous SE wall is far from perfect when you look closely. The visible parts of the foundations, consisting of small, poorly laid blocks, look awfully sketchy for stones weighing up to fifty tons. One end of this wall, adjoining the platform's east wall, consists of a low, horizontal monolith apparently cut to form part of a gateway – but not for this structure. A gate makes no sense here, and the stone is not flush with or fitted to the rest of the south wall; neither are the stones of the west wall, which meet the south wall haphazardly at the corner.

All this is part of the multi-dimensional puzzle of Ollantaytambo's main ruins. Dr. Joseph Hollowell, an independent scholar of the site, made observations suggesting that many of the huge stones were taken and repurposed from some earlier temple, which he believed was destroyed by a landslide. He proposed that the remains of this earlier structure would be found beneath the square of Mañaraki, although modern use makes it difficult to test this hypothesis. Hollowell also observed that the sheer quantity of big blocks in and around the site, and also at the quarries, rules out any original plan for building atop the mountain spur; there simply was no place to put them all.

Scattered around the space in front of the six monoliths are stones standing on temporary platforms, finished stones with a brilliant polish on their inner faces, and stones with T-shaped grooves cut in one face – all testimony to the obsessive perfectionism of at least one phase of construction. The T-grooves would have been coupled with similar cuts on an adjoining block, then filled with molten bronze to key them firmly together – as if they weren't sturdy enough already. Some Inca structures wear both suspenders and a belt, as if the builders intended them to outlast the end of the universe. One theory goes that when the bronze contracted as it cooled, it pulled the two adjacent stones together, tightly closing any gap that remained between them. The technique is also observable in a few scattered stones at the Qoricancha in Cusco, and is very much in evidence at the ancient pre-Inca ruin of Tiwanaku at Lake Titicaca. This has led some observers to propose a connection between these two sites, so very far apart in both time and geography. However, J.P. Protzen, who has studied both sites, says the two stonework styles are in general very different. However, he does note a strong similarity between Tiwanaku stonework styles and what appears to have been one of the oldest structures at the site (*see #7 below*).

It appears that different phases of building and perhaps different architects succeeded each other. There are many other signs of remodelling and radical changes of plan at Ollantaytambo. Something happened to interrupt the whole project – perhaps the Inca civil war, perhaps the Spanish conquest, perhaps a rebellion of the inhabitants, as has also been suggested. Or perhaps it was simply the death of Pachacuti, whose estate this was.

To the left of the six monoliths, on the south side of the plaza, stands the head of the *Great Ramp* (6) which was built for hauling blocks up to the site. From here you can look WSW 3.5 air km (2.2mi) across the Urubamba Valley to the source of the rhyolite blocks, the quarries of *Cachicata*, located in a great rockfall at the foot of *Yana Urco* (Black Mountain). Some 50 huge stones lie abandoned between the ruins and the quarries of Cachicata. This is an aspect of Ollantaytambo especially worthy of our admiration; the stones were dragged about 6km (3.75mi) overland from these quarries. Somehow the Inca engineers maneuvered the blocks over the steep banks and across the surging current of the Urubamba River. Then they hauled them up the long ramp, the remains of which are most clearly seen from the fields between the ruins and the river. Near the bottom of this ramp, a few feet from the modern road, lie three so-called "tired stones" – huge masonry blocks on their way from the quarries which never reached their destination. They are partly finished, and one has marks showing clearly the Inca method of splitting stone. The architect Vincent Lee has proposed a theory which may answer the puzzle of how huge stones, the largest of which weighs 52 tons, were maneuvered up the ramp and around a sharp left turn into the temple compound (*see p.129*).

The six monoliths plus the two adjacent sides form the retaining walls of a platform extending from the spur above. This was truly the ceremonial heart of the site, where ceremonies and celestial observations were performed. It offered a clear view for miles, both up and down the Urubamba Valley, and also up the Patacancha side valley. This view included part of a snowcapped ridge extending west from the major mountain *Wakay Willka*, hence visual connection with a powerful *apu*.

At the NW end of the platform an inconspicuous line of *Green foundation stones* (7) almost flush with the ground is the scant but superb relic of a building that once stood here. Its small blocks are so flat, smooth and square that the joins are barely perceptible to the touch, and their style, cut from a rare type of green andesite whose source has never been located, is nothing like Inca work. Stones from it are found scattered about the site, and one is actually in the foundations beneath one of the great monoliths, all of which testifies that this thoroughly demolished construction was pre-Inca. But built by whom? J.P Protzen points out that the stonework style, just in this one architectural remnant, is strikingly similar to that of a structure at the site of Tiwanaku on Lake Titicaca. Which, of course, raises a lot more questions than it answers, since Tiwanaku occupation has never been confirmed in this region.

North of the temple is a complex of cruder buildings, apparently a *Residential Complex* (8), and beyond that, a massive outer *Defensive Wall* (9) protecting this complex on the gentler west slope of the mountain. The wall and houses were built with far less care and in a totally different style than the nearby temple, and are thought to represent a military headquarters and defenses dating from Manco Inca's occupation of 1536-37, which lasted eight months.

A path leads through the wall's one gateway and up the mountain to a walled site – not visible from the main ruins – which tradition calls variously *Intiwatana* or *Incawatana* (Place of Tying up the Inca) (10). This name is certainly recent, post-Conquest. There are four man-sized niches side by side, each with holes bored at about the right height for tying up the wrists of a seated man, hence the popular name. But it is mere racy speculation to suppose that the site was used in this way.

If they did tie people up here they certainly gave them a wonderful view. The niches face south through a narrowing of the Urubamba Gorge known as *Wayrajpunku* (The Wind Gate) to a magnificent sweep of Wakay Willka (a.k.a. Verónica) (5,950m / 19,516ft).

Return to the top level of the *Pumatallis* terracing and follow it NE towards the cliff to reach a trail leading east along the edge. This will take you to a set of colcas (11) perched high above some terracing and the Patacancha Valley. A pair of long staircases descends through the terraces, returning you to the valley bottom.

One of Ollantaytambo's striking features is the astonishing variety of stone to be found there. Most of the bedrock at the site is a highly fractured metamorphic rock, but the big cut stones are from the Cachicata quarries on the south bank of the Urubamba, and smaller colored stones seem to have been imported from all over, many of them probably recovered from the river. There are also anomalous outcroppings, one of them a carved, andesite boulder at the foot of the southern staircase, singled out by the Incas for special treatment and known as the *Waca (Sacred Rock)* (12). Llama bones and figurines plus serving vessels have been found here, suggesting that the rock was regularly "fed" animal sacrifices. Archaeologist Steve Kosiba contends that this site is the culminating waca in a series of seven on the Inca road to Ollantaytambo, most of them similar anomalous andesite boulders with carved bench features, surrounded by different rock types. The series starts halfway down the Huarocondo Gorge and includes the sites of Ñaupa Iglesia (*see p.167*), a former waca at the Pachar bridge, and the Inca fort at Choqana (*see p.168*).

The floor of the Patacancha Valley below the ruins is worth exploring. Just east of the Waca, you come to the *King's Bath* (13), an unusual Inca fountain because, unlike most others, it was enclosed within a roofed structure. The authors of *Incamisana* suggest that this bedrock fountain was originally carved by pre-Inca peoples, then taken over and remodeled by the later Incas. (This section and those below owe a debt to Kenneth Wright et al for their book *Incamisana; see Bibliography*.) The building, which still contains traces of Inca plaster work, is fronted by large, double-jamb niches with windows, indicating high ceremonial importance. The water supply to this site (and sites number 14 and 15) enters from the north through an underground channel and presents us with something of a mystery: it hovers 1.5m (5ft) above the ancient ground level (the nearby Patacancha River flooded massively in 1679, covering the site with 1-2m of sediment). Lacking a supporting wall, how the channel functioned during Inca times remains unclear.

Adjacent to the King's Bath is the *Outdoor Bath* (14). This is a massive, 20-ton boulder moved here by the Incas and then carved as a perfect combination of nature and Inca artistry, where the water's graceful, arcing plunge into well-designed receiving pools would have set the scene for Inca water veneration ceremonies. The boulder's upper surface is flat, with three finished water channels ending in jet spouts. A fourth channel was started but remained unfinished when the Incas abandoned the site. The feeder channel splits in two, and each fork splits again; together, these four channels embody the Inca concept of complementary dualism. The idea of paired opposites (Sun and Moon, male and female, inner and outer) has been essential in Andean culture from ancient times through the present day. Examples of duality abound at Ollantaytambo, including the two-part design of the site's core area, with urban and religious districts separated by the Patacancha River.

The *Baño de la Ñusta*, the so-called *"Bath of the Princess"* (15), is an exquisite example of Inca sculpture in bedrock – featuring the ubiquitous step-motif portrayed in both two and three dimensions – adapting the environment to form a small waterfall, almost certainly a place for ceremonial bathing. Archaeologist Arminda Gibaja found 11 ceramic offerings buried nearby, most of them in male-female pairs, another classic example of Inca dualism. (Bath of the Princess *and* Prince?) A few steps to the north is what the *Incamisana* authors call the Lip Fountain, a private bathing area. While not quite as striking as its Princess neighbor, the hydrology here is no less impressive: the carefully shaped lip at the channel's end ensures that the water falls in a jet, even under low water conditions, and was created by shaving nearly 2.5cm (1in) off the entire face of the stone.

Both of the above fountains receive water from the *Water Channel* (16), which brings water from the nearby Patacancha River. This channel may have been in a slightly different spot in Inca times, with the modern version being a colonial re-routing.

About 100m (330ft) along the cliffs north of the Bath of the Princess is an area called *Incamisana* (a Quechua-Spanish hybrid word meaning

Place of the Inca's Mass). The whole area was clearly devoted to the veneration of water and features extensive *bedrock sculpting* (17). The base of the cliffs has been tooled and scrolled with artful carving, much of it niches and bedding work for walls which were destroyed or never actually built. Its purpose was undoubtedly ceremonial, an effort to energize and sanctify the rock and the nearby water temple. Some of the most impressive niches are the four small identical double-jamb ones high up on the cliffside on two surfaces at 90° to each other. One pair of these is on a separate, movable stone. Arminda Gibaja found this lying in a nearby waterway in 1980 and realized it was a perfect fit on the cliff; it was later restored to its rightful position. Many of the sculptures are invisible from the valley floor, a shame for today's visitor since the cliffs are now roped off and inaccessible. These include a *paqcha* – four linked squares thought to be small ritual water channels; a perfectly cut, 1.7m^2 (18ft^2) grid in the floor of a carved alcove; and a throne carved into a rock wall known as the Condor Temple, which is named for the gigantic condor form which some people see in the mountain above it.

The surviving walls of the *Green Stone Water Shrine* (18) stand at the base of these cliffs. Once a sizeable bath or water shrine, its entranceway is strikingly different from most Inca structures this size, but similar to those of many other baths, being offset rather than dead center, such that you could not see into the building from outside but had to enter it in zigzag fashion through a narrow access. This would have ensured privacy for those within. Also striking is its water supply channel, which is still visible carved into the bedrock of the cliff behind, and divides into two channels just above the shrine. One branch fed a large outer bath which can still be seen built into the north wall of the building; the other probably fed a bath inside the shrine, although any traces of it remain buried beneath rubble.

The mountain that looms over the Patacancha on the opposite side of that valley is called *Pinculluna* (Mountain of Flutes). You can see a string of ruined buildings clinging to its steep slopes. They are long and narrow with openings set high in the uphill wall and others low in the downhill wall, a first-in-first-out storage system for what were maize granaries. The upper openings were used to tip in the grain, the lower ones to remove it. Horizontally across the mountainside to the right are some smaller, square structures which were also storehouses, these ones of a dark, windowless design intended for potato storage. The yellowish tinge to the walls of these and other buildings at Ollantaytambo comes from a hard coating of sun-baked clay with which the walls were adorned.

The inaccessible location high on a windy hill is logical, because the cool, windy conditions would help preserve the stored food in buildings that were well designed for ventilation while also protecting it from intruders. The granaries were also visible for miles around, a constant reminder to the drafted labor toiling below that working for the Incas had its payoff: peace, shelter and a full belly.

In recent times an interpretation of Ollantaytambo that has become fashionable, almost dominant, proposes that a formation in the cliffs of Pinculluna, represents the face of Wiracocha, the old god and culture hero of the Incas. The great terraces west of the temple are characterized as a "pyramid," the temple and its terraces are perceived as being built in the form of a llama, the mountain above the temple site as a condor, and so on. These ideas can be found in the work of Fernando Elorrieta (*see Bibliography*). While Elorrieta's book offers some interesting observations concerning solar alignments and man-made features, the grand overarching symbolic scheme proposed here seems fanciful to this author.

TWO WALKS NEAR OLLANTAYTAMBO
Walk I: Cachicata

The quarries of *Cachicata* are worth a visit for those curious about Inca construction methods and make an excellent day-hike. (From the Inca bridge, 7km/4.4mi one way to Choquetacarpo, +920m/3,050ft, 8-10 hours round trip, *see map p.165*) They are located between

700-900m (2,300-2,950ft) above the valley floor, about 3.5km (2.2mi) SW of Ollantaytambo as the crow flies, and can only be reached on foot or horseback. The highlights include the Inca bridge outside town (*see p.170*), a set of mysterious carved "needles", several cylindrical tombs known as *chullpas*, and the extraordinary gate of Intipunku that perfectly frames Wakay Willka (Verónica). See Trekking on **www.peterfrost.org** for directions.

Walk II: Pumamarca

This is a small, nicely preserved Inca ruin, up the Patacancha Valley from Ollantaytambo. (6.1km/3.8mi one way, +550m/1,800ft, 4-5 hours round trip plus time at the site.) There is a campsite with a covered area and bathrooms at the ruins. The high surrounding wall with its numerous zig-zags (very effective for defense) suggests a fort, as do the heavy-duty bar-hold niches at some of the entrance doors – the site may have been a defensive outpost for Ollantaytambo. But the food storage structures are located outside the walls. Does this make sense if the building was a fort? Puzzling. There is a nice *kallanka*-type building within the walls and the overall layout is classic Inca save for one building which apparently had three floors, an unusual feature for an Inca building. The stonework is *pirca* style – uncut fieldstone set in adobe. 300m (1,000ft) south of the ruins, before the road, are two buildings which appear to be *chullpas*.

See **www.peterfrost.org** for the Pumamarca trail and map.

CHAPTER FOUR

INCA TRAILS TO MACHU PICCHU
Hikes Into the Inca Lost Province

HISTORY OF THE INCA TRAIL

The whole of Peru was once criss-crossed with Inca and pre-Inca highways. Sometimes they followed the valleys, but just as often they traversed the high mountainsides, tracing impossible pathways and following narrow ledges above the bottomless gorges of the Andes. The trails were built for men on foot and lightly-burdened llamas. Frequently their gradients gave way to stairways, tunnels and long zig-zag trajectories down steep faces.

Most of these highways were useless to the European invaders. Horses balked at the steps and got stuck in the tunnels. Carts and carriages could never pass. The roads of the coast and the valleys became colonial highways, which were allowed to deteriorate in a way the Incas would never have accepted, but kept in use. Many are roadways to this day. But the highland trails were abandoned to the natives, mostly to crumble and vanish over the centuries, even though many an Andean footpath quite suddenly becomes a staircase of huge, carefully-laid slabs, worn down by generations of mules and herders, but still solid, enduring.

One such trail followed the gorge of the Urubamba River. The main highway turned north out of the valley just below Ollantaytambo to cross the Panticalla Pass leading to the jungle settlement of Amaybamba. Perhaps this was the only highway still in use by the time of the Conquest, for the Spaniards never discovered the trails that continued on down the valley to a point where it is becoming a gorge and will soon be a canyon. The Incas built a string of settlements onward from here down both banks of the Urubamba, and pushed secondary highways down both sides of the gorge far beyond Machu Picchu.

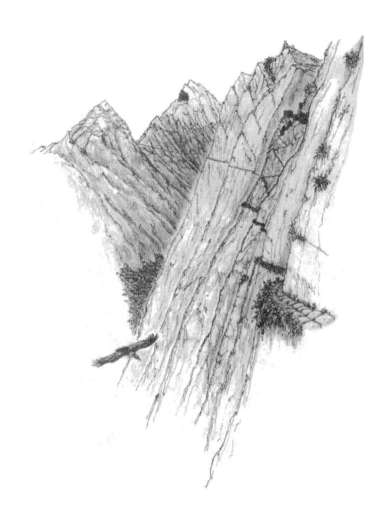

The main Inca highway from Cusco took a different route altogether, however, beginning with a turnoff from the main northbound Inca artery, the *Chinchaysuyu* highway, somewhere in the vicinity of Zurite, traversing NW through the mountains between the Pampa de Anta and the Urubamba Valley, and meeting the Cusichaca Valley at the well-preserved Inca site of Paucarcancha, just upstream from Wayllabamba where modern trekkers feed into this route and continue along it, the royal highway to Machu Picchu – the famous Inca Trail. Keep in mind as you hike the "Inca Trail" that everything before Wayllabamba was an Inca side trail to the Sacred Valley, not the main route from Cusco.

The route was rediscovered by Hiram Bingham in 1915 when he returned to Peru to make further studies and clear the ruins at Machu Picchu. His guides took him to other ruins to the south and east, and he discovered traces of an ancient road linking the city to a string of lesser settlements in the direction of Cusco. The highway was traced and explored in more detail in 1942 by the Viking Expedition, sponsored by the Wenner Gren Foundation. Its leader, Paul Fejos, made important discoveries – most notably the stunning site of Wiñay Wayna – and published his conclusions in the United States.

By this time the trail had ceased to be the exclusive territory of archaeologists and scientists. A handful of rugged travelers each year were struggling along its 50 or so kilometers, a trail far more overgrown and difficult to follow then than it is today. And in the years since, the Inca Trail has become a celebrated and popular hike, known to backpackers all over the continent. There are thousands of Inca trails, but there is only one Inca Trail.

Why? Few relatively short hikes in the world can offer such variety of scenery, so many staggering views, such a mix of jungle and high sierra. Certainly no other walk known to man will lead you along an ancient highway from one secluded ruin to another, each in a breathtaking setting, each almost perfectly preserved, offering shelter, solitude and views that no pen or camera can ever adequately record. And of course, no other hike in the world ends with a climactic descent into Machu Picchu.

THE QHAPAC ÑAN
The Highway of the Inca Empire

"In the memory of people, I doubt there is record of another highway comparable to this... The roads constructed by the Romans in Spain, and any others of which we read, are not to be compared with it." Pedro Cieza de Leon, 1553.

The Inca Trail to Machu Picchu is but a tiny segment of the once-mighty *Qhapac Ñan* (*Road of Power* or *Royal Road*), roughly 40,000km (25,000mi) of Inca highways. This pan-Andean network traversed coastal deserts, mountain passes, *altiplano* and forests, uniting parts of modern Argentina, Bolivia, Chile, Colombia, Ecuador, and Peru. In 2014, UNESCO added the entire surviving Qhapac Ñan its World Heritage List, making it the only site to span six countries.

Four road arteries left the Plaza de Armas in Cusco (*see map p.79*), meeting innumerable smaller branches along the way. As usual, the Inca drew heavily upon the construction techniques of earlier cultures. Thick, interlocking blocks of stone defined the paths, which were as much as 20m (65ft) wide on the plains, less than a meter in steep terrain. Many sections are engineering marvels, with superb drainage, tunnels, bridges (*see p.289*), and thoughtful landscape integration. Travelers encountered ceremonial sites and well-spaced supply depots and lodgings known as *tambo* (the invading Spaniards were overjoyed to find numerous such storehouses to ransack).

The practical uses of the Qhapac Ñan were endless. Metals, obsidian, wood, plant medicines, skins, feathers, sea shells and salt were traded across the Andes. Messenger runners (*chasqui*) relayed information coded into knotted cords (*quipu*). Inca armies paced its length, conquering new territories and subduing rebellions. Andean priests walked it for ritual purposes, occasionally parading children destined for sacrifice.

The Qhapac Ñan's value wasn't just material: it had a strong unifying effect on Andean peoples. Through it, Cusco's social organizing and engineering prowess extended to all imperial citizens. Every town could lay claim to a stretch of Inca road and was likely responsible for its upkeep. And should its

> inhabitants be harboring rebellious sentiments, they could easily visualize a column of Inca soldiers marching down it. The Inca Empire would have been impossible without this network: the abrupt Andean topography demanded roads to tame it and unite its inhabitants.
>
> — Leo Duncan

Walking the Inca Trail it is impossible to doubt that the entire experience was planned – there was nothing happenstance about the stunning combinations of scenic and man-made beauty. The Incas wanted those who walked this way to reel in awe as they crested the passes and rounded the corners. They designed the trail as a dramatic narrative, with a series of troughs, slow build-ups and climaxes, each greater than the last, until the stunning finale, when travelers looked down from Intipunku upon Machu Picchu, shining on its stone isthmus between two great peaks far above the Urubamba River.

Fundamental to this experience were the near and distant views of snowcapped peaks and the astounding array of Andean natural environments, over high cold *puna* close to ice and snow, past grasslands, wildflower meadows, waterfalls, tunnels, shifting layers of forest, all compressed by swift altitude changes into a short revelatory journey of learning and transformation.

The Inca Trail and Machu Picchu are rarely, if ever, considered in this light, as a complete work of art – perhaps because there was no single work of art among Old World civilizations on anything approaching this scale. And yet in this author's view it was exactly that, rather like a gothic cathedral, with its intended purpose: to create a complete transformational experience of sacred landscape for elite pilgrims on the way to Machu Picchu, a sacred city.

The entire Inca Trail lies within the 32,592ha (80,536 acre) Machu Picchu Historical Sanctuary. In 2004, concerns about erosion and damage to

THE INCA TRAIL

© P. FROST 2016

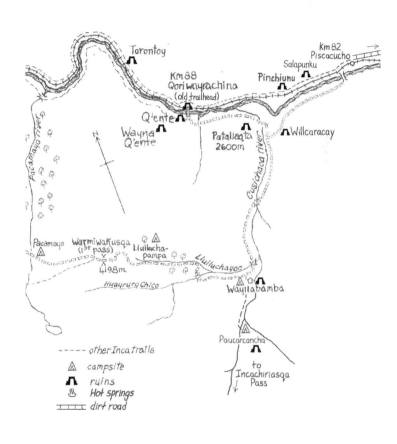

Torontoy

Km 88
Qoriwayrachina
(old trailhead)

Salapunku

Km 82
Piscacucho

Pinchiunu

Q'ente

Wayna
Q'ente

Patallacta
2600 m

Willcaracay

Pacamayo river

Cusichaca river

Pacamayo

Warmiwañusqa
(1st pass)

Llulluchapampa

Llulluchayoc

4198 m.

Huayruro Chico

Wayllabamba

Paucarcancha

to
Incachiriasqa
Pass

- - - - other Inca trails

△ campsite

⋔ ruins

♨ Hot springs

▥ dirt road

archaeological sites prompted the Peruvian government to impose major restrictions and regulations on the trail: permits are required, and only 500 people per day are allowed, roughly 300 support staff and 200 paying hikers. (Why is the trail now so heavily regulated? See the Exploring *Cusco Museum* at www.peterfrost.org to learn more about this and the early history of the hike.) Permits often book out 4-6 months in advance for the high season; tour operators can check availability for you. Tourists must book with a certified Inca Trail operator, though groups of up to four can do an independent trip (no crew, no porters) with an authorized freelance guide (see *General Information*, www.peterfrost. org). Camping is only permitted at specific sites.

WALKING THE INCA TRAIL

Length, Elevation, and Time. 43km (27mi); +1,530m (5,020ft) to the highest pass from the trailhead; 4-5 days including Machu Picchu. Five-day trips are preferable if you can afford it because you see fewer hikers. Ecoinka (*see p.42*) offers a five-day itinerary that spends the first and second nights at their comfortable campsites at Km. 82 and the ruins of Paucarcancha, respectively.

Fitness. Any active, experienced and acclimatized hiker can tackle the Inca Trail, especially with the assistance of porters.

Weather. The best months are May through September. April and October are transitional months, sometimes with fine weather; November through March, count on some rain (be prepared anyway); January – yuk! The trail is closed in February for maintenance. Local lore holds that the best weather occurs in the last few days before full moon. In the author's experience this is indeed true.

Tip: For the altitude and all-around energy, take coca leaves and an activator (*see p. 48*)

Nature: In the tropical Andes, altitude is biological destiny, and small changes in the former produce radical transformations in the latter. The Inca Trail passes through an astonishing variety of environments during its short journey to Machu Picchu, many of which are mentioned in the trail description below.

Scientists have recorded 374 bird species in the Sanctuary (nearly 5% of all known species), most of which may be seen along the Inca Trail. Ground animals are fairly rare, though white-tailed deer are not uncommon. *Vizcacha*, the rabbit-sized Andean rodent, may sometimes be seen leaping around areas of jumbled rockfall, while the jewel in the crown of wildlife sightings along the trail is the Andean bear (a.k.a the Spectacled Bear, so named for the distinctive pale rings around its eyes) – an endangered cloud-forest species, which is sometimes sighted along the Inca Trail and even at Machu Picchu (see YouTube for amazing videos of the latter).

Plant *aficionados* will find a bewildering variety – some 250 species of orchid have been identified in the Sanctuary, along with countless bromeliads, begonias, mosses, ferns, and others, too numerous to list. Orchid specialist Benjamín Collantes found 59 species of orchid, including ten new to the Sanctuary and three new to science, while simply walking along the banks of the Urubamba River from Km. 88 to Km. 104.
(See "Nature and Wildlife" in the Bibliography for field guides.)

MAIN SITES ALONG THE INCA TRAIL

Not all tour operators will stop at every spot. The higher-end ones give you more time at the various ruins sites along the way and have more knowledgeable guides.

1. **Km 82 - Piscacucho:** The trail starts at Km 82 at the small community of Piscacucho (2,670m/8,760ft), where you present your trail permit and cross the footbridge that leads into the trail. The hike begins in arid cactus and agave canyon-floor habitat.

2. **Willcaracay and Patallaqta:** Following the trail some 5.5km (3.4mi) along the Urubamba River, you come to the ruins of Willcaracay (2,750m/9,022ft). This was probably an elite compound belonging to the overseers who managed production at *Patallaqta* (2,625m/8,610ft), the big ruined settlement that you see in the Cusichaca Valley far

below you. Patallaqta (Terrace Town) stands on the mountainside high above immense banks of agricultural terraces, on the west bank of the Cusichaca River. This well-preserved and major Inca ruin was not part of the string of elite ceremonial centers that you will see later on – yet it was vital to their existence, because it produced the food on which they depended. Combined with *Q'ente*, further downstream, and other sites higher up the Cusichaca (Bridge of Joy) Valley, this area produced three or four times more food than it consumed. Unlike Machu Picchu and the other Inca Trail sites, this one was settled by earlier cultures before the Incas arrived, with human occupation beginning at least 2,000 years ago, through to the present day.

Patallaqta was not a high-prestige settlement. A visit to the ruins provides a contrast to some of the sites to be seen later on. The residential compounds are built with uncut fieldstone, in a strictly repetitive architectural style, characteristic of the type of site where transient *mit'a* labor contingents were housed. But the solid stonework, the attention to urban planning, and above all the quality and beautifully contoured style of the terracing betrays the hand of first-rate royal architects and engineers, most likely those of Pachacuti's *panaca*.

Below the ruins, near the banks of the Cusichaca River, stands a small site called *Pulpituyoq* (Pulpit-having – a hybrid Spanish-Quechua word). This curved building, constructed around a huge rock, was Patallaqta's *waca*.

3. **Wayllabamba:** Continuing on for 4.5km (2.8mi), you will pass Wayllabamba (3,000m/9,840ft), the last village along the trail and a popular campsite. Beyond Wayllabamba, the trail leaves the Cusichaca River and follows the Llullucha River.

A spectacular six-day, 60km (38mi) Inca Trail variation will also lead you to Wayllabamba. The High Inca Trail, as it's sometimes called, combines the Inca Trail and Salcantay trek (*see p. 207*) and allows you to experience the connection between Machu Picchu and the sacred mountain of Salcantay. The route requires an Inca Trail permit and licensed operator. Day One initially follows the standard Salcantay route, passing through Mollepata and starting in Soraypampa, then diverges before the Salcantay Pass, taking you NE instead of NW to a campsite at 4,600m (15,100ft) at Ichupata. This campsite is very cold all year round; come prepared and well acclimatized. Day Two you ascend to the 4,900m (16,076ft) Incachiriasqa (Where the Inca Was Cold) Pass on the shoulder of Mt. Salcantay and then descend into a valley to the next campsite. On Day Three you pass the community of Pampacahuana and the ruins and campsite of Paucarcancha (3,150m/10,335ft) to connect with the classic Inca Trail at Wayllabamba. Apus Peru (*see p. 42*) and Enigma (*see p. 41*) both offer this route.

4. **Unca Forest:** About 2km (1.2mi) up the Llullucha from Wayllabamba, the trail winds steeply upwards above the left bank through a thick wood for a little over 1km (0.6mi). This is a shady, humid woodland of *Unca* (*Myrcianthes oreophila*), a tall, smooth-bark tree, and one of numerous micro-environments within the sanctuary. It is a fragile habitat which supports various endemic bird species and is highly endangered by deforestation throughout the Peruvian Andes.

5. **Llulluchapampa:** As you emerge from the woods the route traverses a brief belt of Andean dwarf forest following a section of stone highway which is essentially, as Peruvians say, *bamba* – a piece of "Inca" trail built in recent times. When you arrive at a broad sloping area of open grassland with steep mountain slopes on either side you have reached Llulluchapampa (3,600m/11,800ft, about 2 hours and 2km/1.3mi from the Unca forest. *Llullucha* = small plants; *pampa* = flat area.) The upper end of this pasture offers good opportunities for spotting a variety of birds found in the *puna* zone, plus white-tailed deer, or even the rare Andean *taruca* (a small barrel-chested deer with spiky little antlers).

6. **Warmiwañusca:** The high altitude grassland on this next leg is excellent for viewing Andean raptors, like the Black-chested eagle, the mountain *caracara* and the aplomado falcon. Condors are rare but sometimes seen.

The trail ascends high-altitude slopes of *ichu* bunch grass for two hours and 1.6km (1mi) from Llulluchapampa to the *Abra de Warmiwañusca* (Dead Woman's Pass; we have no record as to the origin of this name). This is the first pass and the highest point of the trail at 4,200m (13,780ft). Notice traces of ancient steps at the head of the pass, the first unmistakable signs that you are following a pre-Columbian highway. If visibility is good you can see two high passes ahead of you from here. The one on the right is your destination. You can pick out the two small lakes near the pass and the circular ruin of Runkuracay below them.

7. **Pacamayo River:** Descending 2.1km (1.3mi) from Warmiwañusca, a new stone trail winds down the steep slope to the *Pacamayo* (Hidden River, 3,600m/11,800ft, 1.5 hours from Warmiwañusca). It is not Inca, but in this case, construction was justified because of the problem of loose rock and erosion on this section. As you near the valley floor you see the waterfalls of the river Pacamayo tumbling down the mountain to your left. You begin to find real Inca stone steps built into the mountain as your route zig-zags up its slopes to Runkuracay at 3,780m (12,400ft), 1 hour and 0.7km (0.4mi) from Pacamayo. The woodland of this valley is primarily *polylepis* (local name *q'ueña*), whose gnarly trunk and branches, small leaves and flaky red bark makes it one of the most characteristic native species of the high Andes.

8. **Runkuracay:** Hiram Bingham got the name *Runkuracay* from his local native porters. Victor Angles has suggested that, since the word *runku* doesn't exist in (Cusco) Quechua, Bingham must have misheard them, and the name should be Runturacay, meaning "egg [shaped] building." The late Alberto Miori pointed out that the building is round, not egg-shaped, and that *runku* does indeed exist in the Ayacucho/Apurimac Quechua dialect (close neighbors of this region). Thereby, the name translates as "basket [in shape and/or function] building." And there's also *runp'u*, meaning "ball, or anything circular/spherical in shape..." Gets complicated, this Andean toponymy.

The circular shape of the main structure at Runkuracay is unusual for a large Inca construction. The two concentric walls of the enclosure form two long, curved chambers and four small ones, all giving onto a central courtyard. The outer walls are massive and solid, and have no windows, but the eastern quarter of the courtyard is open, giving a magnificent view over the Pacamayo Valley. The site might have served as a lookout point (most of the sites in this region command the landscape visually for kilometers in every direction), and also as a tambo – a place where travelers lodged, animals were corralled and cargoes were relayed.

9. Second (Runkuracay) Pass: The trail climbs on from Runkuracay for an hour, 0.5km (0.3mi) toward the second pass, named after the ruins. Once again it follows the left hand flank of the mountain, climbing between the twin lakes of *Yanacocha* (Black Lake); you see the lower one first, on your left, and the other behind you on the right as you near the second pass, the *Abra de Runkuracay* (3,924m/12,870ft). In clear weather the view ahead from here is fabulous – a breathtaking sweep of snow peaks, dominated by the 6,000m (19,680ft) Pumasillo massif, the Puma's Claw.

This pass is actually the summit of a ridge, stretching 40km (25mi) from the peak of Salcantay to Machu Picchu and the Urubamba River. You will be criss-crossing it for the rest of the hike. This is often a good place to spot the Great Sapphirewing, one of the largest and most dazzling hummingbirds of the sanctuary. As you descend from Runkuracay, the trail becomes more and more obviously an Inca highway. After about half an hour you can see ahead of you, clinging to a spur, the ruins of Sayacmarca.

10. Sayacmarca: *Sayacmarca* (3,525m/11,560ft, 1 hour and 1.3km/0.8mi from *Abra de Runkuracay*) was discovered by Hiram Bingham in 1915. He called it *Cedrobamba*, meaning "Plain of Cedars." But since it is not a plain, nor are there any cedars, Paul Fejos, who explored the area in 1940, gave it a new Quechua name meaning "Dominant [or Inaccessible] Town." The complex is built at the end of an abrupt

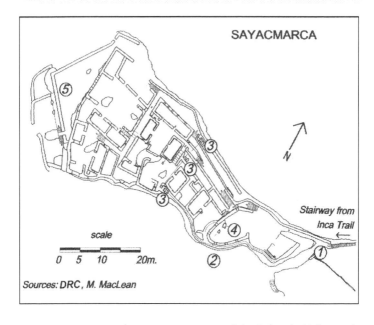

promontory commanding a sweeping view of the Aobamba Valley, with the snowcapped Pumasillo in the distance.

The layout of the settlement is maze-like and tightly organized, almost cramped. There must have been some special motive or mindset behind the choosing of this site, because there is a small plateau nearby to the NW known as *Ch'akicocha* (Dry Lake), which, from our perspective, would seem a much better location for a town. It has a more accessible water supply, and far more space for building. But it does not overlook its surroundings in the same way as the site that was chosen. This was surely the overriding factor for the Incas – Sayacmarca was not, in military terms, a defensible site: its water supply was easy to cut off, and it could be bombarded with missiles from the nearby mountain slope. What it does have in common with all other sites along the Inca Trail is a commanding view of the landscape.

A line of observation platforms ran between here and Machu Picchu, and it seems likely that the Incas used a signalling system to send information – warning of the approach of important people, for example – up and down this line. Sayacmarca may also have served as a center from which to control travel and cargo along the two main highways visible from this point (the second of these being the trail that led down the valley directly south of Sayacmarca, to the Aobamba Valley).

These are the utilitarian reasons for the location of Sayacmarca. But the deeper motives were metaphysical and are harder to explain. The truth is that there was no real economic or strategic rationale for building Machu Picchu or the Inca Trail and its sites. The land is so rugged and steep it is hardly worth farming, and there were no significant mineral deposits. The quality and type of construction cannot be accounted for by a military threat, and in fact the settlements were so remote that they made no economic sense at all. If they had, they would never have been abandoned.

Machu Picchu and the Inca Trail make no sense to our rational minds, but our hearts can readily understand. The Incas worshipped the natural world – particularly the snowcapped mountains which are visible from all the major sites – and tried to communicate with its spirits. They were willing to make an enormous investment in the veneration of landscape. The man who had all this built was a warrior and imperial conqueror; this was his other face, the hidden aspect of Pachacuti.

IN THE RUINS. The water supply (now defunct) ran down a cleft in the mountains behind, filling a large natural cistern. An aqueduct, probably consisting of a hollowed U-section log, then brought it onto a tall stone buttress (1) at the head of the ruins. The channel continues along the precipitous south wall of the complex (2) and descends through a series of three ritual baths (3). A fourth bath has been discovered outside the ruins, beside the trail shortly before the access stairway.

The unusual tongue-shaped building that dominates the site (4) has a curious feature: all of the trapezoidal openings on the west side have four pierced ring-stones set into the outside of the wall, one at each corner. Since the prevailing winds were from the west these might have been used to secure screens that would cover these openings when the wind was blowing hard.

At the lower end of the complex a broad triangular plaza (5) opens onto a wonderful vista of the Aobamba Valley. To your right, NW, you can see the Inca Trail crossing the flats and potential campsite of *Ch'akicocha* (750m/2,460ft from Sayacmarca), and winding around the mountain flanks toward the third pass. The trail is surprisingly distinct due to the white granite blocks used in its construction. Recognizing that too much beauty is intolerable, the authorities have considerately built a conspicuous stone-and-concrete latrine a few meters from the Inca Trail, in the middle of this view.

Directly below Sayacmarca stand the small ruins of Conchamarca, a cluster of three houses standing on a finely constructed stand of stone terraces. These were only discovered in the early nineteen-eighties and were not cleared until much more recently.

11. **Upper Cloud Forest:** This next part of the trail starts at Sayacmarca and skirts the fringes of the cloud forest, a zone of nocturnal fogs, made temperate by increasing proximity to warm air from the Amazon lowlands, which rises to 3,400m (11,150ft) at this point. Some of the most colorful bird species of the Inca Trail can be seen here, including the dramatic Scarlet-bellied mountain tanager. Parts of this trail section are flanked by steep banks clad in damp vegetation, a sort of terrestrial coral reef thick with mosses, lichens, ferns, orchids, bromeliads, and dotted with bright flowers. From here onwards, in fact, all of the trail is a riot of exotic plant life.

12. **First Tunnel:** 750m (2,460ft) from *Ch'akicocha* you come to a 20m (65ft)-long tunnel, which takes advantage of a natural cleft in a rock face too steep and solid to pass around. The Incas widened and cut steps into the cleft.

13. **Third Pass:** The third and final pass (3,650m/11,975ft, 1.5 hours and 3.5km/2.2mi from Sayacmarca) is really just the point at which the trail recrosses the long ridge that it previously crossed at the second pass, and is so gentle you may hardly notice it. Here you emerge onto a stupendous view of the Urubamba Valley. The ruins of Phuyupatamarca lie below you to the left. Looking south from here on a clear day you will see, starting from the left, the tip of snowcapped Palcay (ca. 5,600m/18,370ft) then the massive bulk of Salcantay (6,264m/20,546ft); 35km (22mi) to the west stand Sacsarayoc and Pumasillo (6,000m/19,680ft) and then a string of lesser snow peaks away to the west; then if you turn all the way around, there is Wakay Willka (a.k.a. Verónica – 5,750m/18,860ft) 15km (9.3mi) away to the NE.

14. **Phuyupatamarca:** *Phuyupatamarca* (3,580m/11,740ft, 15 minutes and 250m/820ft from the third pass) was another of Hiram Bingham's discoveries. His name for this one (Cloud-level Town) is fitting because, at night, clouds tend to settle around this ridge. There are many agricultural terraces here, possibly enough to have made the site self-sufficient. Once again we find ritual baths – a fine principal bath (1) at the outskirts of the ruins beside the road leading into the complex, and a chain of five almost identical baths (2) descending in a line along the pathway below. These have recently been cleared and restored to working order.

At the top of the site stands a large platform of bedrock (3) which has been leveled off by hand – an amazing feat when we consider the tools the Incas had to work with. The base of a fine double-jamb entranceway can be seen here, and this was evidently the beginning of a structure that was destined to be the most important in the complex. But we can see that it was never completed, because there is no sign of the heaps of cut stones that we would inevitably find had there been finished walls which later collapsed.

Above the ruins stands a ledge littered with rocks that may have served as a quarry. There you can see a block of stone about three meters long with three deep grooves cut into it, suggesting that someone was in the

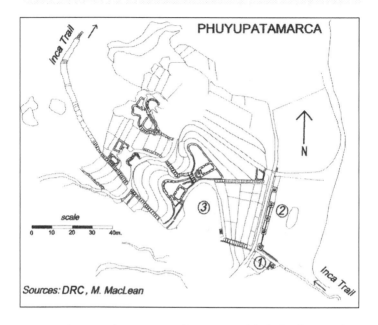

PHUYUPATAMARCA

Sources: DRC , M. MacLean

process of carving this stone into four separate blocks by the pounding technique described in Chapter Two (*p. 126*). The cliff edge was once crowned with a long wall at this point – the bedding-cuts in the rock can be seen clearly.

Each of the small groups of buildings in the ruins features a semi-circular or semi-ovoid structure, resembling a low, single-storey tower. Some of them have sinuous, irregular shapes that seem molded to follow the outlines of the rock on which they are built, and all of them look outwards over the immense Urubamba Gorge. These miniature towers are a unique feature of Phuyupatamarca.

From this point onward the steep and seemingly endless descent to Wiñay Wayna and then Machu Picchu takes you through ever-changing layers of cloud forest, yielding innumerable distinct types of vegetation to the astute observer.

Where the trail exits from the ruins on the west side you come to two flights of steps pointing downward into the jungle. The first of these is a mind-boggling granite staircase which continues the main Inca trail towards *Wiñay Wayna*, *Inti Pata*, and Machu Picchu. First uncovered in the early 1980s, the stairway is wide and impressive, with parts of it cut into solid bedrock. Near the top you find a cave, and a kilometer or so beyond that another, both with walls and niches built inside them. The second of these probably served as a small rest stop and shelter. A lookout platform stands close by. From this point, in clear weather, you look down upon the ruins of Wiñay Wayna and the somewhat jarring rooftops of the adjacent modern visitor center – all some two air kilometers away.

15. **Second Tunnel and Inti Pata:** The trail passes through another steep tunnel, cuts across the mountainside and eventually joins a modern pathway that descends near a line of electricity towers. The original Inca trail continues horizontally from here, leading to the huge fan-shaped agricultural terraces of *Inti Pata* (Sun Terraces, 2,850m/9,350ft), another site first encountered in modern times during Hiram Bingham's explorations of 1915. This is the longer and more beguiling route to the visitor center and the ruins of Wiñay Wayna. It leads to a small ceremonial complex at the very top of Inti Pata, passes stone storehouses descending long stone stairways to the distant lower end, where you find another small platform and temple complex. The terraces are both massive and intricate, another startling testament to Inca design, architecture and engineering. You will have to make this descent either way, but this is the longer route. The shorter way down is direct but dusty, following the modern trail that zigzags below high tension power lines in a vertical drop of approximately 300m (1,000ft), to emerge at the visitor center (2,650m/8,692ft, 2 hours and 3km/1.9mi from Phuyupatamarca). The campsite here, packed onto narrow terraces, is somewhat crowded and noisy but very popular due to its location a short hike from Machu Picchu.

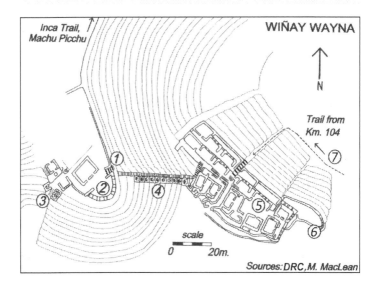

Sources: DRC, M. MacLean

16. **Wiñay Wayna:** The ruins of Wiñay Wayna lie 250m (820ft), about five minutes walk, off the trail around the hillside to the right (south) at this point. The site is named after an orchid genus (here, *Epidendrum crassilabium* and *E. secundum*) with red, violet or yellow flowers that was once abundant in this area and is still to be seen. The plant blooms year-round, hence the Quechua name, which means "Forever Young."

The ruins here were discovered in 1941 by Paul Fejos during the last days of the Viking Fund Expedition. He had time only for rudimentary survey and clearing work. The Peruvian archaeologist Julio C. Tello conducted further investigations in 1942. The ruins are built on the steepest of mountain slopes, flanked by ancient farming terraces. Due east from here, the land plunges into the Urubamba Gorge and then soars upward to the shining glaciers of Wakay Willka (Verónica).

IN THE RUINS. As you take the path from the visitor center to the ruins you pass from the mundane to the divine, encountering one of those sudden, sensational first views that the Incas seemed to delight in creating. A magnificent sweep of curved terracing leads the eye down to a cluster of steep-roofed buildings perched at the end of a steep spur, while in the background a high waterfall sprays down the mountainside through dense cloud forest vegetation.

The trail leads into the complex along a broad terrace with a long, curved wall to one's right, which ends at a huge doorway (1). Ascend the steps leading through this doorway to enter a large round-walled structure (2) that commands the site in much the same way as the similar structure at Sayacmarca does, and the unfinished enclosure at Phuyupatamarca would have. Look back to see the mighty *apu* Wakay Willka (Verónica), framed dead center in the doorway – certainly not an accidental alignment. Wiñay Wayna is evidently a ceremonial site connected with this mountain.

Walk to the rear of this area to find a small fountain complex, the first and most secluded of the descending baths, which suggests that this area was restricted to the highest ranking residents.

Returning to the entrance, a straight flight of stairs takes you down past a unique set of ten ritual baths (4). They are almost identical. Historical data confirm that ritual bathing or cleansing was an important feature of Inca religious observance. The element of water itself was also worshipped. Ritual baths are a feature of every major Inca site, but they are particularly numerous on the Inca Trail sites – and they become more numerous the closer one gets to Machu Picchu. This is another factor among many which support the view that the Machu Picchu/Inca Trail network held a special spiritual significance for the Incas.

If you follow the steps downhill past these waterworks you reach the dwelling area. Here there is a small square (5) overlooked by two open-fronted buildings, which might have been a communal area where the social and economic transactions of the community took place. At the lower extreme of the dwelling area you emerge onto a tiny, startling platform (6) (careful!) poised over two hundred meters of nothing – a vertical farewell to earth. To your right a waterfall sprays down the cliff face; overall, a breathtaking view in an astounding Inca site.

The one-day Short Inca Trail (*see Alternative Inca Trails below*) from Chachabamba at Km. 104 crosses the opposite side of this ravine, passes close to the waterfall, then enters the terraces of Wiñay Wayna at (7).

17. Enchanted Forest: Leaving Wiñay Wayna, you are on the last leg of the trail, with 2.5 hours and 4.4km (2.75mi) to go to Machu Picchu. The trail traverses fairly steadily across open mountainside at first, and then, rising and falling, enters an enchanted forest, scattered with huge tree ferns and giant begonias with sprays of cream-colored flowers when in bloom, and so large it's hard to believe they are related to your humble pot plant back home; careful observers will note many new plant species here and a different type of cloud forest habitat, with larger trees.

18. Intipunku to Machu Picchu: The trail passes through a ruined gateway flanked by remains of buildings: *Intipunku*, the Sun Gate, ca. 2,700m (8,860ft) and 3.1km (1.9mi) from Wiñay Wayna. (*Birdwatchers:* right by these ruins on the east side of the ridge is a great viewing spot). You have reached the city limits. Walk to the far side of the ruin and you see the climax of your journey, one of the world's breathtaking views. The tall peak of Wayna Picchu lies directly ahead. Before it, spread impressively over the ridge below you, lies the lost city of the Incas, Machu Picchu.

INCA TRAIL ALTERNATIVES
The Cusco region offers countless hiking routes. Below are a few that will either take you directly to Machu Picchu or can easily be combined with that visit.

Short Inca Trail
This is a one-day hike to Machu Picchu starting at railway Km. 104 and passing through Wiñay Wayna on the way. This requires an Inca Trail permit and must be done with an authorized operator or independent guide. It is closed in February. Distance is about 4km (2.5mi) to the visitor center at Wiñay Wayna and about 8.5km (5.3mi) total to Machu Picchu.

Visitors spend the night in Aguas Calientes and return to visit Machu Picchu the next day. The trail begins at the bridge at railroad Km 104, where there is a visitor checkpoint. Shortly thereafter the trail passes through the very interesting ruin site of *Chachabamba*. This differs from other Inca Trail sites, being built on level ground right by the Urubamba River. Its central feature is a large carved boulder with a three-sided structure built on top of it. The site features no fewer than 14 ritual baths in four separate groups, one at each corner of the site. Archaeologist Margaret Maclean suggested that this shrine was associated with the nearby river, which was itself a sacred feature of the Inca world. From here the trail begins to climb steadily around an open (and sometimes very hot) mountain slope into the ravine below Wiñay Wayna. After passing a spectacular waterfall, you climb through the ruins of Wiñay Wayna (*see p. 204*) and join the main Inca Trail, continuing to Machu Picchu.

The following don't require an Inca Trail permit:

Salcantay Trail

Starting from Mollepata, the classic three-day, 30km (18.8mi) trail takes you through Soraypampa, over the spectacular Salcantay Pass, and then down a long descent to the jungle climate of Challhuay before finally ending in Santa Teresa. From here, you can take transportation to the hidroeléctrica (hydroelectric station) and walk or take the train to Aguas Calientes to reach Machu Picchu. The route also passes the suddenly popular glacial Humantay Lake just above Soraypampa, which many agencies now offer as a day trip. It is possible to hike here independently without doing the whole Salcantay trail (*see below*).

There have been rumors for years that a permit, separate from the Inca Trail one, may be required to do the Salcantay hike at some point. Check **www.peterfrost.org** or with any travel agency.

Hiking It. Options here run the gamut from luxurious inn-to-inn experiences to schlepping all your own gear and sleeping in a tent. Mountain Lodges of Peru (*see p. 41*) offers a series of swanky lodges and a seven-day itinerary that lets you acclimatize and enjoy the route at a very reasonable pace. Any number of other less expensive tour operators can arrange a more standard version of this trek, carrying your gear on mules and housing you in tents; be warned that nearly all of them have a difficult and exhausting itinerary for Day Two. A somewhat easier alternative is to choose an agency that camps the first night further along the trail at *Salcantaypampa*, such as Explorandes (be sure to be well acclimatized if you choose this as you will be sleeping at 4,145m/13,600ft), or an agency which camps at the midway point on day two (Huayraqmachay), such as Apus Peru. Clients of Salkantay Trekking (**www.salkantaytrekking. com**) spend their first night in glass igloos with incredible sky views. A step above hiking independently is the economically priced Refugios Salkantay, (**www.refugiossalkantay.com**) run by hospitable local families who provide food and lodging along the way (you must carry your own day pack and guide yourself, however). Many tour operators offer an interesting, five-day variation on the classic route which takes in the ruins of Llactapata, ending at the hydroelectric station outside Aguas Calientes. Finally, you can hike the entire trail or just to Humantay Lake by yourself. See **www.peterfrost.org** for directions.

Inca Jungle Trek

A 3-4 day, multi-sport adventure option, involving biking down the paved road from Abra Málaga to the town of Alfamayo, rafting, hiking along a section of Inca trail (but not *the* Inca Trail), and ziplining at Cola de Mono (*see p. 45*). Ultimately you end up in Aguas Calientes before exploring Machu Picchu the next day. Most tour operators can arrange this for you. No trail permits required.

TWO SHORT HIKES NEAR AGUAS CALIENTES

I) Trail to Putucusi

East of Machu Picchu on the north bank of the river stands the small rounded peak of Putucusi (2,500m/8,200ft), free entrance. The summit affords nice views of Aguas Calientes and a panorama of Machu Picchu. The climb is steep, difficult, and definitely not for those with vertigo or fitness issues; moreover, at the time of writing, the ladder and rope which once scaled a sheer cliff face on the route have been removed for maintenance, making this a dangerous (especially when wet) rock climbing route. Closed until further notice on **www.peterfrost.org**

When the ladder is restored, find the trailhead by following the train tracks north out of town (away from Ollantaytambo, towards Machu Picchu). On the right-hand side of the railroad behind the Sumaq Hotel, a small trail begins to descend. Follow this for around 10 minutes to arrive at an abandoned control point. Three-hour round trip.

II) **Trail to Mandor Ravine & Waterfall**

From the old railroad station at *Puente Ruinas* (the bridge on the road up to Machu Picchu), walk downstream along the railroad tracks towards the *hidroeléctrica*. About 3km (1.9mi) beyond Puente Ruinas station, Mandor Ravine enters the Urubamba Gorge from the north bank of the river. Look out for the coffee and banana plants along the way. About twenty minutes' climbing up this ravine brings you to the 12m (40ft) Mandor waterfall, an exceptionally lovely spot. There is currently a small entry fee. *Birdwatchers*: early in the morning or at dusk, this walk features a lot of birdlife, including, if you are lucky, the spectacular Peruvian national bird the Cock-of-the-Rock (*Rupicola Peruviana saturata*). 6km (3.8mi), 3-4hrs round trip.

CHAPTER FIVE

MACHU PICCHU
The Fabled City

HISTORY

For centuries the Lost City has been the most durable and evocative of myths about ancient Peru. El Dorado. Paititi. Vilcabamba. The names have lured treasure hunters, adventurers and explorers ever since the Conquest. In early colonial times the jungle swallowed up hundreds of gold-hungry Spaniards and thousands of their press-ganged Indian porters. All in vain. They found nothing, except the Amazon. But the irony was that there *were* lost cities buried in forested eastern slope of the Andes. The 20th century has seen the discovery of more than one: Gran Pajatén in northern Peru; Espiritu Pampa in Vilcabamba; and, most famous and awe-inspiring of all, Machu Picchu.

Hiram Bingham, known today as the scientific discoverer of Machu Picchu, was actually seeking Vitcos and Vilcabamba the Old, the remote last strongholds of Manco Inca and his sons, whose locations were at that time unknown. Today we have virtually watertight evidence that he actually did find the latter site, without realizing it, when he visited Espiritu Pampa near the Apurimac River, some 100km west of Machu Picchu (*see Vilcabamba; Chapter Eight*). But Bingham only saw part of the ruins at Espiritu Pampa, and eventually came to dismiss them as insignificant. He later solved the conceptual problem of having found unknown Machu Picchu while searching for historic Vilcabamba by declaring that Machu Picchu *was* Vilcabamba.

Bingham was a historian, a Yale graduate, and later a U.S. Senator. He first came to South America in 1908 to participate in the first Pan-American scientific congress in Santiago, Chile. Early the following year, he traveled through the Andes and saw his first remote Inca ruin when he joined an expedition to the spectacular site of Choquequirao, above the Apurimac canyon. He was fascinated by Peru and returned in 1911 as leader of the Yale Peruvian expedition, whose goals included surveying the 73rd meridian; climbing Coropuna, a mountain near Arequipa then thought to be a candidate for "highest peak in the Americas"; and searching for the lost Inca capital of Vilcabamba. He had read some of the sources on the history of the last Inca refuge and had become curious about its location.

In Lima Bingham obtained more clues from the historian Carlos Romero. Then later, in Cusco, he learned from Albert Giesecke, the rector of the Cusco university, that there were many Inca sites down the Urubamba Valley below Ollantaytambo and unexplored ruins on the ridge above Mandor Pampa on the Urubamba River. Alberto Duque, who lived downstream from Mandor Pampa, gave him similar information.

Bingham therefore decided to follow the Urubamba, using a new mule trail down the river and bypassing the more familiar route over Abra de Málaga to the region thought to harbor Vitcos and Vilcabamba the Old. On July 23rd, 1911, he camped at Mandor Pampa, the flat strip of valley floor that curves around the north and west flank of Wayna Picchu and Machu Picchu. Next day a local farmer and innkeeper who knew the ridgetop ruins, one Melchor Arteaga, guided Bingham over the perilous river crossing and grueling climb for a reward of one silver *sol*.

Two local *campesino* families were farming in the ruins and had helpfully cleared the central part of the site (which was therefore not completely overgrown, as Bingham later claimed), so the fortunate Yankee was able to see some of what was there. But Bingham was not unduly excited at first by Machu Picchu; he spent five hours at the ruins, took some pictures, made a rough sketch map, and jotted a few laconic notes in his diary. That was all.

The value of his find slowly dawned on him. Next day, on July 26th, while waiting on a lost mule, he began a letter to his wife: "[Machu Picchu] is far more wonderful and interesting than Choquequirao. The stone is as fine as any in Cusco! It is unknown, and will make a fine story." He was hitting his stride and there would have been more, but the letter suddenly ends: "They found the mule!" He would not return until the following year.

Before setting off, he wrote in his journal: "Agustín Lizárraga is the discoverer of Machu Picchu." Lizárraga was a farmer who lived at San Miguel bridge, just downstream from Mandor Pampa; Bingham had seen his name chalked on a rock at the ruins.

Perhaps Bingham did not think to delay at Machu Picchu because it was completely at odds with Spanish historical accounts of terrain and other details at Vilcabamba – and that was the prize he was after. Later, Bingham would forget those inconvenient topographical details and proclaim that Machu Picchu *was* the lost Inca capital of Vilcabamba the Old.

He sent three members of his expedition back in September of 1911 to clear and map the ruins while he pressed on with his goal of a first ascent of Coropuna. But in his preliminary report on the findings of the Yale Peruvian expedition the following year, he devoted only seven lines to Machu Picchu, and more than two pages to some prehistoric human bones he had discovered in a glacial deposit near Cusco, which he thought were of epoch-making significance.

Even when Bingham returned to Peru a year later, with the Yale/ National Geographic Expedition of 1912, Machu Picchu still was not specifically mentioned as an objective. He was more interested in Peruvian geography, and in his prehistoric bones. But further investigation suggested these were relatively recent, so he at last decided to throw most of his expedition's energies into months of clearing and excavating at Machu Picchu. Typically, he spent just two weeks there getting his crew started, then set off on new explorations. He returned for a spell in mid-August, departed again to cope with political problems in Lima, and returned again in November to wrap up the expedition. Bingham was an excellent photographer, and in these three visits he assembled a vast collection of seven hundred photographs. Today, some scholars regard this collection of early photos as one of Bingham's most valuable scientific contributions.

Bingham's photos knocked the proverbial socks off the folks at National Geographic, and in April, 1913 the magazine devoted an entire issue to Bingham's Peruvian expedition (still without mentioning Machu Picchu on the cover), and soon afterwards both Bingham and Machu Picchu were famous. Some of these pictures can be be seen at the Inka Museum and the Casa Concha Machu Picchu Museum in Cusco (*see Museums, p. 49*), the Sanctuary Lodge cafeteria at Machu Picchu, and on the National Geographic website.

Photos were not the only thing he took. He amassed a voluminous collection of archaeological material, mostly bones and potsherds, plus some metal items, including some silver, but no gold. There were few museum-quality pieces, and due to the absence of gold many people in Cusco believe to this day that "Bingham stole all the gold." A more charitable and perfectly plausible explanation is that when the Incas abandoned Machu Picchu they took all their gold treasures with them. The only known gold object recovered there was a plain wristband, apparently an offering, recovered during excavations beneath the lower esplanade in the 1990s.

Permanent export of antiquities was already illegal in Peru by 1912. But Bingham had permission from the government to take his collection to Yale – as an indefinite loan. In the early 2000s this situation became a bone of contention between Yale and the Peruvian government, a dispute ultimately resolved with the repatriation of the collection to a museum set up for it by the UNSAAC, the aforementioned Casa Concha.

Hiram Bingham was extraordinarily lucky and hilariously blind to his luck. He longed for fame, and today, over 100 years later, with all that we have learned since then, one laughs to read of his manic pursuit of spurious bones and first ascents (he bagged the wrong peak), right after he had become the first scholar to see Machu Picchu.

During his explorations in 1912 and 1915 he located a string of other ruins and a major Inca highway (now known to us as the Inca Trail) to the south of Machu Picchu. Later still, in 1941, the Viking Fund expedition led by Paul Fejos discovered the important site of *Wiñay Wayna* (*see Inca Trail; Chapter Four*) above the Urubamba gorge, about 4.5 km due south of Machu Picchu, enlarging both the scope of Machu Picchu and the mystery surrounding it.

In recent years the issue of Machu Picchu's discovery has been fraught with claims, counterclaims and controversy. Even before local farmers visited the site in the early 1900s, it seems others may have been there. Explorer and researcher Paolo Greer located a map of the region dated 1874 by one Herman Göhring, a German cartographer under contract to the Peruvian government. Machu Picchu appears on it, clearly marked in about the right spot on the Urubamba River. Whether Göhring actually saw Machu Picchu himself is doubtful, but Greer also found a record of one Augusto Berns, another German who was living at the spot where Aguas Calientes now stands during the 1880s. The slightly shady Herr Berns attempted various doomed ventures in the valley before floating his most intriguing scheme in 1887, a company with prominent stakeholders in Lima whose stated mission was to plunder a nearby Inca ruin he had found, which he called "Huaca del Inca." This ruin was almost certainly Machu Picchu.

Whether any of the proposed pillage took place remains uncertain. But what *is* certain is that, 24 years later, Hiram Bingham became the *scientific* discoverer of Machu Picchu – the first person to go there with scientific aims and leave us a serious record of the site.

As with most scientific discoveries, numerous people were involved. Carlos Romero, in Lima, Giesecke and Duque, Bingham's informants in Cusco – none of them had visited Machu Picchu (an attempt by Giesecke only months before Bingham's expedition had been defeated by bad weather); Lizárraga had, but his goal was probably treasure. Melchor Arteaga knew the ruins, and there were *campesinos* actually living there. None were aware of the site's historic importance.

Bingham remains a controversial figure in Peru today, partly because of his somewhat ruthless pursuit of his goals, his carting off crateloads of archaeological material, and his purchase of looted artefacts from elsewhere to supplement his meager haul of museum-quality items from Machu Picchu. But perhaps most of all it was because *anyone* who makes a major scientific discovery is destined to be controversial. Like him or not, in the end it *was* Hiram Bingham who, rather hesitantly, announced Machu Picchu to the world.

After that day at Machu Picchu in 1911, Bingham continued onward, locating the Inca sites of Vitcos and Vilcabamba the Old at Espiritu Pampa (*see Vilcabamba; Chapter Eight*) shortly afterwards. These were the sites he had originally been seeking, the remote last strongholds of Manco Inca and his sons. Ironically, he at first identified both ruins correctly. But somewhat later, now dazzled by the response to his spectacular find on the Urubamba gorge, he reversed himself on the second site, declaring that Machu Picchu was the location of Vilcabamba the Old.

Butterfly motif from ceramic plate, found at Machu Picchu

Bingham's mistake was understandable. He only saw part of the ruins at Espiritu Pampa, which were thoroughly buried in dense vegetation – and who would imagine that there were not one, but two major lost cities in the forest northwest of Cusco?

Today no one believes Machu Picchu was Vilcabamba the Old. Firstly, there is so much high-quality construction and design that must have taken many years and employed a vast labor force in its construction at Machu Picchu, whereas Manco's capital was mostly a post-Conquest city, built hurriedly with limited resources. Secondly, Machu Picchu is purely an Inca city; there are no traces of the Hispanic influence one would expect to find at Vilcabamba. Furthermore, we know that the Spaniards actually discovered Manco's capital and burned it, before its location was lost to memory, yet there are no clear signs of destruction at Machu Picchu; even the setting fails to conform to historic Spanish accounts of the terrain around Vilcabamba. The name itself (Vilcabamba means Sacred Plain) flatly contradicts the hypothesis, given the precipitous terrain around Machu Picchu. Finally, and most convincingly, the true site of Vilcabamba the Old *has* been confirmed – at Espiritu Pampa, by the Savoy expeditions of 1964 (*see Vilcabamba; Chapter Eight*).

So Bingham revealed an enigma even deeper than he imagined. Machu Picchu was not Vilcabamba the Old.

Then what was it?

THEORIES OF THE LOST PROVINCE

A popular and alluring myth portrays Machu Picchu as some kind of Andean Shangri-la perched alone on its remote crag, and it is easy to believe this if one sees only Machu Picchu itself, without walking the Inca Trail. But many more discoveries, large and small, have been made in the region since 1941. Taken as a whole they support a view of Machu Picchu as the ceremonial (and possibly administrative) center of a large and quite populous region – not a lost city, but an entire lost province.

The school of thought fostered by Bingham held that the city existed primarily for strategic and defensive purposes. He pointed to the outer wall (by the main ruins entrance) and inner walls, the latter flanked by a deep trench (#7 on site map) as evidence of fortifications. There was also the apparently strategic drawbridge to the west of the ruins, and the lookout platforms atop Wayna Picchu and the peak of Machu Picchu.

However, Mecca is also surrounded by walls and has closely guarded gateways, yet it is not a fortress. The studies performed in the 1980s on the skeletons shipped to Yale by Hiram Bingham in 1912 found no warrior types among them, and relatively few weapons were found. Modern evidence and interpretation leans strongly to the view that Machu Picchu was essentially a site of spiritual and ceremonial significance, perhaps with important agricultural functions. Its strategic purposes, if any, were secondary.

During the 1980s, the eminent U.S. archaeologist and ethnohistorian J.H. Rowe discovered a document dated 1568 attributing ownership of all the lands on this stretch of the Urubamba River to the Inca Pachacuti. This showed that Machu Picchu had been essentially the private property of that Inca emperor, built and populated by his royal family. This detail did not initially tell us very much, but recent years have yielded illuminating studies of Inca royal estates, or palaces, as some describe them. As the archaeologist Susan Niles has pointed out, nearly all of the famous sites that visitors come to Cusco to see were Inca royal estates: Pisac, Chinchero, Ollantaytambo, Huchuy Cusco, Tipón, Choquequirao, to name some. They represent the summit of Inca architectural and artistic achievement, set in some of their most glorious landscapes. But most of these royal lands were also strategic locations, powerhouse population centers, engines of trade and agricultural production designed to consolidate power and generate wealth for the Inca emperor and his family. Machu Picchu was none of those things. Why did Pachacuti order this massive investment of human labor, design, architecture and engineering on this far-off forest ridge, in this remote, politically and economically insignificant corner of his empire?

Few people in history were as bonded to their landscape, economically, politically and spiritually, as were the Inca. Indeed, those modern distinctions meant nothing to them; the three were one and the same. In the Andean world, Mother Earth, her rivers and her mountains, the *apus*, ultimately owned and endowed everything that grew and lived upon them. Certain humans were privileged to control and administer this bounty. During the 15th century, that privilege belonged to the Incas and their grand network of allied nobilities. They held what Chinese dynasties called "the Mandate of Heaven."

How did they demonstrate this? In many ways – and one of them was to effectively control visual and physical access to the most powerful precincts of the Andean landscape: the high mountains, the mighty rivers. At Machu Picchu so many of those sacred elements came together; not for nothing did archaeologist Johan Reinhard label Machu Picchu the "Sacred Center." We find here a direct physical link to Salcantay, the mountain due south of Machu Picchu, 6,264m (20,546ft) high, and to this day venerated as the most powerful *apu* west of Cusco. An immense ridge 40km (25mi) long begins at its summit, eventually reaches the point where Machu Picchu reclines in a saddle beneath the dramatic exclamation point of Wayna Picchu, then falls swiftly into a deep, forested canyon. These features alone would have guaranteed Machu Picchu's ritual importance, but there was much more: the Willcamayu (today the Urubamba), the Incas' most sacred river and viewed as the earthly counterpart to the celestial river known to us as the Milky Way, made a huge snaking loop which almost surrounded the city. Moreover, the encircling crescent of mountains north of the river was the western tail of another long ridge, extending from the sacred snows of the scarcely less important *apu* Wakay Willca (now Verónica) and ending in its own signature mountain west of Machu Picchu, now known as San Miguel. Even today, the most jaded visitor cannot fail to sense the extraordinary beauty and power of this setting.

Here, where sacred river embraced sacred mountain, the Inca landscape's most vital features were imbued with spiritual meaning. Having found the place and added it to his expanding realm, it was perhaps inevitable that Pachacuti would build some elaborate expression of Inca magnificence there. Ownership of this sacred landscape signaled the Inca's close bond with the Andean gods. The emperor may have brought the chiefs of allied tribes there as honored guests, to be suitably awed by his achievement – and we see some evidence that he did *(see the lozenge-shaped rocks, p. 233, and obsidian shards, p. 235).*

No good theory exists without a rival. Richard Burger and Lucy Salazar of Yale University propose a counter-theory of Machu Picchu as a kind of Inca "Camp David" (the secluded retreat where U.S. presidents relax and occasionally meet with other leaders). In this scenario the Inca emperor moved his court from highland Cusco to Machu Picchu's agreeable climate for an extended period during the cold winter months. These two interpretations of Machu Picchu are not diametrically opposed; they are differences of emphasis. The Camp David theory acknowledges Machu Picchu's intense concentration of religious architecture, while the Sacred Center theory allows that it may have served as Pachacuti's occasional retreat. But this author finds highly implausible the notion that the emperor would spend months in isolation far from the Inca capital, leaving his empire and throne at the mercy of rival ambitions. He aligns with Reinhard and others in locating the site's primary inspiration and purpose in an Inca ritual landscape, where the emperor was an occasional visitor.

If we accept the standard dates of the reigns of the Inca kings, we can speak of the construction dates of Machu Picchu with reasonable confidence. Most scholars accept that the Inca expansion began around the year 1438, after Pachacuti's defeat of the invading Chanca tribe. (Although some scholars are sceptical of the 1438 date of the Chanca war and the beginning of the Inca expansion, putting it further back in time.)

Various chronicles tell us that for strategic reasons (to pre-empt the retreating Chancas) this region was the first to be settled in the headlong rush toward empire. The building style of Machu Picchu is "imperial Inca," which supports this thesis, and, unlike many other Inca sites, this one bears no sign of pre-Inca occupation. Nor are there clear signs of post-Conquest occupation. So Machu Picchu may have been built, occupied and abandoned in the space of less than one hundred years. The rest is speculation. And who can resist speculating when faced with something as affecting, and yet impenetrable, as the mystery of these silent stones?

DAILY LIFE IN THE SACRED CITY

Hemming states that Machu Picchu has only 200 habitation structures, leading him to estimate a permanent population of about a thousand people. However, as an Inca emperor's royal estate, housing for the leader's considerable entourage would have been needed during his visits. The currently accepted paradigm suggests, therefore, that a caretaker population of about 300 people swelled to a thousand or more when the emperor arrived.

In the 1980s Cusco archaeologists Alfredo Valencia and Arminda Gibaja surveyed the area, including the major nearby sites, and calculated production at about 28 metric tons of maize per year, assuming only maize was cultivated. This does not add up to a great abundance of food. The terraces at Machu Picchu were dry farmed, not irrigated, and though the region is rainy for much of the year, this would have inhibited dry season farming of secondary crops. If each inhabitant needed ¼ kg of maize per day, the 28 ton figure gives us food for only just over 300 people. Even if production were twice that, they still fed only 600 people.

Soil samples from the main terraces revealed abundant evidence of maize pollen, while other sectors showed signs of medicinal plant production and *hierba mate*, known as Paraguayan tea. There are clues in the 1568 document that the population in this area were growing food to be burned in ritual sacrifices in addition to cultivation for human consumption. So it is clear, at least, that Machu Picchu must have been supplied with food from elsewhere – probably a variety of sites, including the major production center of Patallaqta near Km. 88, which visitors can see during the railroad journey (*see box, p. 225*).

Some archaeologists have proposed that a principal function of the Machu Picchu region was to create a reliable supply of coca leaves for the priests and royalty of Cusco. Today, Machu Picchu itself is too high to grow coca, but old documents show that the Incas had developed many crop varieties—since lost—that would flourish at altitudes far above where they grow today. The Incas built many agricultural centers which seem to have been designed and used for plant adaptation, and this Inca settlement may have been partly designed as a center for the adaptation of coca to higher altitudes, but this is only speculation; soil samples have not revealed any evidence for it. In either case, Machu Picchu was probably a conduit to Cusco for coca grown lower down the Urubamba Valley.

Studies done on Bingham's collection at Yale in the 1980s, especially on the skeletal material, revealed a great deal about Machu Picchu's population of regular folks. The 177 burials were neither elites nor laborers, but mostly people of middling status from the servant classes, apparently a multicultural crowd from all over the Inca empire, and they were fairly healthy, showing few signs of childhood disease. They were well nourished, but their diet was very high in carbohydrate and was more than 60% maize, a staggeringly high intake suggesting that both sexes were imbibing plenty of corn beer. The population was a normal one of infants, children and adults evenly distributed between the two sexes. This last finding thoroughly debunked a popular myth derived from the mistaken 1912 identification of the skeletons as 75% female—and ruined a great story; guides may no longer tell us, as they once did, that Machu Picchu was the last refuge of the Virgins of the Sun.

One enduring mystery is why the Spanish never heard of or visited Machu Picchu. Along with its outlying sites, it remains the most perfect surviving example of Inca architecture and planning because it was never looted and destroyed. The same 1568 document that attributes Machu Picchu to Pachacuti also tells us that the valley floor below Machu Picchu was being farmed at that time, and perhaps visited occasionally by Spaniards, but 34 years after the Conquest the farmers may have been only dimly aware of the overgrown site on the ridgetop 700m above them.

This "lost" aspect of Machu Picchu is easiest to understand if we suppose that the place was abandoned during the years of crisis that immediately preceded the Spanish Conquest, when first an epidemic, then a catastrophic civil war plunged the Inca empire into chaos and must have severely stretched its resources. At such a moment the hard-pressed Inca elites of Cusco may have been obliged to shut down this remote and costly religious center.

Another theory concerning the abandonment of Machu Picchu is that it ran out of water. The cut stones of an unfinished supplementary water channel (#2 on site map) still lie scattered about, and this has been interpreted as a failed attempt to increase the water supply. Yet the premise of this argument is undermined by core samples from the Quelccaya ice cap south-east of Cusco, showing that the climate in southern Peru was actually getting wetter during the early 16th century, so this theory does not quite...hold water. The channel construction was probably intended to redistribute rather than increase water supply.

One last detail: a Spanish document of 1562 states that the rebel Incas of Vilcabamba had "burned and pillaged all the Indian houses" of this area, probably to establish a secure zone between themselves and the Spanish in Cusco, and to prevent the Spaniards discovering and using the access routes from Machu Picchu to Vilcabamba. So Machu Picchu could also have been abandoned at a later time, during the period of Inca resistance.

RECENT DISCOVERIES

Over the years, explorations in the area around Machu Picchu have added some details to our picture of the site. The most extensive finds have been made just across the river to the northeast, on a sloping plateau about 100m above the valley floor known as Mandor Pampa. Its outstanding feature is an enormous wall about 3.5m high and 2.5m wide (11.5 x 8ft), and more than a kilometer (0.6mi) long, which runs straight up the mountainside, toward a distinctive pointy peak known as Yanantin. This was apparently a multi-purpose wall built to protect adjacent agricultural terraces from rockfall off the nearby slope, carry a water channel, and be used as a raised causeway through the forest. It may also have served to demarcate two areas with separate functions.

At this writing that area is overgrown with vegetation, but the wall can still be seen in the forest across the river northeast of Machu Picchu. Other finds there include quarries, circular buildings, a large number of stone mortars (emphasizing the utilitarian nature of this area), and a large observation platform to the west. The area was most likely where many of the laborers responsible for the construction of Machu Picchu would have lived.

Around 2010 an area of terracing with superb walls and buildings, was found on the north slope of Wayna Picchu, near the Urubamba River, located on an Inca trail which climbs to Machu Picchu through the site now called the Temple of the Moon. Named Incaracay, it includes a temple structure which archaeologists Mariusz Ziolkowski and Fernando Astete identified as a solar and Pleiades observatory.

In the early 2000s Alfredo Valencia and the Wright Water Engineers team investigated the forested eastern slope below Machu Picchu, finding extensive areas of terracing and a year-round spring channeled through a series of five well-made fountains – still fully functional after minor maintenance – which could have served as backup in case of problems with the site's main water channel.

There was also a superb stairway leading up from the river. For years the park authorities have tantalized us with hints that this and other trails will be opened to the public as hiking routes out of Machu Picchu, an alternative to the bus. Nothing doing so far.

GETTING THERE. For road transportation to Aguas Calientes, see p. 21. For train transportation there, see p. 24 for logistics and the adjacent textbox for a description of the magnificent route. For the bus from Aguas Calientes to Machu Picchu or to walk up there, see p. 59. For where to stay, where to eat, where to boogie etc., see p. 59.

THE TRAIN JOURNEY

The experience of visiting Machu Picchu is not limited to the site itself; it also includes one of the world's great train rides. Most travelers board the train at Ollantaytambo, 1¾ hours by road from Cusco; however, some trains depart from Poroy, a 30-minute drive through Cusco's congested and chaotic outskirts, later passing through Ollantaytambo. The usual time for the journey from Poroy is about three hours. From Ollantaytambo it takes about 1 ½ hours. (*For details, see Rail Transportation, p. 24*)

From Poroy

The first part of the route winds through farmland past the fertilizer and explosives factory of Cachimayo to your right, followed by Izcuchaca, a cross-road and market town on the Cusco-Lima highway. Now you are crossing the Pampa de Anta, a high plateau where Inca armies are said to have defeated the Chanca tribe at the beginning of their expansions, and where later the rebel Gonzalo Pizarro was defeated, captured and beheaded in 1548. Far off across this plain to the west, the huge Inca terraces of Zurite *(see p. 266)* hug the base of the next range of mountains. Huarocondo stands close to the head of the Huarocondo Ravine, which you now descend to meet the Urubamba Valley. The railroad zigzags through a switchback at the lower end of the Huarocondo Valley, then joins the Urubamba Valley at Pachar. Here the ruins of Inca storehouses cling to the steep mountainside above you to the left, and the futuristic plastic bubbles of the cliff wall hotel dangle on the vertical cliffs beyond the river at right *(see Natura Vive, p. 45)*. At Pachar the railroad turns westward, passing by ruined Inca forts and huge areas of terracing before stopping to collect more passengers at Ollantaytambo.

From Ollantaytambo

After the train leaves Ollantaytambo, look behind you to the right, across the terraces, to see the impressive remains of the Inca temple and the

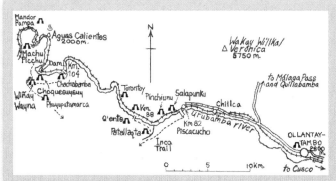

long ramp used for dragging stones up to the site. Soon the railway enters the beginnings of a gorge which grows ever narrower and deeper as you pass Chillca. You may catch occasional glimpses of snowcapped Verónica (5,750m/18,865ft) to the right. Look out for the striking endemic Andean torrent ducks all along the river to Machu Picchu, often seen perched in pairs on boulders in the stream.

You soon pass Piscacucho, Km. 82 on the railroad, where you may see hikers crossing a suspension bridge across the river which marks the beginning of the famous Inca Trail to Machu Picchu. As you approach Km. 88 the extensive ruins of Patallaqta can be seen on the mountains across the river on the left. Soon a modern suspension footbridge across the Urubamba, built on Inca foundations, comes into view below the train tracks.

After a short tunnel you see rows of solid Inca terracing across the river, the ruins of Q'ente. The vegetation grows more prolific – you are leaving the highlands and entering the mountainous cloud forest, known locally as the "eyebrow of the jungle" (*ceja de selva*). Across the river you can see a restored Inca trail that parallels the Urubamba all the way to Km. 104, where another suspension footbridge crosses to the ruins of Chachabamba and meets the trail climbing to the ruins of Wiñay Wayna (*see Chapter Four*). There it joins the main Inca Trail to Machu Picchu.

The next landmark is the ruin of Choquesuysuy, above the river on the opposite bank. Immediately thereafter comes the hydroelectric project whose diversion dam and tunnels carry water beneath the mountain to emerge at a point 14km (8.8mi) downstream, taking advantage of an 800m (2,625ft) drop to generate 180MW of hydroelectricity. Next comes your final stop, Aguas Calientes (a.k.a. Machu Picchu Pueblo), a town that has mushroomed ramshackle-tourist-trap fashion into the required overnight stop for Machu Picchu. The Enter/Exit-through-the-Gift Shop strategy deployed at the station obliges you to pick your way through a thicket of market stalls in order to reach the terminal for buses to Machu Picchu, by the old Aguas Calientes train station.

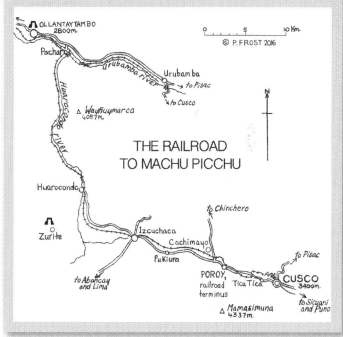

MACHU PICCHU

to Wayna Picchu and
Temple of the Moon

scale

0   50 m.

N

1. House of the Terrace Caretakers
2. Water Channel
   Unfinished Water Channel
3. Agricultural Sector
4. Inca Trail from Cusco
5. Watchman´s Hut
6. Ceremonial Rock
7. Dry Moat / Main Drainage Channel
8. Main Gate
9. Sun Temple
10. Main Fountain
11. Royal Mausoleum / Pachamama Shrine
12. Palace of the Princess
13. Open-fronted Building /
    Fountain Caretaker´s House
14. Royal Palace
15. Quarries
16. Temple of Three Windows
17. Principal Temple
18. Semi-circular Balcony
19. Sacristy
20. Intiwatana
21. Sacred Rock
22. Common (Hurin) District
23. Unfinished Temple
24. Arrow Stones
25. Mirror Stones
26. Condor Temple
27. Intimachay

▲ Echo stone

Sources: DRC, Valencia,
Wright Water Engineers, Bingham

Modern Trail
from Entrance

Map continues
on following page →

To the Inca Bridge

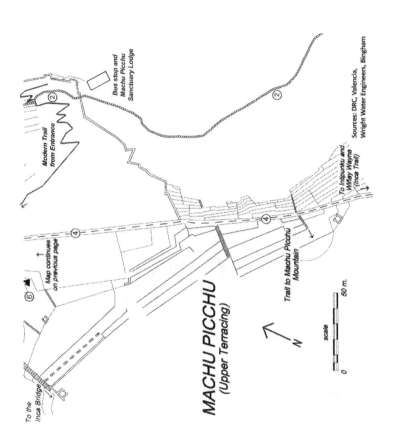

Bus stop and
Machu Picchu
Sanctuary Lodge

Modern Trail
from Entrance

Sources: DRC, Valencia,
Wright Water Engineers, Bingham

To Intipunku and
Wiñay Wayna
(Inca Trail)

Map continues
on previous page

Trail to Machu Picchu
Mountain

MACHU PICCHU
(Upper Terracing)

N

scale

0   50 m.

To the
Inca Bridge

Visitor's note: Nowadays Machu Picchu can be extremely crowded, with brutally long waits for buses: lines begin forming in Aguas Calientes as early as 4am. March, April and November tend to be the quietest months. Try to avoid visiting between July 28th & August 10th, when Peruvian national holidays are in full swing. "Cusco Week" leading up to Inti Raymi (June 24th) is also busy; it's best to enjoy the festivities in Cusco and visit Machu Picchu afterwards. *Important!* bring your original passport with you to Machu Picchu, as this is a requirement for entry.

Since 2014, there have been reports that the DRC will impose strict new regulations for visiting Machu Picchu. These include having to hire a guide, being limited to one of three routes through the ruins, and having time limits at some of the highlights and within the site itself. These rules had not been implemented as of publication; check **www.peterfrost.org** for confirmation. However, a one-way policy was implemented in 2016 such that visitors are not allowed to backtrack. If you miss something you wanted to see, you will have to exit the ruins and wait in line to re-enter. Also note that there are no toilets within the ruins, so be sure to use the facilities by the bus station before entering. Two visitor time slots were introduced in 2017: one from 6am to 12pm, another from 12pm to 5:30pm. Visitors must leave at the end of their timeslot.

Machu Picchu Historical Sanctuary is the official name of the 32,592ha (80,536 acre) national park created in 1981to protect Machu Picchu and its surrounding archaeological sites and natural environments. It includes all of the Inca Trail.

Conservation Note: One of the charms of Machu Picchu is its great variety of wild flowers, including many varieties of orchid. But they are fewer every year because of irresponsible collecting by visitors. Please don't pick them! And don't buy them from people offering them for sale at the train stations.

IN THE RUINS. Hiram Bingham studied and excavated at Machu Picchu, later classifying the ruins into sectors, naming some of the buildings, and so on. His categories are often quoted as gospel by local guides and guidebooks. But Bingham himself noted that words like "temple" and "palace" are used tentatively, and merely record the impressions conveyed by a careful examination of the buildings. If his conclusions often appear wide of the mark to modern archaeologists, we nevertheless still need some way of designating the different sectors. Since nobody has come up with a better system than Bingham's, here goes:

The walking tour is about 1.5km (0.9mi) in total, and today there are two main routes into the site. The more level and physically easier one enters through the *Houses of the Terrace Caretakers* (1). Taking it will lead you to many of the same highlights. However, the slightly more strenuous route is well worth the effort, as it offers a magnificent overview of the site from a high vantage point.

To do this, take the stone Modern Trail that climbs to the left shortly after the ticket entrance. After a couple of zigzags you cross the remains of what was one of Machu Picchu's most vital, if overlooked, features: the *Water Channel* (2) that ran about one kilometer from where water seeped from the mountainside to the south, into the heart of Machu Picchu. Since there was no water source in the urban area, the Incas engineered abundance from scarcity here, generating a supply of 70 liters per person per day at high flow. A small miracle of durability, carefully engineered, sealed with clay, and graded so that excess water would spill off where it would not cause erosion, the channel still runs perfectly today.

You get your first panoramic view of the site as you emerge from the woods onto a series of terraces near the top of the *Agricultural Sector* (3), just below where the *Inca Trail from Cusco* (4) enters Machu Picchu from the south-east. You can walk 1.5km (0.9mi) to the Intipunku (Sun Gate) on the Inca Trail from here (*see p.248*).

It is amazing that these terraces were found standing firm and upright on this vertiginous ridge, 400 years after they were abandoned to the forest. Excavations have revealed that the Inca engineers carefully prepared the subsoil of terraces and plazas for drainage by recycling the vast quantities of stone chippings left by their stone masons into thick, permeable foundations before filling in the topsoil that would be used for planting crops. They also built innumerable subterranean buttressing walls in crucial places to prevent subsidence. It was all this invisible engineering that made the terraces so resilient.

Continue climbing until you reach the large terrace prominently featuring the *Watchman's Hut* (5), so called because its location really does provide the best overall view of Machu Picchu – and is the spot where people gather *en masse* in the early morning to bag that classic photo.

This terrace is conspicuously strewn with lozenge-shaped stones roughly 45cm (18in) in length. Surprisingly perhaps, it was not until a few years ago that site archaeologist Piedad Champi inspected these stones more closely and saw that most of them were not from Machu Picchu. They were brought from nine different sources in the Cusco region, placed in clusters according to place of origin, and set upright on a bed of white sand. A singular discovery, suggesting a very specific purpose to this place. This author's interpretation, for what it's worth, is that the stones were brought there as offerings, perhaps by chieftains from those regions, and placed here to symbolically unite those territories with Machu Picchu. Since the terrace is close by the main Inca highway and just outside the urban center, this would be a natural place for a final offering before entering the sacred city. Subject tribes of the Incas did something similar with sand or soil from their territory in the main square of Cusco (*see p. 81*), so there is a known Inca precedent for this kind of thing. And it reminds us of the profound significance of Machu Picchu, at least during Pachacuti's reign

Close by these stones stands a large piece of carved bedrock designated today as the *Ceremonial Rock (6)* – a suitably generic label for a feature whose exact function and meaning in the Inca world is now lost to us. Hiram Bingham called this the "Funerary Rock" because his team found burials not far away, and because it has a large flat surface, where he suggested corpses were eviscerated and laid out to become naturally mummified. However, another take on the stone suggests that, looked at from the south-west, its pointed tip replicates a mountain on the eastern horizon, and so is of interest to "echo stone" collectors. Echo stones are recurring characteristics of Machu Picchu, and some other Inca sites, which appear to replicate—and thus visually connect us to—outstanding features of the surrounding landscape. The more obvious ones are marked with a symbol on the site map. Observant visitors may spot others.

The Lay of the Land. Look northwards from the terrace to get an overview of the site you are about to see up close. The precipitous mountain dominating the site to north is Wayna Picchu, the Young Peak. At the very summit is a carved arrow stone, almost identical to #24 below. An Inca stairway leads up the mountain, which is adorned with incredibly steep terraces, a bedrock tunnel, one small building, and what appears to have been an astronomical observatory featuring two standing stones. Unlike the terraces elsewhere, these ones consist almost entirely of stacked rock, with no upper layer of soil. If anything was grown here, it had to be something that would thrive in that context. Orchids anyone?

Behind you is Machu Picchu Mountain, the Old Peak. The compact city spread out below you consists of two distinct sectors, separated by a large, grassy esplanade. This layout corresponds to the classic Inca custom of dividing their elite settlements into Upper (Hanan) and Lower (Hurin) moieties, with the Hanan sector both physically and socially higher than the Hurin; distinctions clearly marked here in architectural styles and functions. It would have looked different in Inca times. Those steep-pitched gabled roofs would have been neatly and thickly thatched, some of the buildings would have been stuccoed (a few traces of this have survived) and perhaps brightly painted with designs in red or yellow mineral oxides. The walls of new-cut granite – today mostly grey with lichen and algae – would have been pale, almost white, their crystal and mineral flakes glistening in the sun. A shining city on a hill, indeed.

In the foreground to the left, just beyond the city's main gate, stands a jumble of natural boulders which served as a stone quarry for the masons. Before the Incas arrived, all of the broad mountain ridge must have been like this, though it was also buried under dense forest; the small patch of boulders is all that remains of the land's original form, while the surrounding sculpted landscape embodies the Inca-period transformation.

Descend the stairway leading from the NE corner of this upper terrace, and continue as it rejoins the main Inca Trail and curves through the agricultural terraces toward the main gateway into the urban sector. The two sectors are delimited by a deep cut in the mountainside with a solid wall beyond it, uninterrupted but for this one gateway. Hiram Bingham interpreted these features as defensive and called this trench the *Dry Moat* (7). But modern investigations show this to be a key engineering feature of Machu Picchu; drainage channels feed into it underground from both sides, carrying stormwater away from both the city and the agricultural terraces to run harmlessly down the channel through large rocks stacked underground.

As you descend the last two steps leading to the city's *Main Gate* (8), notice what you see straight ahead: Wayna Picchu, the striking mountain that towers over Machu Picchu to the north, and was undoubtedly a vital element of the sacred landscape, hangs there perfectly, dead-center within that door frame. That was the Inca pilgrim's view in the supreme moment when she crossed the threshold from Machu Picchu's periphery into its inner heart.

This is a hefty gateway built of massive blocks with a substantial lintel, featuring on the inside a detail often found in major Inca sites: a bar-hold niche on either side, where matching vertical stone posts could be used to lash a horizontal bar across the doorway, which may have been a simply symbolic barrier, a sort of *No Entry* sign, but was also capable when necessary of securing a heavy wooden door.

Just inside this gateway, Hiram Bingham's team excavated a small cache of obsidian (volcanic glass) pieces, doubtless an offering. Instead of the usual sharp flakes which were used as cutting tools, the pouch contained stones worn rounded and smooth by river action – so they were of ritual rather than utilitarian value, and they came from Chivay in the Colca canyon, far to the south. Yet another reminder that Machu Picchu was born of imperial expansion, not merely local concerns.

Walk northwards along the corridor, past two-story Inca buildings with separate entrances, above and below, for each story, then down a stairway past the foundations of a well-carved double-jamb doorway that was either destroyed, or simply unfinished.

Unfinished structures are almost as common as finished ones at Machu Picchu. The entire site was the product of a brief supernova of Inca expansion that lasted around a hundred years, from the early 15th to early 16th centuries, and its construction heyday may have been even briefer. In the Inca system of royal inheritance, Machu Picchu would have belonged to Pachacuti during his lifetime, then after his death, around 1470, his *panaca* would have maintained ownership of his royal lands while losing its authority over the general population. With a new emperor in power priorities changed, and the panaca, unable to draft the necessary armies of laborers, engineers and architects, may have abandoned or severely curtailed the construction of its dreamlike settlement around this time.

You reach the head of the stairs which descend to one of the iconic areas of Machu Picchu, the *Sun Temple* (9) and the Royal Palace. This is a detour from the path which continues north past some of the best known highlights – but to see this area do it now and then double back, because you may find it impossible to access here later in the circuit.

Descending the stairway you pass the north wall of the Sun Temple. There is an entrance-like opening here, on the north-east wall of the temple, which presumably was not really a doorway because it has no steps leading down to the next level. It has holes drilled about the jamb, much like a rather similar opening at the Qoricancha in Cusco *(see Chapter One)*. Speculative interpretations portray these holes encrusted with precious stones or with snakes crawling through them, or perhaps they were used to suspend something within the opening, but in truth there is no reliable interpretation as to their purpose.

Just below this stands the *Main Fountain* (10), the third, the largest, and the best carved of a series of 16 ceremonial baths that tumbles from the main water channel, winding and bifurcating its way through the heart of the urban sector. This chain of carefully constructed miniature waterfalls and splash basins is one of the site's outstanding features. Most have a distinctive individual design, and all except the first and last of them are accessed from the main stairway.

The Sun Temple itself is best viewed from below or from a vantage point on one of the terraces above it. The assigned route takes us around the base of the temple, giving us an all-around view of this amazing structure, set into bedrock so artfully that work of man and work of nature seem one and the same. Its rounded, tapering tower features the most extraordinary stonework of Machu Picchu. It contains niches for holding sacred objects and offerings, and the centerpiece is a great rock, part of the actual outcrop onto which the temple was built. Archaeo-astronomical studies carried out in the 1980s by David Dearborn and Raymond White have shown how this temple was used as an astronomical observatory. The rock in the center of the tower has a straight edge cut into it. This is precisely aligned through the facing window to the rising point of the sun on the morning of the June solstice. The pegs on the outside of the window may have been used to support a shadow-casting device, which would have made observation simpler and even more accurate. The purpose of another almost identical window in this building, which faces roughly SE, has not been determined. Some guides will say that it is oriented to the December solstice sunrise, but they are mistaken.

Set beneath the Sun Temple's rock outcrop is a small natural cave that the builders enlarged and clad with some of the site's finest stonework. Bingham designated it the *Royal Mausoleum* (11). He found no burials here but reasoned that it may once have housed a royal mummy. We know that the Incas often housed their dead in caves, and it does seem possible that, being so exclusive, it once sheltered the mummy of Pachacuti himself during his posthumous peregrinations around his former domains. An alternative interpretation one often hears nowadays is that it was dedicated to earth worship, the *Pachamama Shrine*.

Now you ascend again, past a small but exquisite two storey-building designated, in one of Bingham's more fanciful indulgences, the *Palace of the Princess* (12). It seems more likely to have been the dwelling or place of preparation for ceremonies for the temple priests.

Pass through a passageway whose imposing double-jamb entryway features the typical bar-hold niche design for securing doorways, then turn right along the rear wall of the Sun Temple, a truly outstanding piece of stonework stretching northward such that it naturally leads the eye towards the dominant peak of Wayna Picchu. And when looking back from the far end of the wall, the orientation towards Machu Picchu Mountain is equally striking.

The terrace above the Sun Temple's rear wall here carries the water channel into the heart of the urban sector and splashes into the first fountain of the series you initially encountered when descending the stairs. This fountain was beautifully carved and perfectly placed just across the stairs from the royal palace so that the emperor had first use of Machu Picchu's water during his sojourns – further testimony to a carefully designed master plan behind the building of Machu Picchu. (Curiously, the very last bath at the lower end of the fountain chain is, though simply constructed, the only other one with private access, limited to two adjacent dwellings.)

Next to the first fountain stands a jarringly incongruous entryway to (or exit from) the Sun Temple precinct, a jumble of careless masonry, at odds with the exquisite stonework all around it. This is just one among many scattered examples of rough construction at Machu Picchu, *(see also, for example, the semi-circular balcony, #18)*. A possible explanation for these

238

crude travesties of the other stonework is that they pertain to a later period of Inca construction, after the death of Pachacuti, when priorities – and skilled masons – had shifted elsewhere under the new emperor, Topa Inca.

Next to the Sun Temple, just above the main fountain, is an *Open-fronted Building* (13), which has been restored and its roof thatched as an example of how these structures looked in Inca times – although Inca thatch was much more perfectly laid. (In his monograph *The Lost Half of Inca Architecture*, Vincent Lee proposes that the ceilings of Inca structures were highly decorated, with a rattan mat woven in elaborate geometric designs stretched between the roof poles and the thatch). This has also been called the *Fountain Caretaker's House* – but it's unlikely to have been a house at all, since it is open to the elements on one side. The thick stone pegs high up in the wall are thought to have served as hangers for heavy objects.

An interesting (but unverifiable) proposition derived from the characteristics of four structures clustered in this sector (the Main Fountain, the Sun Temple, the subterranean "Royal Mausoleum," and the Open-fronted Building) suggests that these represented four temples to the four elements of Water, Fire, Earth and Air, respectively.

Cross the stairway here to enter the *Royal Palace* (14), so called because of the relative roominess of the buildings, and also for the huge rock lintels (weighing up to three tons) which generally characterized the homes of the Inca potentates. It is also the only compound featuring attached, more rustic buildings; probably servant quarters. This must have been where the Inca Pachacuti resided when he came visiting his sacred precinct (unless some fabulous marquee was set up for him on the spacious esplanade). It's a modest dwelling for a mighty emperor, but small quarters are typical of Inca sites. Its courtyard holds two large buildings facing each other, one of which seems to have been private quarters with a bed space built into the floor, and an adjoining alcove which might have been a toilet. The other can easily be visualized as a room where the Inca dined and received guests.

Two small, open-fronted structures occupy the other two sides of the courtyard; one of them has two small mortar stones carved in the bedrock at its entrance. Now, what were they about? What was being ground in these small receptacles in the emperor's courtyard? Wild speculation: special herbs, perhaps psychotropic plants used by the elites in their ceremonies.

You have now completed the Sun Temple loop off the main route. Climb the stairs and pick up your circuit again at the *Quarries* (15), a large jumble of natural rock. Close inspection here reveals signs of Inca stone cutting in progress. Ignore the partially split rock bearing a line of wedge-shaped cuts where tools were hammered in to form a crack. This is an erroneous 20th-century demonstration of how they used to think Incas cut stone (*for more recent knowledge, see p.125*).

Follow the ridge NW away from the quarry, with your back to the staircase, to arrive at one of the most interesting areas of the city. There is a small terrace garden here, planted exclusively with indigenous species. Here also stands the *Temple of Three Windows* (16). Its east wall is built on a single huge rock; the building's trapezoidal windows are partially cut into it. The large stones of the south wall have pulled slightly apart, allowing us to peer between them and see that not only did the rising joints fit perfectly all the way through but that the adjoining faces were cut in helical profile, like the surfaces of an airplane propellor – an incredible technical challenge – which would have prevented them from shifting laterally (but not, as you see, from pulling apart due to ground movement.)

Bingham based a grandiose theory on this temple, speculating that the three windows symbolized the three caves from which the mythical Ayar brothers, the founders of the Incas (*see p. 63*), stepped forth into the world and that Machu Picchu therefore represented the origin place of the Incas. Modern scholars dismiss this theory, locating this mythical origin place near Pacarictambo, south of Cusco. Close inspection reveals that the temple once had five windows, two of them having later been transformed into niches.

On the open side of this three-walled building stands a stone pillar which once supported the roof. On the ground by this pillar is a rock bearing the *chacana* (step symbol motif) common to so many other Inca and pre-Inca temples.

The huge corner-stone at the north end of the building is unfinished and shows clearly how the masons were pounding away the face of the wall after it had been erected to leave the smooth surface we are accustomed to seeing. There is even a shallow groove in the end face of the stone which told the workers how far they were supposed to cut.

Next to this site is the *Principal Temple* (17), another three-walled building with immense foundation stones and artfully-cut masonry and an enormous rear horizontal stone, which we might interpret as an altar. In the ground at the western end of this building stands a kite-shaped bedrock stone pointing south, which is said to represent the Southern Cross (an echo stone), and would indeed be a perfect replication of what one would see in the night sky there at certain times of year.

At the western edge of this square, overlooking a drop onto steep terraces, stands a small *Semi-circular Balcony* (18) whose base is of beautifully carved and fitted stones, while the upper portion is rough and crude, another apparent example of late-phase construction at Machu Picchu.

The Principal Temple is so named because of its size and quality, and also because it is the only temple with a kind of sub-temple attached to it, (around the NW side, to the rear of the Principal Temple). Bingham called this the *Sacristy* (19) because it seems a suitable place for the priests to have prepared themselves before sacred rites. A stone which forms part of the left-hand door-jamb has no fewer than 32 angles in its separate faces, far more than the inordinately famous 12-sided stone on *Hatunrumiyoc* street in Cusco. The doorway of this temple is oriented directly towards the Inca site of Patallacta, on a ridge off in the distance to the west.

Ascending the mound beyond this temple leads you to what was probably the most important of all the many shrines at Machu Picchu, the *Intiwatana* (20) or "Hitching Post of the Sun," so-called because the Incas are said to have symbolically "tied" the sun to such stones during those critical solstice sunrises to prevent it from wandering any further away down the horizon.

The term was popularized by the American scholar Ephraim Squier in the 19th century, long before Machu Picchu was known. Every major Inca center supposedly had such a stone, but – other than the inadequate "sun-hitching" explanation – nobody has ever proposed a plausible theory of how they were used. It seems possible that the stone served for making astronomical observations and calculating the passing seasons, and most people today cite this version, describing it as a "sun-dial." However, an equally plausible explanation suggests that it could have been a *huanca*, an Inca "ownership stone," which represented the human owner of the site in that person's absence. In this theory, the Intiwatana represented Pachacuti himself; when the emperor visited the site he would have ritually sat or stood upon it in order to reaffirm his possession of Machu Picchu.

Another mystery at this spot: the pointed stone with a shallow arrow-shaped flange (24) at the south edge of the Intiwatana is almost identical in shape and orientation to three other carved stones at Machu Picchu (*see also p.244*).

Johan Reinhard has shown that the Intiwatana was at the centerpoint of alignments of important solar events and sacred peaks. The tip of Wayna Picchu lies due north, while the peak of Salcantay (not visible from this point) is due south. Viewed from here at the equinox the sun rises over the peak of Verónica (Wakay Willca) and sets behind nearby Cerro San Miguel, across the river to the west, on whose summit Reinhard, Astete and Vera discovered an Inca platform with a small standing stone. At the December solstice it sets behind the distant snow peak of Pumasillo, the highest peak in the snowcapped range to the SW, which is visible from here on clear days. Reinhard also suggests that the Intiwatana was itself a stylized representation of Wayna Picchu, creating a similar play of shadows across its face with the passing of the day and the seasons.

There was at least one other "Intiwatana" in the vicinity, located near the hydroelectric power station, visible on the valley floor down to the west. This second stone was probably situated to make a specific astronomical alignment with the main one. The Machu Picchu stone itself is a sculpture of surpassing beauty. It is the only one in all Peru which escaped the diligent attention of the Spanish "extirpators of idolatry" and survived in its original condition… at least until a camera crew dropped a crane on it during the filming of a beer commercial in 2000, chipping off the southern corner.

The group of buildings east of the level grassy esplanade in the center of the ruins comprises another, slightly more utilitarian sector of the city. At the north end of this sector, farthest from the entrance to the ruins, you find two three-sided buildings opening onto a small plaza, which is backed by a huge stone generally called the *Sacred Rock* (21).

An intriguing aspect here is that the outline of this great flat rock erected at the northeast edge is shaped to form a visual tracing of the mountain skyline behind it. Then, if you step behind the *wayrona* (open-fronted structure) on the southeast edge and look northwest, you find another rock that echoes the skyline of the small outcrop named Uña Wayna Picchu in the same way.

Inca culture was oral, and many spaces must have been designed for performing the poetry and song through which information was transmitted. It is easy to imagine this plaza as such a place, with the audience seated in the square or in the shelters and the bards standing on the stone ledge that skirts the sacred and acoustically useful rock like a narrow stage.

Walking back toward the main entrance along the east flank of the ridge you enter a large sector of mostly cruder constructions that has been labeled the *Common (Hurin) District* (22). This area is labyrinthine and the paths through it split into several alternative routes. Although there are few outstanding features like the Sun Temple, there are many intricate and fascinating details of design, construction and stonework, which make it well worth snooping around here. At this writing one is more free to wander and explore in this part of the site than elsewhere.

The major feature at the north end of this district is the *Unfinished Temple* (23). Huge, rustic but well-fitted stones form the outer terrace walls of this complex, where raw, uncut bedrock stones stand at the center, probably intended for carving and surrounding with cut stones.

A curiosity to be found at the southern end of this sector is a pair of *Arrow Stones* (24), both very similar to one that is carved into bedrock next to the Intiwatana (#20) and to another carved into bedrock at the summit of Wayna Picchu. The arrow point on all four of these stones indicates due south. Aside from the abstract notion of "south," what lies due south of Machu Picchu? The summit of Salcantay, the highest snowcapped peak of the entire region, a mere 19km (12mi) as the condor flies, and *the* major feature of the Inca sacred landscape in this region. Perhaps the reference encoded in these arrow stones was none other than Salcantay.

At the end of this sector you come to a building with two curious disc shapes cut in high relief into the bedrock of of the floor, the so-called *Mirror Stones* (25). Each is about two feet in diameter, with a low rim carved around the edge. Bingham called these mortars for grinding corn, but they are flat with a shallow flange, not at all like typical mortar stones. Nowadays a signpost here informs us these were mirrors, the idea being that they were for observing celestial events, although quite how this worked is not clear.

THE CELESTIAL ANDES

One source of the well-regulated order of the Inca empire was its calendar system. Based on a complex integration of solar, lunar, stellar and even biological cycles, the Inca calendar provided an orderly basis for all aspects of Inca life. Agricultural and herding activities, the celebration of state and provincial rituals, and the performance of public works for the Inca were all coordinated with clockwork precision by calendar specialists in Cusco and in other administrative centers throughout the empire.

The astronomical knowledge of the Incas derived from regular, naked-eye observations of celestial events. Astronomical cycles were probably preserved on the knotted-string recording devices called quipus. The center for the collection, storage and interpretation of the astronomical information, and for the coordination of provincial calendars throughout the empire, was Cusco. Stone towers, or pillars (called *sucanca*), were set up at the appropriate places on the horizon around Cusco to mark the points of sunrise and sunset on the days of the solstices, the equinoxes and days when in Cusco the sun stood straight overhead, in the zenith, at noon (October 13 and February 13). Observations of moonrise and moonset at the horizon (solar) pillars, as well as the recording of the phases of the moon, were combined with the solar observations to provide month-like units of time and an overall greater precision in the annual calendar.

The Inca knowledge of the stars and constellations was as rich (and as complex) as that of any other ancient civilization. The morning and evening stars (Venus) were recognized and named and were accorded a special room for their worship in the Qoricancha. The principal stars and constellations of the Incas were located within or near the Milky Way; the Inca called this bright path of stars *mayu* ("river"). In Inca cosmology, the "river" of the sky had its earthly counterpart in the Urubamba River, along which are located Pisac, Ollantaytambo and Machu Picchu. According to their vision, the two great rivers of the Inca universe, the Milky Way and the

Urubamba, were joined at the edge of the known universe in the waters of a great cosmic sea which encircled the earth. The Milky Way was thought to have its source in the cosmic sea, from which it took water into the sky. As the Milky Way passed through the sky at night, it deposited moisture in the sky which fell to the earth in the form of rain, replenishing the waters of the Urubamba River.

The Incas recognized two major types of constellations along the *mayu*, the celestial river. One type, similar to the constellations of western Europe, traced familiar shapes in the sky by conceptually joining together neighboring bright stars. These constellations included such shapes and objects as bridges, storehouses, crosses, and animals. For example, the constellation which we know as Scorpius was considered by the Incas to represent a great serpent (the tail of Scorpius) which was changing into a condor (the head of Scorpius). One of the most important constellations of the Incas was the cluster of stars known to us as the Pleiades, in the constellation of Taurus. The Pleiades were considered to be a "storehouse" (*colca*), and they were observed regularly to help determine the times of planting and harvesting the crops.

The other type of constellation identified by the Incas was called *yanaphuyu* ("dark cloud"). These constellations, virtually unknown in traditional European astronomy, are seen in the dark spots and streaks which cut through the bright path of the Milky Way. The "dark clouds" are explained by modern astronomy as fixed clouds of interstellar dust within our galaxy which block our view of stars in the direction of the dark spot. These deep black, seemingly amorphous clouds in the Milky Way took shape in the Inca imagination as a veritable menagerie of Andean animals; these include a snake, a toad, a *tinamou* (a partridge-like bird), a mother llama with her suckling baby stretched beneath her, and a fox. The dark cloud constellations can best be seen when the Milky Way stands more or less overhead and when there is little or no light from street lamps or the moon.

— **Gary Urton**

NOTE: We are not speaking only of the dusty records of a long-lost culture here. Much of the above information was compiled from interviews with modern-day *campesinos*, who are still using many of the elements of this system. For more information, see Gary Urton's book *At the Crossroads of the Earth and the Sky*, U. Texas Press, 1988. Cusco also has a good planetarium near Sacsaywaman *(see Learning and Courses, p. 32)*.

Just across the next staircase you come to a deep hollow surrounded by walls and niches known as the *Temple of the Condor* (26). Bingham called this the "Prison Group" because there are vaults below ground and man-sized niches with holes that he suggested were used for binding wrists. But our concept of "prison" probably did not exist in Inca society; punishments tended to involve loss of privileges, physical suffering or death. Some early Spaniards reported pits full of snakes or pumas into which offenders were dropped to see if they would survive, but this hardly constitutes a prison. More likely, the complex was a temple, perhaps dedicated to the dead. A rock at the bottom of this hollow bears a stylized carving of a condor, with the shape of the head and the ruff at the neck clearly discernible. If you face this carving and look up you see a splayed rock formation which some interpret as the wings of the condor.

The condor was associated with the spirits of the dead, and there is an underground cavern here containing a large niche perfectly proportioned for holding a mummy. The aforementioned "punishment" niches were also probably used for that purpose.

There is a small cave known as *Intimachay* (27) above and to the east of the Condor Temple. It was identified in the 1980s by archaeo-astronomers Dearborn & White as a solar observatory marking the December solstice. The cave is faced with coursed masonry and features a window carved partially from a boulder that forms part of the front wall. This window is precisely aligned so that the rising sun's light illuminates the back wall of the cave at the time of the summer solstice. Mariusz Ziolkowski and Fernando Astete also demonstrated that a side window here is aligned to the summer solstice, and the so-called "lunistice," the northernmost rising point of the moon's orbit.

WALKS CLOSE TO THE RUINS
Intipunku

Above the ruins to the southeast you can see a notch in the ridge, with a small ruin at the center. This is Intipunku, the Sun Gate. The trail you see traversing the mountainside from this point is the last section of the Inca Trail, arriving from Wiñay Wayna and other sites further south. It is well preserved and makes for a fairly easy climb, taking typical walkers about an hour and a half to walk the round trip (3km/1.9mi, +200m/650ft) – but allow time for enjoying the view of Machu Picchu from Intipunku, which is magnificent. To get there simply follow the Inca Trail (#4) leading from the upper terraces.

The Inca Drawbridge

A trail winds back from the heights of the ruins, starting west of the Ceremonial Rock (#6), leading along the west flank of the mountain behind Machu Picchu. This trail grows narrower, until it is cut into the side of a sheer precipice. Follow it until you come to a spot so abrupt that the ancients had to build a huge stone buttress to create a ledge for the path to cross.

Puma-head pot handle, found at Machu Picchu

They left a strategic gap in the middle of the buttress, bridged by logs which they could withdraw to block intruders. Beyond this point the trail quickly peters out, becoming unstable and extremely dangerous. The path has been fenced off shortly before the bridge ever since, years ago, a hiker tried to cross it and fell to his death. To the bridge and back is an exciting one-hour walk demanding a cool head for heights.

Machu Picchu Mountain

Note: Climbing either Machu Picchu Mountain or Wayna Picchu, described below, carries an additional cost. Tickets are limited and there are only two morning time slots per day; these must be booked well in advance, often months in the case of the latter. The former is less busy and doesn't usually sell out.

1.3km (0.8mi) one way, +520m (1,700ft). This route has some very steep stairways and difficult spots. It follows an Inca pathway winding eastward up through the woods on the north flank of the mountain until it meets the ridgetop. Here it turns westward, still climbing along the ridge until it reaches the summit, where the Incas built a series of platforms. The beginning of this trail is a set of sunken stairs that climbs through the terraces to the west of the Inca Trail (#4) towards Intipunku *(see map, p.230)*. The trail winds diagonally to the left, up the north flank of Machu Picchu Mountain. When it reaches the ridgetop it turns sharply to the right, following the line of the ridge until it ends at an Inca platform on the summit. This is a tough climb. Allow at least three hours round trip.

Wayna Picchu/Temple of the Moon Circuit

Hardy visitors like to climb this towering granite peak overlooking Machu Picchu from the north. The path is very steep; it's the original Inca path, stepped in places. Approach it with caution, but don't be put off by the peak's fearsome appearance. It's not as exposed as it appears from a distance.

As you near the top of Wayna Picchu you pass through ancient terraces so inaccessible and so narrow that their value for agricultural purposes would have been negligible. Hence, it's thought that these were probably ornamental gardens, bright patches of color on the mountain to be admired from the city below. About an hour to an hour and a half gets the average person up the trail of 1km (0.6mi) and 110 vertical meters (360ft) to the peak for a stupendous view of the ruins, the road, the valley, the mountains – everything. It is possible to continue down from the peak to the Temple of the Moon.

The Temple of the Moon is located inside a cavern halfway down the north face of Wayna Picchu. It contains some of the most impressive stonework of the entire Machu Picchu complex. There is a large and magnificent gateway just beyond the temple, with a long, narrow building tucked into the rocks behind it. Another, more roughly worked subterranean temple lies a few steps downhill from there. This gateway and cave complex was an important ceremonial center, and a major threshold to Machu Picchu via a trail leading down to the river, which still exists but is not open to the public at this writing.

According to Fernando Astete, resident archaeologist at Machu Picchu, an early manager of the ruins hotel gave this place its fanciful name, which then stuck. It almost certainly has nothing to do with the Inca uses of the site, since this is not a good place for observing the moon. Human remains were found here. These caves may have been a place of venerating the Inca mummies.

The main Inca pathway which leads to the temple forks off the main trail to the left, about one third of the way up to the peak of Wayna Picchu. It takes about two hours round-trip to reach the temple. Note that parts of the trail are quite exposed, with a long sheer drop-off to one side. Not really dangerous, but scary.

From the peak of Wayna Picchu an Inca stairway leads down the north face of the mountain, arriving at the Temple of the Moon. It is incredibly steep, and broken in places. About five minutes down from the peak there is a place where the stairs have collapsed, and ropes and a ladder have been installed to make it easier for daredevils to descend. Even so, this can be a heartstopping experience for the average person.

If you reach the Temple of the Moon this way, you can return via the easier route which climbs around the north flank of the mountain to rejoin the main trail up Wayna Picchu.

CHAPTER SIX

THE HIGH PLATEAU NORTHWEST OF CUSCO

Chinchero-Maras-Moray-Quillarumiyoc-Limatambo

MODERN ROUTES THROUGH THE INCA HEARTLAND

The Incas had every climate and ecological zone from torrid rainforest to bleak, desolate puna within a day or two's march of their capital; the modern visitor can reach these locations in even less time. Just northwest of Cusco lies a highland area, colder and windier than the sheltered valley of the city. It is flatter, too, forming a rolling plateau between the Cusco Valley and the middle Urubamba Valley to the northwest, which is known as the *Pampa de Anta*. This is an agricultural belt of mainly potato, wheat and barley production; yellow and seemingly barren in the dry season when most visitors see it, in the rainy months it becomes a multicolored mosaic of red earth squares interspersed with fields in every shade of green and yellow.

The first stretch of the railway to Machu Picchu crosses this *altiplano*, and a major road parallels it, climbing out of Cusco then descending onto this plateau heading west. It divides shortly after Poroy, the right fork heading towards Chinchero and Urubamba, the left toward Limatambo, Abancay, and the coast.

CHINCHERO (27km / 17mi)

"Don't it always seem to go/That you don't know what you got 'til it's gone."-
— Joni Mitchell

This part of the chapter may be but a requiem for Chinchero as we know it. A project that has been talked up, argued about, promised

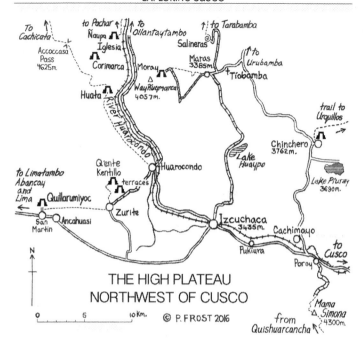

THE HIGH PLATEAU
NORTHWEST OF CUSCO

0   5   10 Km.   © P. FROST 2016

and postponed for nigh on 40 years at this writing is finally coming to hideous fruition: the Chinchero international airport. So called, that is. Some experts say that it can never be the truly international airport with direct flights to Cancún that some locals dream of, owing to the challenging altitude (3,750m/12,300ft) for takeoffs and landings. In any case the cultural, environmental, architectural and financial price is far too high in many people's opinion. Yet the Cusco city airport remains stubbornly inadequate to the volume of traffic it must carry these days, and a witches brew of politics, dubious financial interests and scarcity of viable airport sites in the region has propelled this nightmare beyond the point of awakening from it. Sprawling, speculative strip development began erupting without restraint along the highway through this once-traditional country town long before anyone stuck a shovel in the ground at the airport site, and it can only get worse. We can but hope that the authorities find the political will to throw a broad and permanent *cordon sanitaire* around the archaeological and colonial areas of the old town.

Chinchero was the Pampa de Anta's chief center of population in Inca times. It may have been a considerable city; some historians think that before the Inca expansion it could have been the capital of a small state belonging to the Ayarmaca ethnic group. Later it was chosen by Topa Inca, the second great Inca emperor, son of Pachacuti, as the site of his country estate. "Estate" meant something rather more impressive in the Inca world than our idea of a European monarch's country residence. Topa's lands extended beyond Maras and Moray in the west, to Urquillos on the Urubamba River in the north, to the hills east of Lake Piuray, and probably to Qorimarca, an elaborate Inca site near Cachimayo, in the south – an area of perhaps 200-250km^2 (77-96mi2), although we can't be certain he personally controlled all the land within its borders.

Topa's palace once spread over a commanding rise at the head of a valley which leads down and away northeast to Urquillos on the Urubamba River. The colonial church, plaza (not to be confused with the modern town square right next to the highway) and the palace ruins stand on the slopes east of the highway, with the white bell tower of the church clearly visible from the modern road. On a clear day the views from Chinchero are tremendous: to the west and NW stretches a vista of rolling plateau farmland, ringed in the distance by the dramatic snowcaps of the Cordilleras Vilcabamba and Urubamba. In the not-too-distant future this view will be replaced by takeoffs, landings and the new airport.

The grand destruction of Chinchero began at the orders of Atawallpa, the ruthless emperor who had barely won the rulership when he was ambushed, captured and ultimately killed by Francisco Pizarro. In the preceding civil war between two Inca leaders the descendants of Topa Inca had sided with the loser, Huascar. After Huascar's defeat, Atawallpa's generals set about exterminating the allies of their defeated rival. In this massacre Topa's royal palace was devastated, all ranking family and their servants were slaughtered and Topa Inca's mummy was burned (an extreme act of retribution by Inca standards, signalling the obliteration of a great bloodline). Chinchero's destruction was far from total, as we see when visiting the town today, but it did continue under Spanish rule. In the colonial era the town dwindled into a village and remained a backwater until the Cusco-Urubamba road was completed. (See the *Exploring Cusco Museum* at **www.peterfrost.org** for a word sketch of Chinchero before the road.)

Today, many people visit Chinchero for its handcraft market, which is particularly active on Sundays and is the best known in the area after that of Pisac. This market is located in the plaza in front of the church, and the produce market is at the foot of the hill. These days the handcraft market carries similar items to that of Pisac, though there are fewer vendors. However, the setting here is spacious, it is easier to wander off into open, uncrowded areas, and shopping here feels relaxed.

Chinchero has been the birthplace of a revival movement in the Andean weaving tradition. The original co-operative project (today there are many others here and throughout the region) was the Center for Traditional Textiles of Cusco, which has a big location in the town and a store/museum in Cusco (*see p. 60*).

IN THE RUINS. (Entrance by BTC.) Not only ruins, the remains and layout of Topa Inca's royal palace survive alongside the old colonial town, church and bell tower to form a unique and intriguing attraction for visitors. (This section owes a debt to Stella Nair for *At Home with the Sapa Inca*, her original and informative work on Chinchero; *see Bibliography*.)

To reach the handcraft market, main square, church, and ruins (entrance by BTC), follow the street *Manco II* from the highway, next to the large red *Parque Arqueológico Chinchero* sign.

The town's handcraft market is located in the square. This seems to have been a restricted area adjacent to Topa Inca's palace complex. Its best-known feature is a wall of 12 huge niches, facing onto the square in

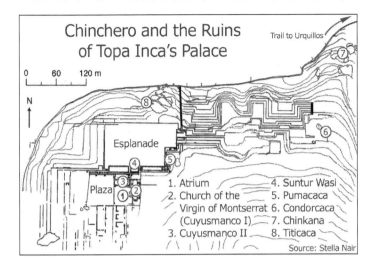

Chinchero and the Ruins of Topa Inca's Palace

Trail to Urquillos

0 60 120 m

N

Esplanade

Plaza

1. Atrium
2. Church of the Virgin of Montserrat (Cuyusmanco I)
3. Cuyusmanco II
4. Suntur Wasi
5. Pumacaca
6. Condorcaca
7. Chinkana
8. Titicaca

Source: Stella Nair

its massive east terrace wall. Nine of them appear to be original, while the three at the wall's northern end are cruder ones added at a later date to fill in the front entrance of a great *cuyusmanco* hall belonging to Topa Inca's palace. The emperor's original plans seem to have included two plazas, the royal residence, storage facilities, and fountains, but the Inca's death cut short his grand plans for Chinchero; much of the estate was never completed.

The site museum on the west side of the plaza (SST) is located in the old home of Brigadier Mateo Pumaccahua (*see below*). Displays include Inca *aryballos* jars, farming and weaving tools, and colonial era wooden door locks with wooden keys. Most signage has English translations.

Climb the stairway from here to reach the raised *Atrium* (1) of the *Church of the Virgin of Montserrat (Cuyusmanco I)* (2), built on the foundations of another Inca great hall in the same royal architectural style known as *cuyusmanco*. The Atrium, beneath which lie several ruined Inca buildings, was created in colonial times by filling in an Inca courtyard here. The church (entry by donation, daily 8am-12pm,

1-5:30pm) is well worth seeing for its elaborate restored murals and ceiling decoration dating from the 17th century. Above the main entrance on the outside is a later mural depicting the defeat of Tupac Amaru's native uprising of 1780 by the Spanish, with the help of one Mateo Pumaccahua, a descendant of Chinchero's native aristocracy; both were descendants of Inca nobility who fought on opposite sides in the rebellion. Thirty years later Pumaccahua found himself on the wrong side of another war against the Spanish crown and, like his former adversary, was executed.

Inside the church, facing the main entrance, an early mural depicts the Virgin of Montserrat and includes a scene of angels sawing off the top of a mountain (perhaps a wish-fulfilment vignette for the Spanish clergy, who doubtless prayed for the power to do exactly that during their ultimately unsuccessful effort to suppress native mountain worship).

Walking north along the west wall of the church, notice the fine surviving stonework of the Inca structure on which it was built. By following this wall to the north end of the building you can see embedded around the north-facing colonial doorway the remnant outline of the enormous open entrance characterizing the high-status *cuyusmanco* style hall that once stood here. This doorway was oriented such that its entrance could be seen from the vast esplanade extending east-west across the terraced area below this sector.

Perpendicular to this building, just across the north-oriented passageway here, stands the remains of *Cuyusmanco II* (3), mentioned above, whose grand entranceway faced the more private and exclusive Plaza. According to early sources the emperor would have positioned himself sequentially in front of both cuyusmanco entranceways during grand occasions, to be seen first by the elites and then by the masses. The enormous openings of these buildings and the difficulty of seeing into their dark interiors from outside would have highlighted their exclusive nature.

Descending the staircase leading north, you find yourself overlooking a series of elaborate buildings that faced the vast esplanade. One of them, what Nair calls the *Suntur Wasi* (4), seems especially private and splendid, with double- and triple-jamb niches and openings looking out onto the esplanade; it has the feel of a reviewing stand or "royal box" where Topa Inca and his entourage might have watched festivities and parades. Turn east along the upper terraces above the esplanade, to visit a series of carved stone wacas around Chinchero's stupendous terraces. The first of these is the *Pumacaca* group (5), a cluster of bedrock outcrops with the inevitable stone benches, shelves and abstract geometrical shapes that characterize Inca stone carving. One of the outcrops is a double platform facing the esplanade, with two now eroded and vandalized pumas around the base, one small (young) and one larger (adult). This symbolism leads Nair to suggest that this was a viewing platform for Topa Inca and one of his sons, the chosen heir. This is the only rock outcrop in the vicinity that receives numerous visitors.

350m (1,150ft) further east along the highest terraces you come to *Condorcaca* (6), an enormous rock, carved over most if its surface, which one presumes to be bedrock, but according to Nair was dragged into this position from elsewhere. She believes this because the rock has tilted at a steep angle where the ground underneath it has subsided, which is not what you'd expect with bedrock. Sceptics might say it would not have been possible to drag a stone this size, but it's no bigger than some of the Sacsaywaman stones, so why not?

Condorcaca has sunken seats facing the local *apu* known as Antakilke and one facing west towards Salcantay, the giant peak associated with Machu Picchu. Near the base of the stone is an indistinct carved puma, two cuplike indentations, perhaps for liquid offerings, and the outline of a condor which gives the rock its name. There is a smaller rock nearby, also heavily carved but lacking in distinctive shapes that can be identified.

Downhill from here stands *Chinkana* (7), a gigantic, mansion-size boulder covered in carvings, including stairways, benches, tunnels, niches and innumerable enigmatic shapes. It features a deep niche facing east towards the Inca highway from Urquillos — perhaps it once housed a mummy — and what seems to be a little conference room or meeting place with seats carved in a circle at the top of the outcrop.

It stands where the Inca highway ascending from the Urubamba Valley entered Chinchero. A series of small waterfalls coursed alongside it down the terraced slope; it may have been a shrine where travelers paid their respects and left offerings as they arrived at the royal palace.

Here you can return westwards along the Inca highway towards the esplanade, with a final carved rock outcrop, *Titicaca* (8), prominent on the skyline ahead. To reach it you climb the Inca stairway which once provided the grand entrance to Chinchero for visitors arriving from the Urubamba Valley. For those passing below it seems mainly natural and unworked, but for those entering it from the Chinchero precinct above, it appears completely different. A narrow fissure with a carved stairway leads to what was once an elaborate hallway carved in bedrock lined with man-made stone walls, now mostly gone.

A pleasant hike descends from Chinchero to Urquillos in the Sacred Valley along an old Inca road (3-4 hours, 9km/5mi). See **www.peterfrost. org** for instructions.

MARAS-SALINERAS (56km / 35mi)

Maras is a colonial era town, once a prosperous place, which later fell into decline. Now it is on the upswing again, with tourism traffic and a mini boom in Maras gourmet salt. It is worth a stop after Salineras or on the way to Moray for the many carved stone doorways on the former colonial mansions of the main street. The big colonial church has some interesting Cusco school paintings, but it is usually closed and it can be hard to find someone to open it for you.

The remarkable site known as *Salineras* (SST) lies on a righthand turnoff before Maras in a ravine 3.5km (2.2mi) to the north. Thousands of handbuilt terraces, watered by a saline underground stream, collect salt by evaporation. The dazzling, salt-encrusted terraces make an extraordinary sight, especially for photographers. These have been worked since pre-Hispanic times – there are small Inca ruins close by. Each salt pool is owned by and passed down through local families; they dig out the sun-dried salt by hand, load it onto donkeys, and sell it to a collective for resale. The product contains many additional minerals and is sold as gourmet salt the world over.

A dirt road takes you there via the well-marked Maras turn-off, to the left from the Chinchero-Urubamba highway, but there's no public transport there. However, there are taxis which will take you to Salineras from the Maras turn-off on the Urubamba highway (*see Transportation, p 21*). If walking on your own, the best way to go is to start from Maras and walk straight down the valley, which lies a few kilometers uphill from the Salineras.

To descend to the Sacred Valley from the salt pans (2km/1.3mi, elevation -150m/490ft), it is easy to follow the steep, switchbacked trail north and down the left side of the valley to the small village of Pichingoto. Walk through the village, pass a cemetery, turn to the right to follow the river, and you soon meet a footbridge (*Puente Arcoiris - Rainbow Bridge*) over the Urubamba. Cross it and follow the trail another 500m (0.3mi) or so to the main valley highway at Tarabamba.

You can walk to the Salineras from the Sacred Valley (*see map, p. 165*), essentially the walk described above, except backwards. Take an Ollanta-bound colectivo (*see Transportation, p. 21*) and get off at Tarabamba. Walk SW down a dirt road towards the river, take the first right and then the next left, and cross the Urubamba River on the *Puente Arcoiris*. Pay your Salineras entrance fee at the ticket booth, then follow the directions above in reverse.

MORAY (56km / 35mi)

The plateau around the town of Maras lies on a shaky bed of salt and soluble minerals. Its soil is highly calcitic, rich in calcium sulphate and carbonate, and in places the land has collapsed from long exposure to rain and groundwater into a honeycomb of subterranean erosion and potholes. West of Maras at Moray, a series of great sinkholes, or *muyus* as they are called in Quechua, formed and was later transformed by ancient people into a cluster of vast earthworks, with regular layers of terracing flowing harmoniously into the landscape. Moray is beyond different – it is truly unique. There is no great ruined settlement here to awe visitors, but as an enormous work of art surrounded by a stupendous mountain landscape, Moray offers deep satisfaction to the contemplative traveler.

The landscape transformation here began long ago, spanning several cultures. Pottery fragments from the Chanapata culture – dated around the time of Christ – have been found here. Ceramics from the later Wari, a "middle horizon" civilization dating between 650 and 950 A.D., were found on the bottom six levels of the main muyu, but there is no clear evidence of Wari construction at Moray. Immediately before the Incas, the Ayarmaca people occupied the area and likely began to construct terraces at Moray. But what we see at Moray today is Inca (with a little reconstruction by the government of Peru, c.1990). The construction and design are clearly imperial Inca, both in layout and durability. After the Inca expansion Moray was incorporated into Topa Inca's royal estate of Chinchero; Moray was

Moray
three main depressions

probably refined and enlarged at that time. The smaller depressions were terraced, a large horseshoe-shaped extension was added to the main depression, and all were fitted with vertical-drop water channels.

The nearby villages have a rich mythical tradition about Moray. A very old man told anthropologist Gary Urton that the terrace walls were once covered in plates of gold and silver to trap and reflect celestial light. Another told him that the Inca Wayna Capac is alive and dwells underground beneath the largest bowl.

Among guides and visitors, the story took hold years ago that Moray was an Inca agricultural research station. The author pleads guilty to promoting this theory in these pages, starting in 1979 and through all later editions; however, he didn't invent it – it is based on the research of anthropologist John Earls.

Earls discovered that an air temperature gradient of +15°C (27°F) can exist between the highest and lowest levels of terracing, which he proposed made it suitable for testing new crop strains in the different microclimates at each level of terracing. Noting the usefulness of a single locality with naturally controlled variations where many different crop strains could be developed, Earls suggested that this may actually have been Moray's function. Today this idea has hardened into conventional wisdom.

However, the indefatigable hydrology researchers Ruth and Kenneth Wright, authors of studies at Machu Picchu, Tipón and most recently Ollantaytambo, have performed intensive studies at Moray. Their 2011 publication (*see Bibliography*) makes a strong case that the terraces and geology were quite unsuitable for agricultural purposes. The area only receives annual precipitation of about 50cm (20in) of rain, meaning that any agricultural terraces would have required irrigation – but the Wrights show quite conclusively that irrigation wasn't used here. Evaporation of irrigation water would have reduced the soil temperature gradient to a paltry 1-2°C. Also, the terraces lack hydraulic structures to deal with overflow irrigation water, which, had irrigation been deployed, would have badly eroded the steep, soluble slopes that the Incas went to such lengths to stabilize. Some observers point to the vertical water channels running down the faces of the muyu terraces as evidence that irrigation was used. In fact, though, the terrace hydrology was not conducive to circulating irrigation water (more on all of this below); these channels may instead have been part of a ritual water system.

A further objection to the experimental agriculture theory is that the soils at Moray are highly calcitic, which would have made crop variants suited to these soils somewhat atypical and therefore not useful in other localities. Pollen samples taken by the Wrights and others failed to yield solid evidence for the planting of maize and quinoa here during Inca times. And in fact this type of agricultural research could have been conducted more easily on the slopes of the numerous tributaries of the nearby Urubamba River.

If everyone's favorite theory has evaporated along with the irrigation water, what then was Moray? The Inca, with their profound sense of landscape, would no doubt have been intrigued by these deep, impressive muyus. Inca terraces, such as those at Chinchero, Pisac and Machu Picchu were built not only for agricultural or structural purposes but also for aesthetics and landscape veneration. Moreover, the highly unusual sinkhole formations might have touched the nerve of Andean sensitivity to large scale manifestations of complementary opposition; they loved high mountains and they loved their opposites, often deep river gorges. Here they found unusually perfect "anti-mountains": huge, inverted-cone shaped empty spaces in the earth. The Inca seldom resisted the urge to honor such phenomena architecturally – especially, perhaps, when the place came into the possession of Topa Inca, a mighty emperor with all the power to satisfy such impulses.

Closely bound to the Inca notion of sacred landscape was the veneration of water. Emerging springs were viewed as a point of contact between the human/material world (kay pacha) and the underworld (ukhu pacha), and the Inca-built environment featured many other expressions of the spiritual significance of water. The Wrights suggest that the Incas built the terraces of Moray both to consecrate the location and to serve as a temple for water ceremonies. Many *wacas*, or notable terrain features, are scattered about Moray and the nearby hills, and the construction of these high quality terraces is consistent with the Inca spiritual approach to landscape. High areas between the muyus, and the now-ruined structures upon them, were likely the sacred precincts where priests conducted water ceremonies. Water or *chicha* poured into the canals would have descended terrace-by-terrace and then finally into the natural subterranean drainage tunnels of the earth. The symbolism of liquid passing over the stonework to be consumed by *Pachamama* would have greatly appealed to the Inca.

GETTING THERE. You can reach Maras and Moray by bus from Cusco (*see Transportation, p.21*), or by mountain bike or ATV tours (*see p. 43 & 45 respectively*).

Explorer's note: The walk between Maras and Moray is about 5km (3.1mi), and takes about 1½ hours. This is also a nice bike ride. Follow the main road out of town heading towards Moray. On the town's outskirts by the modern cultural and handcraft complex the road makes a right angle turn heading southward uphill. Leave the road at this curve, following a trail which heads straight onwards (west). The trail continues west across open country all the way, deviating only when it zigzags through one of three ravines along the way. Cross the first of these, a small one which you meet just 300m (980ft) or so from the trailhead; then the second, a bit larger, about 750m (2,460m) further on. After about 3km (1.9mi), you pass the only farmhouse on the route, noticeable for its trees, shrubs and small ponds. About 350m (1,150ft) beyond this point you meet a crossroads, the only spot where you might take a wrong turn. Take the right fork and continue for about 700m (2,300ft), where you rejoin the main road. Follow the road through the last small ravine and arrive at Moray. You'll find quite a few vehicles here until about 3:30pm, and so a good chance of catching a ride back to the main Cusco-Urubamba highway.

Explorer's note: At the bottom of the hairpin bend in the road on the way to Moray, there is a small *waca* called *Pacchac*, meaning "water source" (site signage says *Pulpituyoq*). These are three carved rocks, plus a fourth one just across a stream. The three first rocks have carved tables, liquid receptacles, and niches that are still in use today for ceremonies involving water and offerings. The fourth rock has been partially carved on its NE face to resemble an enormous pulpit.

IN THE RUINS. (Entrance by BTC.) Drawing again on the Wright studies, we note that the true engineering marvel of Moray is hidden out of sight beneath the bottom of the muyus, where the Inca builders must have gone to great lengths to prevent salt accumulation and erosion from rain and groundwater. The builders probably created an "inverse filter" by filling the natural drainage cavities at the bottom with large rocks and then placing progressively smaller stone layers on top; finally, the topsoil layer was perfectly graded. No subsurface excavations have been done to verify this, but it is the likeliest explanation since we know, based on their terrace construction, that the Incas understood inverse filters. It is a testament to the Incas' engineering abilities that now, roughly 500 years later, the flat bottoms of the *muyus* remain perfectly intact. This is a remarkable achievement for such a geologically unstable area.

The *muyus* are all interconnected, and you can visit most parts of the site at will. To orient yourself as you enter the site, north is to your right, towards the snowcapped mountains beyond the Sacred Valley. The easternmost and largest muyu, known as *Quechuyoc* (Warm Place), has fifteen levels of terracing. The building foundations on the level horseshoe-shaped esplanade to the south were likely once an administrator's residence. Notice that the single line of vertical water channels that survives here, as in each of the other three muyus, lacks a corresponding partner on the opposite side of the terraces. This means that irrigation water would have had to travel 360° around the terraces, part of that flowing upslope – an impossible feat – or it simply would have pooled and overflowed on the other side. If Moray had indeed been an agricultural center, the Incas would have built matching water channels on the opposite side and sloped the terraces downward towards them.

The three other muyus are smaller and less well preserved. The tiny sinkhole high above the others to the SW, and invisible from below, is locally known as Ñustahispanan (Where the Princess Pee'd), a.k.a. *Kuichi Muyu* (Rainbow Muyu) – a curiosity common in Inca legend: a spring rose at this spot, and Inca myths often attribute this to a royal lady having urinated there. Many small wacas are scattered around the terracing here.

Adjacent to and west of the main muyu of Quechuyoc lies *Simamuyu* (Grassy, or possibly Tongue-having Muyu). The ridge extending between these two muyus holds the remains of ceremonial buildings and a platform where water ceremonies may have been conducted. The long stone walkway extending southwards from the ridge was likely an aqueduct as well as a path. *Intiwatana* is the northernmost muyu, the familiar name suggesting that an Inca "calendar stone" may once have stood on this spot. These terraces were long open for locals to graze their livestock and have suffered erosion as a result. The flat raised area between *Intiwatana* and *Simamuyu* features the overgrown remains of buildings set on a tiered platform, incorporating the remnant of a double-jamb doorway. The quality of the surviving stonework here suggests this may once have been the ceremonial heart of the site.

Explorer's note: For a bird's-eye view view of all four muyus, make a half-hour climb to the middle of the three peaks of *Wañuymarca* (Town of the Dead), the mountain which looms over the ruins to the south. It is also possible to take a vehicle close to the top and walk to the summit from there.

PAMPA DE ANTA AND POINTS WEST

By taking the left fork after Poroy to Abancay instead of heading north to Chinchero, you come to the Pampa de Anta, a broad plain hemmed in to the north and south by mountain ranges. The road passes the terraces of

Zurite and the scenic ruins at Quillarumiyoc. It then climbs gently to the 3,740m (12,270ft) Vilcaconga Pass, marking the watershed between the Apurímac and Urubamba river systems. The highway plunges in a radical series of zigzags 1,140m (3,740ft) from the pass to the Inca ruins at Tarawasi, crossing along the way the site of a major battle between Incas and Spaniards in 1533. A lofty condor lookout lies west of Tarawasi at the village of Chonta but is well off the main road, difficult to get to by yourself.

For a long day trip taking in Quillarumiyoc, Tarawasi and Chonta, Orellana Expeditions (**www.machupicchuorellana.com**) seems like a good option. Vegetarian Peru Adventures (*see p.47*) offers tours to Chonta and the nearby ruins either as a day trip or as part of their yoga retreats.

A reasonable self-guided day trip could take in Tarawasi and Quillarumiyoc. (You could also tack on a visit to the remarkable carved rocks and *usnu* of Saywite [*see p.306*], but you would need to overnight in Curahuasi, which has beautiful countryside to wander in.) Reach Tarawasi by public transit along the main road (*see p.23*). After exploring, walk 1.5km (0.9mi) SW down the road to the town of Limatambo to catch return transportation. For Quillarumiyoc, get off at the community of San Martín, shortly before Ancahuasi, and walk north through town. To return to Cusco, go back to the main road and catch eastbound transportation.

Explorer's note: During the Inca Empire, the small town of *Zurite* (Melting Snow) was an important center for agriculture and goldworking and was a rest stop along the road to *Chinchaysuyu*. Today, the town is best known for its massive agricultural terraces, some of the largest built by the Inca, and the pretty San Nicolás de Bari church in the main square. This sleepy town is appealing to ruins buffs and those looking for a quiet few hours far off the tourist circuit. To reach Zurite, get off your transportation at the large stone entrance arch on the main highway and wait for northbound transportation. Zurite's massive main terraces and nearby agricultural research station can be reached by walking 2km (1.3mi) down the road from the main square. Also nearby are the tranquil and appealing hummingbird-shaped terraces of Q'ente Kentillo, 2.5km (1.6mi) out of town via a very pleasant walk; ask a local how to get there.

QUILLARUMIYOC (46KM / 29MI)

Just north of the small community of San Martin lies *Quillarumiyoc* (Stone of the Moon), a lyrical and scenic set of ruins and the first important shrine located on the Inca road from Cusco to the *Chinchaysuyu*. The site had both agricultural and religious functions, the latter indicated by the two ceremonial caves, sacred platform, and an exceptional carving supposedly representing the crescent moon. To arrive at the ticket booth by vehicle, get off in Ancahuasi and look for a taxi. Alternatively, public transportation will leave you on the roadside at the entrance to the community of San Martín (*see Transportation, p. 23*), from where you can see the ruins. Simply walk up the road and follow it to the ticket booth (SST). There is a small but interesting museum at the site with lots of pictures of the local attractions (Spanish text only). The only lodging game in town is the *Albergue Turistico* on the town road, which will do in a tight pinch.

IN THE RUINS. Walk NE from the ticket booth through the fields to reach the first terraces at *Nuñunkayoqpata*. Just above this you'll come to a cave, now roped off, in the *Tankarqaqa* sector with faces crudely carved into the walls. Locals still come to do ceremonies here, as evidenced by all the coca leaf offerings tucked into niches in the walls. Along the trail due east from here is the *Quillarumiyoc* sector and the east-facing moon-shaped carving which gives the site its name. This is yet another example of superb Inca craftsmanship: perhaps 2m (6.6ft) wide, multifaceted, smooth to the touch (don't touch it!) and as precise as if designed in AutoCAD. Some archeologists believe that this site was for moon worship. Uphill from here in the *Inkaraqay* sector lies an elevated platform with fine stonework encircling it, on top of which is a rock with the familiar step form *chacana* carved into it. Site signage speculates that this platform was used for animal sacrifice. Just north of the platform, there is a 400m (1,300ft) stone-lined pathway leading uphill to the northernmost part of the site, *Sala Qaqa*. This large ceremonial boulder has a natural cave lined with Inca stonework and niches beneath it.

See Trekking on **www.peterfrost.org** for the Moonstone Trek, a hike starting near Quillarumiyoc and ending in Ollantaytambo.

TARAWASI (75KM / 47MI)

Tarawasi is a small site, about 0.6ha (1.4 acres), just before the town of Limatambo and on the old Inca road to *Chinchaysuyu*. (*See p.23 for transportation.*) The site is most noteworthy for its exceptional polygonal architecture, which forms terraces, a flight of stairs, and an usnu (tiered ceremonial platform). The usnu has many niches, and an upper corner features an unusual low-relief carving reminiscent of an umbrella blown inside out by the wind. Given the usnu and high quality stonework, Tarawasi must have had a ceremonial purpose. Its location along the old Inca road suggests that the site was also a rest stop for travelers. The large buildings across from the highest platform are 18th-century colonial *haciendas* built upon Inca foundations.

CHONTA (100KM / 63MI)

A lefthand turnoff just beyond Limatambo climbs to the village of Chonta, on clear days offering stupendous views of Salcantay and the snowcapped Cordillera Vilcabamba along the way. The village is most easily reached on a tour (*see p.266*), but you could try to arrange a ride in Limatambo. The cliffs near Chonta, high above spectacular vistas of the Apurimac gorge, are home to numerous condors. Their fairly predictable daily routine offers visitors an excellent chance of sighting them: they begin circling in the canyon far below in the early afternoon, gradually ascending until by mid to late afternoon they soar at eye level as seen from one of several viewing platforms. These are between 45mins and 1¼hr walk from Chonta. The lowest, furthest platforms offer the best views, and a small fee is charged for entry.

CHAPTER SEVEN

THE VALLEY ROAD SOUTHEAST
The Road to Collasuyu

THE ROAD LESS TRAVELED

Many travelers take the southeast road or railway toward Lake Titicaca and Arequipa en route to Bolivia or southern Peru. Yet few visitors know of the many fascinating places close to Cusco along this valley, a calm alternative to the much busier Sacred Valley. This chapter describes some of the most interesting spots. Figures in kilometers indicate distances from the city of Cusco. Directions (left, right) are given for people traveling south; if you are traveling north you should, of course, reverse them.

Explorers should find many interesting places along some of the lesser side roads off the main valley. But it is just about essential to have your own transport to do this, unless time is unimportant. These roads carry little traffic.

The best way to see the main valley if you do not have your own transport would be to select two or three places to visit. Then, catch a bus early from Cusco going to Sicuani (*see Transport, p. 22*) and get off at the first place you intend to see, moving on later with the next available transport. The main road is quite busy and buses are available well into the evening. The town of Andahuaylillas (*see p. 281*), with its famous colonial church, is a good base from which to explore the valley.

One useful item to carry if you plan to visit churches would be a powerful flashlight, since some are dark inside and this is the only way to see the paintings clearly. A pair of binoculars is also useful for picking out the details of paintings high up on walls or ceilings.

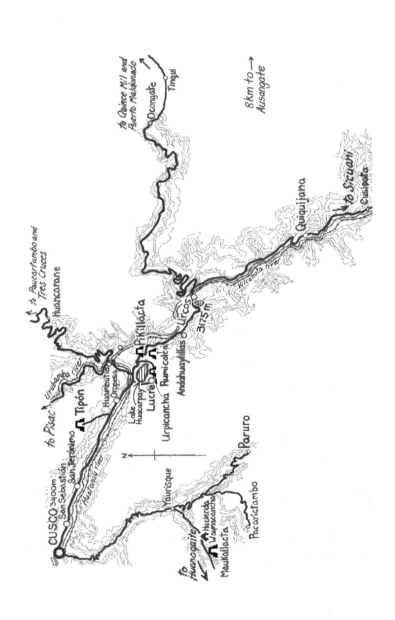

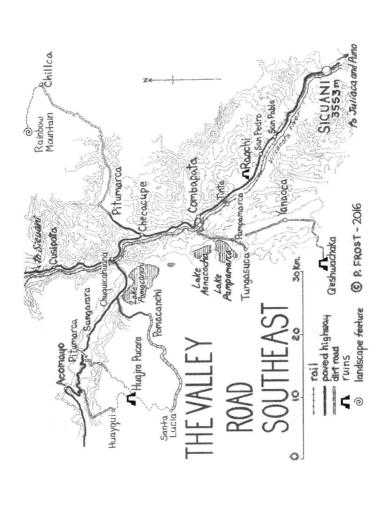

THE VALLEY
ROAD
SOUTHEAST

rail
paved highway
dirt road
ruins
landscape feature

30 Km.

© P. FROST ~ 2016

SAN SEBASTIÁN (5km / 3.1mi)

This town's once-beautiful church suffered a catastrophic fire in September 2016. See www.peterfrost.org for more.

SAYLLA (12km / 7.5mi)

This is your spot if you like *chicharrón de chancho* (fried pork) – a whole village of restaurants devoted to pigging out. And just beyond it, off the highway to left, is *Huasao,* known as the sorcerer's village, where the local specialties are magic, ritual, and the casting of spells.

TIPÓN (turn-off: 23km / 14.3mi)

An Inca site of considerable interest to ruins junkies and those wanting to try *cuy al horno* (baked guinea pig), a specialty in the nearby village of the same name. The turn-off (left) is about 2km (1.3mi) before Oropesa, marked by the standard DRC signboard for archaeological monuments. The site lies 4km (2.5mi) off the highway, much of it fairly steep climbing (about 1½ hours on foot) and can be reached by car up a reasonably good paved road.

On the road to the Tipón ruins lies the Valleumbroso Estate, a colonial manor once owned by the Marquises of San Lorenzo de Valleumbroso, who also owned the mansion on *Marqués* street in Cusco *(see p. 107).* The estate currently houses the offices of the DRC workshop for restoration of colonial art, which can be visited amidst beautiful grounds, architecture and decorated interiors. Well worth a visit; open Mon-Fri, 7am-3pm.

Tipón is an outstanding sweep of sculpted and carefully engineered mountain landscape, designed, as is often the case, both for Inca ritual and ceremonial life and to provide stupendous agricultural production. The early construction was done by the Killke people of the Cusco Valley, who fortified it with a 5m (16ft) defensive wall; this made Tipón, along with Sacsaywaman, one of only two fortified sites in the entire Cusco Valley. It seems to have been an attempt to resist Inca expansion. But as they grew more powerful, it eventually fell into the hands of Inca Wiracocha, father of Pachacuti, who transformed it into his royal estate.

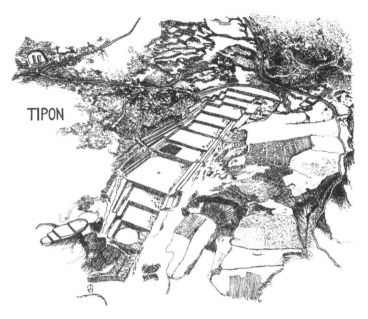

TIPÓN

Two areas, at the northern and southern limits of the site, featured planned residential districts, and massive, regular terrace construction revealing the hand of the imperial Inca. In between lies a vast, jumbled mosaic of hundreds, maybe thousands, of small, irregular terraces. A glance at the site on Google Earth will confirm what an astounding place this once was.

IN THE RUINS.

(Entrance by BTC.) The lower area of Tipón ruins, which most visitors and tours concentrate on, consists of a long series of tall, beautifully-constructed agricultural terraces – some of the finest in existence – running up the head of a narrow valley. Their irrigation water came from two sources: a 1.4km (0.9mi) aqueduct, now defunct, running down from the mountain spur to the west of the terraces; and an abundant underground water source which still emerges silently year-round from the mountainside below the highest terrace, whence it was channeled through an impressive waterfall fountain carved with four separate spouts.

The upper channel is artfully engineered straight down the mountain spur and across a built causeway, snaking its way below ground through a cluster of buildings above the main terraces known as the *Intiwatana* group. Here, ritual baths and large niches in protected spaces indicate an important Inca ritual site, as does an adjacent U-shaped open air temple. This large, intriguing structure of superb stonework once featured huge niches at the rounded end of the U and appears to have offered an open view to the south at the other end.

Explorer's Note: For those who enjoy a bit of hiking and solitude, the other settlement and terrace complex at the upper, northern end of the site is a rewarding excursion. Follow the aqueduct uphill and turn left on a clear trail near the top of the channel. Follow it north until you reach the upper site, which offers intriguing features, copious ceramic scatter, and receives few visitors. Upon the heights above this area, an hour or more of further climbing, stand the remains of an ancient walled enclosure, perhaps a fort, which evidence suggests was built during the Killke occupation of this area of the Cusco Valley.

OROPESA (25km / 15.6mi)
Shortly after the Tipón turn-off lies another to *Oropesa*, which boasts a colonial church with fine murals and a staggering number of small bakeries supplying bread and pastries to the city of Cusco.

LUCRE AND LAKE HUACARPAY (30km / 18.8mi)
Beyond the lefthand turn-off for Paucartambo (*see below*) and the Sacred Valley via San Salvador, the road begins to climb to a small pass. To your right is *Lake Huacarpay*, a beautiful reed-lined lake. Ask to get off at the entrance to Lucre, and from there you can walk south down the road to get to the lake. There are a number of bird observation towers around it

and the 8km (5mi) circuit makes for a pleasant, level stroll. The nearby village of *Lucre* specializes in duck dishes. At Urpicancha, a beautiful spot about 1km (0.6mi) off the main road on the south shore of the lake, there is a small hotel which serves lunches and rents rowboats. Nearby are some seldom-visited Inca ruins known as the *Morada de Wascar* – Wascar's Dwelling – because this is thought to have been the birthplace and country palace of the Inca Wascar, who fought and lost in the civil war against his half-brother, Atawallpa.

PAUCARTAMBO (115km / 72mi)

Paucartambo lies off the highway in a valley above the eastern jungles. The road there is a paved but twisty mountain affair. Drivers should take the left turn into the Sacred Valley about 3km (1.9mi) beyond Oropesa, and cross the bridge over the Vilcanota at Huambutío. (*see Transport, p. 22*)

The town itself is small and out of the way. Expect to rough it if you stay the night. Paucartambo is a picturesque but quiet place, best known for its yearly Christian-on-Pagan festival of the Virgin of Carmen (15th-17th July), a very colorful local *fiesta* with the best traditional dances, and the most varied and exotic masks and costumes to be seen anywhere in the Cusco region. The dances and characters include *saqras* (demons), malaria victims, gringos (warty, evil-looking ones), bear-men, condor-men, black slaves and warlike jungle Indians.

About 50km (31mi) beyond Paucartambo lies *Tres Cruces*, at the eastern rim of the Andes, perched over the last breathtaking drop into the Amazon basin. The Incas held this place sacred for the uncanny optical effects that appear there during sunrise at certain times of year, notably the winter solstice (June). Here you are at 3,600m (11,800ft), looking down over the flat, endless lowlands of the Manu Biosphere reserve; the horizon lies an immense distance away, and on clear mornings observers report multiple suns, haloes, rainbows, a brilliant rosy glow covering land and sky. This phenomenon is at its most intense and frequent during May, June and July.

THE Q'EROS NATION

The Q'eros people claim to be descendants of a mythical founding Inca ancestor, Inkarí, and are therefore inheritors of ancient traditions that they still practice in the remote mountains east of Paucartambo. Their territory lies where the Andes fall steeply into the rainforest, ranging from 4,700m (15,500ft) to 1,800m (6,000ft) and encompassing high *puna* where they herd llamas and alpacas, an intermediate *qeshwa* zone for growing potatoes, and a lowland *yunga* zone where they plant corn and collect forest products. Q'eros families – having homes in all three zones, seasonally working and migrating between them with their animals – are a living microcosm of the Inca world, where skilled management of different altitude zones underpinned the entire civilization.

The Q'eros lived in voluntary isolation for centuries, scarcely known to the rest of Peru, speaking only Quechua, distant from Christian influence and closer to pre-Hispanic traditions than other Andean groups. Then in 1955 they were "discovered" by a landmark multi-disciplinary academic expedition of Cusco University (UNSAAC). The team produced valuable documentation (some not published until 50 years later) and helped one

Q'eros community gain title to its land in the early 1960s, but was also the source of sensationalized Lima newspaper articles about a "living museum from the Inca era." The Q'eros thereby acquired a mystique which has only grown since then, gaining them international renown as ritual specialists and magnets for seekers drawn to Andean spirituality. In 2006 the government designated the five communities of Q'eros "Cultural Patrimony of Peru."

The Q'eros life of herding and farming is punctuated year-round by communal rituals integrally expressing their view of space, time and the world. They live the Andean law of reciprocity, *ayni*, making abundant offerings to their Andean deities in expectation of a good life in return. The largest social event of the calendar is Carnival, celebrated for days on end, and accompanied by the year's chosen song, whose theme might be a sacred bird, plant or flower. Each domestic animal species and gender has its own fertility song and ritual of veneration performed on its own specific day through the year, the male animals being venerated in the male (dry) season and the females in the female (wet) season. Everything in Q'eros – weaving design, music, community layout, worldview – expresses *yanantin*, the union of all male-female dualities (e.g. day-night, above-below) which lies at the heart of Quechua life. In sum, the Q'eros are a living, vibrant, quintessential Andean culture with deep roots in an ancient past.

Today, Q'eros lifestyle and traditions are rapidly undergoing unprecedented changes. Their population has tripled in 100 years, now totaling some 3,000 people in five communities. Once it took days to reach Q'eros, now it is only hours by car. Its people move to towns in search of higher education and urban amenities, or because of dwindling water resources and overgrazing. Few Q'eros farm the *yunga* lowlands anymore, simply purchasing corn when they need it instead– a historic move from self-sufficiency to dependence on the cash economy.

Tourism to Q'eros is a delicate issue. The Q'eros have no community-based tourism model, but if one wants to travel there it is best to stay with a local family (see p. 46), keeping it simple, low-key and respectful. This way the family makes some money while the relationship remains personal. Other visitors are content to meet with the Q'eros in or around Cusco, mainly to learn their famous spiritual practices.

– Holly Wissler

Available for purchase: Kusisqa Waqashayku (From Grief and Joy We Sing). 2007 documentary on Q'eros life by Holly Wissler. DVDs (audio/subtitles in English, Spanish or Quechua) at Café Ayllu on Marqués (see p. 30).

PIKILLAQTA (30km / 18.8mi)

Pikillaqta (Flea Town) stands above the road to the left as you climb past the lake. It is a huge, sprawling site, covering almost 2.5km^2 (1mi^2) – about the size of pre-conquest Cusco – and is of interest primarily because it is the only major ruin of a pre-Inca settlement in the Cusco region. The site was built by the Wari culture, which flourished c. A.D. 600-950. Pikillaqta is in fact the biggest known imperial Wari complex after their capital city in Ayacucho, NW of Cusco. Pikillaqta (entrance by BTC) stands at the narrow southern approach to the Huatanay Valley, and seems strategic in location. The site has a small museum at the entrance whose one notable exhibit is the skeleton and carapace of a Glyptodon, found in 1998 just south of the Cusco airport across the Huatanay River in the district of *Wimpillay*. These giant armadillo relatives went extinct approximately 11,700 years ago, at the border of the Pleistocene and Holocene epochs.

The ruins appears powerful and menacing, with its many hectares of tall, two- and three-story buildings surrounded by an enclosing wall, much of which still stands. And it lies across a rolling slope in a precisely squared-off grid as if it had been designed elsewhere and set down here with utter disregard for the landscape, in striking contrast to the harmonious integration of nature and architecture seen at Inca sites. There is an excellent spot for photos at the high northern corner of the site.

The appearance of control over the valley was symbolic, however, because this was not a military garrison. Neither was it a city, in the ordinary sense of the word. According to U.S. archaeologist Gordon McEwan, who has excavated the site, Pikillaqta was a curious sort of ceremonial center; local vassal lords were brought here for alliance-building feasts and rituals. The only entrance to the entire complex was a narrow street lined with very high walls, stuccoed a dazzling white, so one could see nothing of the surroundings until abruptly entering the site's grand plaza. The effect of arriving there as a vassal of the Wari must have been profoundly intimidating.

At one of the three basic types of structure at Pikillaqta – described by McEwan as "lineage halls" – venerated ancestors were kept in niches, presiding over the festivities. Two nearly simultaneous looting expeditions in 1927 unearthed two very similar sets of 40 tiny turquoise figurines in one of these halls. One set is now one of the major treasures belonging to the Cusco Inka Museum (see p.91), and the other ended up, minus one figurine, in the Museo de América in Madrid. The missing orphan turned up in a private collection and was donated to Yale University Art Gallery in 1942. Another set of 56 figurines, including Wari elites, soldiers and supernatural beings with sacrifices, was found in 2004 by archaeologists Carlos Tuni & Louis Tesar. This set was made of metal, polished stone and spondylus shell instead of turquoise. Replicas can be seen at the Regional Historical Museum in Cusco (see p.110) and the Pikillacta site museum. There is a small display on this 2004 find at the high eastern corner of the site.

Pikillaqta is a puzzling site. The Wari didn't finish building all the sectors, and the ones which were completed were not fully occupied. All of its buildings were covered in a white gypsum stucco – traces of which can still be seen – quarried in the surrounding hills, which must have made it unbearably dazzling in the Andean sunshine. Floors were also of gypsum, 5cm (2in) thick. Many of its rooms were windowless and utterly dark, so that they were once thought to be for storage; but archaeology reveals that these enigmatic spaces were apparently designed for some other purpose.

Turquoise figurines, found at Pikillaqta

Despite today's DRC signage claiming a Wari era population of some 10,000, Pikillaqta's principal archaeologist, Gordon McEwan estimates the site's permanent population would have been less than a thousand; its primary purpose, he suggests, was to accommodate large gatherings during ritual feasts hosted by the elite administrators of this part of the Wari empire. He likens it to a modern office complex, where large numbers of people come and go, but only a handful actually live there.

Beneath the modern town at nearby Huaro, the remains of a major Wari center have been discovered. This settlement was probably the residential site for the people who built and maintained Pikillaqta.

Some violent catastrophe provoked by the stress of a prolonged drought befell the Wari empire while it was still expanding. As a result the Wari deliberately and systematically abandoned Pikillaqta sometime between 850-950 A.D. The Wari filled in partially-built temples with clay and dug up some of the offerings they had buried. Then, after they left, someone came along and torched the place. Perhaps this was the vengeance of the local vassals.

Just up the main highway from Pikillaqta (about 500m/1,640ft) stands *Rumicolca* (Stone Storehouse), the southern gateway to the Cusco Valley. The ruin can be seen to the right of the road. From ground level it looks like a huge Inca work, with its sheer walls of fine-cut stone. However, the tiered stonework on either side of the gate is much cruder. The structure was originally a Wari aqueduct – part of the Pikillaqta complex. The remains of the water channel can clearly be seen along the top. The Incas altered it – probably demolished some sections – and turned it into a great double gateway to the Cusco Valley.

Just down the hill from Rumicolca lie some stone quarries which were the source of much of the characteristic grey andesite which was used in the construction of Inca Cusco. The flat area by the Vilcanota River just south and west of here is the town called *Piñipampa* and is the major center of production for the terracotta roofing tiles of Cusco.

Explorer's Note: The quarries and adjacent settlement, although somewhat overgrown, are worth visiting for fans of obscure ruins. They are a good example of the layout of Inca settlements and stone carving in progress; this is where the "ratchet pebbles" were said to have been discovered (*see p.127*). Foot access is down a 1.3km (0.8mi) dirt road at the very northern edge of Piñipampa, just above the soccer field. Follow the road until it ends at the ridge NE of town, then ascend said ridge to the top. Road access is through Piñipampa around the SE side of the site.

ANDAHUAYLILLAS (37km / 23mi)

Andahuaylillas, a small community just off the main highway to the right, is the most attractive village for miles around. The main square is delightful, with its canopy of trees and the colonial houses surrounding it, some with murals painted on their façades, notably the *Casa de los Medallones*. These odd, anomalous paintings include what appear to be scenes of fur trapping in northern Canada and an old monoplane flying through the woods. The parish house is graced with a proud early-colonial doorway, made of well cut Inca stones in the transitional style, with pumas carved into the massive lintel — the remains of an important Inca temple which once stood here. The major attraction of the village is the church of *San Pedro Apostól* (RBA, 7:30am-5:30pm daily), dating from the early 17th century, which someone in a fit of hyperbole once called the "Sistine Chapel of the

Americas." This is one of the sites on the Andean Baroque Route (RBA), a chain of four colonial Jesuit churches starting with La Compañia in Cusco (*see p.88*) and including three more along this highway. The other two are in Huaro and Canincunca (*see below*). The Andahuaylillas one certainly is a splendid church, with a stunning multicolor and gold-leaf ceiling, beautiful murals and some especially fine colonial paintings. There is no church in the city of Cusco to compare with it. Connoisseurs of European medieval art will find both similarities and striking contrasts in this contemporary Spanish-American colonial art. A free informational pamphlet is available in English at the entrance, along with a DVD (for sale) with information on the entire Andean Baroque Route.

The purpose of covering the inside of this church and others with murals was to evangelize the illiterate natives, often using imagery that harmonized with the indigenous belief system. The Moorish influence evident in the frescoes on the ceiling, for example, evidently appealed to Quechua aesthetic sensibilities, being geometrical and abstract like many Andean textile motifs.

Local guides claim that the painting above the arch is by the 17th-century Spanish master, Murillo. A mural over the main doorway, no doubt designed to instruct the natives, depicts a sumptuously attractive (and crowded) path to hell versus a drearily virtuous path to heaven. The painting in the nave reflects the Cusco school, characterized by a surfeit of gilt ornamentation on top of the paint, whereas the chancel was painted by adherents of Italian Renaissance masters. The entrance to the baptistry to the left of the main door is crowned with a mural whose inscription is written in five languages: Latin, Spanish, Quechua, Aymara and the now-extinct Pukina, language of the Uru and Chipaya peoples of the altiplano. It reads "I baptize you in the name of the Father, the Son and the Holy Spirit."

The sponsor of most of the church's artistic content was a priest called Juan Pérez de Bocanegro, whose image, kneeling before Saint Peter, appears on the pulpit. Many of the paintings were done around 1626-28 by one Luis de Riaño, whose signature sometimes appears.

Also worth checking out is the museum Museo Ritos Andinos, located to the left of the church, entrance by donation. The star attraction here is a rather fanciful extraterrestrial interpretation of an elongated child's skull. The discovery of this skull made international headlines in 2011 when several anthropologists declared it to be of non-human origin. Occam's Razor suggests a simpler explanation: the ritual skull deformation common to many pre-Colombian societies of the Andes. There are also more down-to-earth displays on coca leaves, maize and pre-Inca petroglyphs.

HUARO (44km / 27.5mi)

At *Huaro*, the church of San Juan Bautista (RBA, 8am-5:30pm daily) is another fine colonial church, decorated with beautiful murals and well worth visiting. These works are much later than Andahuaylillas, signed by the artist and head of the project, Tadeo Escalante, and dated 1802. A terrifying painting of Hell, with people facing all manner of tortures, occupies the righthand wall, and the ceiling is entirely covered with floral and animal motifs, among which native Peruvian species feature prominently. There are also scenes of the tree of life and of pleasure, death and dying. The Sacred Stone Museum (daily 8am-5pm, SST) on the south side of the plaza has a collection of carved stones from the surrounding area, some originals, some reproductions.

Excavations at Huaro have revealed the site of an important settlement of the Wari empire, virtually all of it buried beneath the modern town.

The Chapel of the Virgin of Candelaria at Canincunca, just beyond Huaro, and about 1km (0.6mi) before Urcos (47km/29.3mi), is even more heavily decorated with murals than the other churches in this area. It stands to the right of the highway at the small pass from which you can see Urcos and its lake, into which – legend says – a solid gold chain belonging to the Inca Wascar was dumped to save it from Pizarro's ravening wolves. A major *waca* of the Wari people once stood at this pass; much of it was destroyed by the building of the modern highway, but one can still glimpse its foundations where the highway cut was made. Knock on the side door of the chapel and ask the caretaker to let you in. It is possible, via a path to the left (south) of the church, to descend to the lake and take in the pleasant 2km (1.3mi) walking route around it.

TREKKING NEAR AUSANGATE (trailhead: 115km / 72mi)

Shortly after Urcos, a turnoff marks the beginning of the Transoceanic Highway, going all the way to São Paulo in Brazil. The road passes Tinqui, the starting point for the traditional five-six day, 50-60km (31-38mi) circuit of the towering Ausangate (6,384m/20,940ft) (*see Transportation*, **www.peterfrost.org**). The route is home to pumas, vicuñas and condors, plus two hot springs: one at Upis and another at Pacchanta. This is high-altitude trekking, with a three high passes (5,200m, 5,000m, 4,850m / 17,050ft, 16,400ft, 15,900ft), and a minimum elevation of 4,200m (13,780ft) after leaving Tinqui, so prior acclimatization is essential.

On the south side of Ausangate, a second spectacular trekking circuit briefly intersects the traditional route at the Palomani Pass and goes by some of the most hallucinatory mineral-striped mountain scenery on the planet, whose major highlight is Vinicunca, now famous as the Rainbow Mountain of Peru. This landscape was not widely known until a few years ago, when it was discovered almost simultaneously by both tourists and miners eager to get at its valuable minerals. So far tourism has succeeded in protecting this spectacular location from destruction.

Lucky visitors might catch a glimpse of the *chinchay*, the all-but-extinct Andean wildcat. Andean Lodges (*see Trekking, p. 41*) has a series of comfortable lodges along a route that includes Vinicunca and participates in a project to save the vanishing wildcat. This second circuit is accessible through Checacupe and Pitumarca (*see Pitumarca below*). For either circuit, the best season is April to September; December to March are the rainy (in this case snowy) months. The cold and wind can be intense from May through August. Plenty of operators can arrange tours (*see Trekking, p. 41*). Miguel Pacsi is a local guide who can help with horse support for independent hikers on the circuits (tel. 984-668360, mpacsi1@hotmail.com). Cayetano Crispín (tel. 974-327538) runs Hostal Ausangate in Tinqui and can offer advice and route information. Leonidas Mandura (tel. 941-262004) runs the Hostal Ausangate and nearby restaurant in Pacchanta and can organize tours and horse rentals.

Vinicunca (a.k.a. Cerro Colorado, a.k.a. Rainbow Mountain), is offered by dozens of tour agencies as one very long day trip from Cusco, which includes a cruel day hike of 15km (9.4mi) and +700m (2,300ft) – nearly 1,600m (5,250ft) higher than Cusco. CBC Tupay (*see p.45*) offers a more relaxed two-day version of this hike with an overnight stay in a local community. Being remote and inaccessible, a tour agency is the most convenient option for transportation. Independent hikers, see Trekking on **www.peterfrost.org** for directions.

HUAJRA PUCARA (125km / 78mi)

At Chuquicahuana the road turns west towards the towns of Pomacanchi and Acomayo and provides access to the ruins of *Huajra Pucara* (Horned Fort) – local signage says "Wakra." This spectacular and remote Inca ruin clings precariously to a 4,110m (13,485ft) spur above the Apurimac River. If any doubts remained about how important landscape views were to the Inca, a visit to this site will quickly dispel them. The ruins have terraces and other standard Inca features, but the real gem is the platform perched between the site's eponymous pinnacle horns, looking clear across and into the Apurimac Canyon far below. The platform features a steep access stairway, triple-recessed niches, stonework artfully integrated into the adjacent rock, and a lower, secondary platform just a stumble away from canyon and oblivion. Even among Inca sites, few combine such inspiring views with such daring architecture. See it if you can.

HOW TO GET THERE. On foot only. *Guided Trips:* Alain Machaca of Alternative Inca Trails (*see p.42*) offers tours. *By Yourself:* See Trekking on **www.peterfrost.org** for directions.

CHECACUPE (99km / 62mi)

At Checacupe, the restaurant "O,O,O..." (named for the sound you're supposed to make when tasting the food?) along the main highway, with its prominent glass facade, has been recommended for its trout. In the main plaza, a short walk into town to the left of the highway, the Temple of the Immaculate Virgin church is partly built on Inca or transitional walls, worth seeing for those interested in colonial art. The building is often locked; try to get a policeman to find the caretaker for you, or inquire at the municipal building in the main plaza. Just off the main plaza to the north there is a section of attractive, if dubiously restored, Inca ruins along the river, complete with a steel-cable-reinforced hanging bridge.

Explorer's Note: For a quick and scenic – but steep – hike of 1km (0.6mi) and +125m (400ft), cross this bridge out of town and follow the 14 stations of the cross (the stages of the crucifixion) up the ridge, about a 1 hour round trip. The summit affords great views of the valley and the mountains towards Pitumarca.

A 7km (4.3mi) road leads off the main highway NE from Checacupe to the traditional village of *Pitumarca*, accessible via *colectivos* leaving from Checacupe's main plaza or a two-hour walk. A lot of fine weaving comes from this area, which is a major center of alpaca production. Weaving enthusiasts from all over come to visit the area. Food here is very limited, but there are a few basic hostels. About a half-hour walk from the village there are some pre-Inca ruins known as *Machu Pitumarca*.

HERDS AND HERDERS OF THE ANDES

Animal herding in pre-Columbian America was developed only in Peru. Llamas (**Lama glama**) and alpacas (Vicugna pacos) were the domesticated species, the former descended from the guanaco (Lama guanicoe) and the latter from the vicuña (*Vicugna vicugna*), both of which still exist in the wild. The evolutionary ancestor of both the camel and the South American camelids appeared in North America 40 million years ago. One branch of the evolutionary tree went north, crossing the Bering strait and becoming the two Asian camel species, while another went south across the isthmus of Panama and evolved into the camelid family of South America. In the interim, the camel ancestor went extinct in its place of origin.

Hunter-gatherers of the *puna* (the grasslands of the high Andes) began the domestication of llamas and alpacas seven thousand years ago, a process which culminated in the appearance of herding societies five thousand years ago. Since then herding has been a complex adaptive process, especially at the high altitudes where it has been most highly developed, and where today's herders live.

Llamas and alpacas acquired their greatest economic and strategic importance under the Incas. They supplied wool for textiles and meat for consumption, but above all llamas were used for transport. Their load-carrying capacity made the Inca expansion possible. Llamas carried the supplies of the imperial Inca armies to places as far away as southern

ALPACA
EARS: Straight, pointed, shorter than llama's
FACE: Small; short nose; woolly
FACE: long nose; no wool; haughty look

LLAMA
EARS: long and curved
TAIL: often carried high, like a flag

TAIL: usually carried low
LEGS: wool below knee
not much wool

287

Colombia, the sierra of Ecuador, and northern Chile and Argentina.

They played an important part in Andean religion, too. The priesthood kept herds, from which they took animals for sacrifice. In the *Aucaypata*, the central square of Inca Cusco, numerous llamas were sacrificed every day.

The Sapa Inca joined in the festivals of the herders to dance and sing with them. One of the royal symbols of the Sapa Inca was the *napa*, a pure white llama covered with a red cloth, which walked ahead of him during processions. In Inca culture the iconography of llamas and alpacas is diverse, abundant, and esthetically sophisticated.

The 16th-century Spanish invasion brought with it cattle and sheep, which displaced llamas and alpacas to marginal areas, especially the great highland punas above 4,000m, truly the "refuge regions" where modern herders graze them.

There are about 100,000 herding families today, tending to three million alpacas and half a million llamas. Their remoteness has not prevented them from participating in the world fibers market, given that alpaca wool is used in high fashion clothing. Nevertheless, they conserve ways of life and traditions which have changed little since Inca times, although they adopt the modern innovations which interest and suit them.

La Raya is the Experimental Center for South American Camelids. It is the world's principal center for the study of llamas and alpacas. It lies on the route to Puno, 160km from Cusco. Traditional herding regions accessible to a day excursion from Cusco lie on the roads from Ollantaytambo to Quillabamba at the Abra de Málaga (4,000m), and at the Abra de Amparaes (4,200m) on the Calca-Lares road.

– Jorge Flores Ochoa

Today llamas and alpacas are becoming popular in other parts of the world, particularly the U.S. where they serve as pets and pack animals. They are valued for their low impact on the environment compared to horses and mules because their soft hoof-pads do not chew up trails, and their grazing habits are exemplary. Sheep ranchers have also discovered that a few llamas kept with the herd will drive away the coyotes who kill their lambs.

– P.F.

Q'ESWACHAKA: THE BRAIDED BRIDGE

The Inca road system known as the *Qhapac Ñan* (*see p.188*) once spanned the entire empire, crossing innumerable rivers with rope bridges. These were constructed from braided local vegetation and had to be totally replaced on a regular basis as they decayed; nearby villagers would build a new bridge in fulfilment of their *mit'a* public service obligations to the empire. All that remains of this social and engineering accomplishment is the 600-year-old *Q'eswachaka* (Grass Bridge) suspension bridge, which crosses the Apurimac River roughly 21km (13mi) SSE of Combapata as the condor flies. Every year in the second week of June, four local communities gather for a four-day festival and construction party to rebuild the 30.5m (100ft) bridge. Despite a nearby modern road bridge built in the 1960s, locals continue to rebuild Q'eswachaka to maintain their culture and traditions. In 2013, UNESCO added the bridge to its Intangible Cultural Heritage list, and in 2015 Washington, D.C. briefly became home to a replica of it built by the aforementioned communities participating in the Smithsonian Folklife Festival.

To rebuild the bridge, the communities first hold a ceremony to ask permission from *Pachamama*; the old bridge is then cut away, falling into the river. The women braid long ropes called *q'oya* from *ichu* grass and the men string them across the canyon to form the base; the handrails and deck are added after. At each stage of construction, there are ceremonial offerings of coca leaves, potatoes and corn to Pachamama and the Apu mountain spirits. Completion is celebrated with music, *chicha*, and dishes with *chuño* (freeze-dried potatoes). Several tour operators offer visits (*see Cultural and Festival Tours, p. 52*).

Explorer's Note: Following the highway two to three hours beyond Q'eswachaka you reach the town of Livitaca (*see Transportation, p.23*). North of here through spectacular scenery across a tributary of the Apurimac lies the the remote canyon of Chiñiciri, which is dotted with scores of pre-Inca tombs, painted in bright mineral colors, well preserved, and scattered with pottery and textile fragments. The hallucinatory combination of spectacular canyon scenery and ancient mystery makes this a highly rewarding though challenging exploration. It is essential to have your own transport (preferably 4X4) from Livitaca, even better all the way from Cusco, and to find a guide in Livitaca. Bring camping gear.

RAQCHI (119km / 74mi)

The ruins at *Raqchi* (7am-5pm daily, SST) are the last major place of interest on the route within an easy day's journey of Cusco. Any Sicuani-bound bus can drop you off. The site is a short walk from the highway. Raqchi covers a big area, lying to the left of the main highway, about 4km (2.5mi) before the town of San Pedro. The church here looks like the prototype for all those fairy-tale ceramic churches from Ayacucho that are so popular with tourists. The villagers of Raqchi make excellent rustic pottery during the dry season, when the fields are idle. The dirt roading loading NW out of the plaza takes you along a free trail to a viewpoint with excellent views of the site and surrounding area; follow the white arrows.

The site is well maintained and has the feeling of a city park; it's a pleasant place to spend an hour or two just wandering. The star attraction is the *Temple of Wiracocha* towering over the site. If you have time to explore everything, save this showstopper until the end and do the walking tour suggested below.

To the left as you enter the ruins from the village, past the pond, the residence of the nobles or high priests seems to have been located near the hillside. Over there you will find a very fine set of *baths* (1), which has been excavated and restored. The remains of a complex system of water ducts can be clearly seen. Just beyond this lies *Mesapata Usnu* (2). Walking

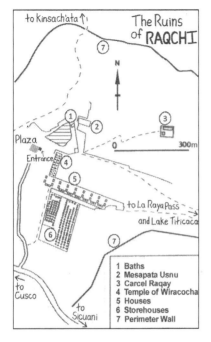

to the south, away from here, you'll come to a field under cultivation and an attractive tree-lined path leading left to the so-called *Carcel Raqay* (Jailhouse) (3). The trail dead ends quickly at a jumble of unrestored stone buildings but provides some much needed shade on a hot day.

The main structure at Raqchi is called the *Temple of Wiracocha* (4). Legend has it that the temple was raised to propitiate the Inca creator god after the area's devastation by the eruption of Kinsach'ata, the now-extinct volcano nearby. (A trail snakes through the forest to the north and leads up to the volcanic crater.) The stone of the district is indeed predominantly volcanic. The building itself is unique in Inca architecture for its sheer size (outer walls 90m/295ft long, 15m/49ft high), and also for its configuration. It consists of a central wall with bases of Imperial Inca stonework and a top section of adobe, with a line of rounded columns on either side of this wall, which once supported the roof. Columns like these are otherwise unknown in Inca structures. Only the bases of these columns remain, though one has been reconstructed. The ruin has been roofed with tiles to protect the adobe from erosion.

Adjacent to the temple are rows of identical *houses* (5) grouped neatly around identical squares: six squares, 36 buildings. Then, toward the road, stand perhaps the most remarkable structures of the ruins: the remains of 200 stone *storehouses* (6). These are cylindrical in shape, grouped in dead-straight rows of ten, and each measure some six meters in diameter by two-and-a-half in height. All of this represents a colossal volume of storage space and is the most impressive remaining testimony in the region to the degree of social organization attained by the Incas. The dividing wall between the houses and storehouses, plus some of the construction under the latter, is pre-Inca, showing once again that the Incas were building on the shoulders of giants. To the dismay of archaeologists, agricultural activity in this area has destroyed many of the storehouses. You can reach the exit road by walking south down the path on the west side of the storehouses.

The entire site of Raqchi, plus a significant area to the east, is contained within an encircling *perimeter wall* (7).

SICUANI (140km / 87.5mi)

Sicuani is mostly a transit town on the way to Puno, Arequipa or Bolivia or a rest stop at the end of a long day of exploring. However, there are some developed hot springs called "Aguas Calientes de La Raya" a half hour south in the community of Occobamba, just before the La Raya pass. The springs are very hot and rarely visited by tourists; there is even a tiny inactive volcano. Take a taxi from Sicuani or get off a southbound bus at the turnoff to Occobamba and walk.

Explorer's Note: The town of Espinar lies 80km (50mi) SW of Sicuani. Its surroundings are home to some incredible Inca and pre-Inca ruins sites, including K'anamarca, Maukallacta (not to be confused with the *other* Maukallacta described below), and Taqrachullo. The former was possibly the capital of the pre-Inca K'ana Nation and contains various limestone buildings with some of their original plaster. Maukallacta is home to dozens of the circular tombs known as *chullpas*, with the tallest reaching 6m (20ft), and is beautifully situated on the shores of the Apurimac River within its canyon. Taqrachullo is SW of here and sits on top of a promontory within the Apurimac Canyon; it has many circular buildings and was likely a control point. The geography of the entire area is awe-inspiring, with rolling hills, sweeping views and dramatic canyonland. The area just SW of Taqrachullo known as *Tres Cañones*, where three canyons merge, is particularly impressive. See **www.peterfrost.org** for more info.

MAUKALLACTA (trailhead: 40km / 25mi)

This is a beautiful, remote Inca site about an hour's walk up from the Cusco-Huanoquite road (*see map, p.270*), a different highway from the Valley Road Southeast which the above sites are on. According to legend, this is Inca Pacarictambo, the origin site where Manco Capac and his siblings emerged from underground to take control of Cusco. Manco's violent brother Ayar Cachi supposedly remains entombed in a nearby cave (*see p.63*). Maukallacta features two very fine double-jamb doorways, extensive drainage channels, and the highlight of the site: an incredible 10x10m plaza with nine triple-jamb niches, highly unusual in Inca architecture. There are also extensive remains of pottery, clay mortars and original adobe walls preserved beneath modern thatch roofs. The site makes for a good day trip from Cusco, one with hardly any other tourists on it. Alternative Inca Trails (*see p.42*) does tours here.

Getting There. (*See Transportation, p. 22*) From Yaurisque, the turnoff for Maukallacta is about 7km (4.4mi) along the road to Huanoquite, immediately after the second bridge after the town. Your taxi then follows a grassy road south for about 500m (1,640ft) to reach the trailhead. Follow the well-marked trail for 1.5km (0.9mi) as it ascends 300m (980ft); the trail is quite steep in places, but there are three shelters to rest in along the way. When the ruins come into view, north lies to your right as you face them.

IN THE RUINS. North is to your right as you hike into the site. The ruins can be divided into the well-restored northern and middle sectors, plus an unrestored southern sector. The trail up ends just below a long wall with 18 niches and two wide sets of stairs leading into the northern sector.

The spectacular plaza with the nine niches lies just right of the large double-jamb doorway. One of the "niches" is actually a door leading into a small area with multiple rooms. Legend holds that this area was the oracular shrine belonging to the founding Inca, Manco Capac, making this tiny room supremely important. In the passage just north of the plaza lies a drainage channel with another doorway, one with bar-hold features carved within. To the north of this water channel passage lies a plaza with finely carved stone walls, some of the best at the site. The rest of this northern sector has some preserved adobe walls with niches and remnants of pottery, plus a bath at its southern end.

The middle sector starts at the large, north-facing double-jamb doorway. Follow the stairs leading up from the door and water channel just above it into a grassy plaza. Explore around this sector to find mortars, pottery and possibly a clay oven preserved beneath modern thatched roofs. Water channels criss-cross this sector to drain the buildings and plazas. There is also a partially reconstructed but fine ceremonial bath up and west from the grassy plaza.

The southern end of the ruins are separated from the rest of the site by a ravine which can be crossed about half way up. This sector hasn't seen much restoration work and is mostly a jumble of stones. It was probably residential as it lacks the fine features of the northern and middle sectors.

The mountain and ridge above Maukallacta to the west can be climbed for excellent views of the site and surroundings. A trail begins at the northernmost buildings of the site. Follow this trail some 70m (230ft) north from the buildings, then follow it as it turns west and then south to ascend the mountain slope. The summit is a tree stump surrounded by a cairn.

Explorer's Note: Puma Orco is a *waca* due east of Maukallacta, a 1.5km (1mi) walk along the nearby road. Brian Bauer writes: "Puma Orco is certainly worth the small walk. I believe it was the Tamputoco *(the mythical origin cave of the Incas – Ed.).* It has a carved top, including two pumas, and some buildings on one side. It is a tiny but nice site."

CHAPTER EIGHT

VILCABAMBA
Refuge of the Rebel Incas

HISTORY

The fate of the last Incas is a mystery that has long intrigued historians and explorers. After the Conquest some members of the royal line chose a comfortable but impotent existence in Cusco under Spanish tutelage; some collaborated openly with the new order. At one point there were two Incas. The Spaniards had their own candidate, Paullu Inca, fighting at their side against the natives under Manco Inca throughout the second rebellion.

But Paullu was blatantly a Spanish puppet. Diego de Almagro had declared him Inca in 1537, stripping the reigning Inca, Manco, of his title *in absentia*. Manco himself was recently installed in his jungle redoubt of Vilcabamba, where he was preparing to mount the guerrilla war that he would pursue doggedly against the Spanish until his death seven years later.

Manco had abandoned Ollantaytambo in July 1537, seeing that the Spanish forces arrayed against him in the Cusco region were now overwhelming. He retreated by way of the Panticalla Pass, with the Spanish under Rodrigo Orgoñez close on his heels. Evidently the Inca had prepared his retreat; he made straight for the bridge over the Urubamba at Choquechaca, by the modern settlement of Santa Maria – the gateway to the remote wilderness of Vilcabamba. (*Note:*Vilcabamba is the name of both a vast region and the ruined Inca city at Espiritu Pampa, known for clarity as Vilcabamba the Old; there is also a third Vilcabamba, a town near Huancacalle, founded by the Spaniards in 1572.)

The Incas already had a foothold in this area: the fortress city of Vitcos, a few kilometers from the river. Manco took refuge there, but

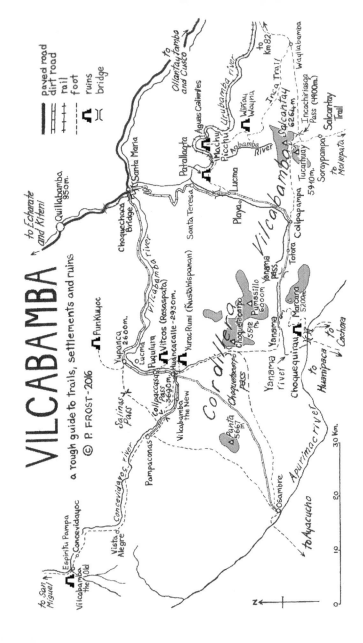

VILCABAMBA
a rough guide to trails, settlements and ruins
© P. FROST - 2016

paved road
dirt road
rail
foot
ruins
bridge

the Spanish were onto him before he could regroup or prepare defenses. They captured the Choquechaca bridge, crossed it, and swiftly took Vitcos. Only the conquistadors' greed saved Manco on this occasion. They discovered loot and women at Vitcos and paused to sack the place, allowing Manco to escape.

The Spanish later had cause to regret this. Vilcabamba under Manco became a legend: a source of fear and unease to Spanish settlers and an inspiration to millions of Inca loyalists in Spanish-occupied Peru; the springboard from which Manco launched the second rebellion and countless lesser raids against Spanish life and property.

Gonzalo Pizarro led a force into Vilcabamba in 1539 in an attempt to crush for all time the rebellious Inca state. Pizarro overran all the main settlements, including Manco's new capital of Vilcabamba. But Manco, in the best guerrilla style, vanished into the jungles to fight another day.

Gonzalo Pizarro's expedition was costly, unproductive and inconclusive. The Spanish found the area of Vilcabamba almost uninhabitable and certainly not worth fighting for. First they tried diplomacy to get Manco out, and when this failed they murdered his captured wife (*see p.173*), burned to death a number of Inca commanders, and finally withdrew, abandoning the problem of Vilcabamba in the hope that it would simply go away. They were, in any case, becoming embroiled in their own civil wars.

But Manco organized the inhospitable territory into a solid native state that continued to harass the Spanish until his death in 1544. In the end, Manco made the mistake of trusting seven renegade Spaniards – disaffected members of the Almagrist faction, wanted by the authorities – and offering them sanctuary. They repaid Manco by murdering him during a game of horseshoe quoits in an attempt to regain favor with the crown. (Manco's soldiers later avenged him by trapping the Spaniards in a building where they had sheltered and burning them alive or spearing them as they tried to flee the flames.)

Manco's appointed heir, Sayri Tupac, emerged from Vilcabamba in 1557 after prolonged negotiations with the Spanish Viceroy. He traded the hardships of a jungle kingdom for a grant of estates and nominal recognition of his title by the Spanish. But the diehards remained in Vilcabamba, and when Sayri Tupac died in 1561 (*see Yucay, p. 164*), raids against Spanish territory resumed under the direction of a tough new Inca, Sayri's half-brother Titu Cusi. Titu Cusi was a skillful diplomat as well as a resolute leader, keeping alive Spanish hopes of a negotiated settlement and fending off their contemplated invasion.

Titu Cusi allowed Christian missionaries into Vilcabamba to appease the Spanish. He dictated a long memoir to one of them, Fray Marcos Garcia, which is a major contemporary source of information about Vilcabamba and the Conquest in general. He died in 1571. A Spanish priest, Padre Ortiz, was accused by the Inca priests of poisoning the Inca, and the unfortunate friar was tortured and beaten to death. His martyrdom, and the killing of a crown envoy to the new Inca soon afterward, provoked the long-delayed invasion of Vilcabamba in 1572. This time the expedition was large, thoroughly prepared, and implacably determined to kill or capture the Inca. They still believed they were after Titu Cusi, whose death had been kept secret, but the Inca was now Tupac Amaru I, yet another son of Manco, half-brother of Titu Cusi and Sayri Tupac.

The invasion, under Hurtado de Arbieto, captured all the major fortifications of Vilcabamba and reached the capital city, which they found a smoking ruin, abandoned and burned by the retreating Incas. Tupac Amaru fled by canoe down the Cosireni River, deeper into the jungle, but this time the Spaniards tailed the Inca doggedly, resolved to put an end, once and for all, to the Inca resistance. They finally came upon him in appropriately pitiful circumstances: huddled over a fire in the heart of the forest; betrayed by some of his captains; almost alone; destitute; defenseless; his followers scattered – the last remnant of an empire that once stretched halfway from the Equator to the Pole now overrun by the terrifying alien warriors.

The royal line of the Incas comes decisively to an end with Tupac Amaru. Viceroy Francisco de Toledo made sure of that. The Inca was taken in chains to Cusco, converted to Christianity with the utmost dispatch, and beheaded in the main square three days later. Members of his family – even collaborators with the Spanish – were exiled, scattered and dispossessed. Not even a Spanish puppet Inca remained. The Incas were finished.

The conquistadors occupied the territory of Vilcabamba and exploited it for what it was worth – which was not much – over the next few decades. They founded the new settlement of San Francisco de la Victoria de Vilcabamba and began to work a couple of silver mines in the area. The remnants of Vilcabamba's native population were conscripted to labor in them. But the mines proved disappointing. Sugar and coca plantations were established, too – but all in all the Spaniards found the humid jungles uninviting, the discomforts many, and the rewards meager. The final dethroning of the Incas meant there were no longer strategic reasons for occupying the region.

By the mid-seventeenth century Vilcabamba was little more than a memory. And its capital city was not even that; its location was entirely forgotten. None of the chroniclers who recorded the invasion, the memoirs of Titu Cusi, and the martyrdom of Padre Ortiz had thought to record the exact site. And now the jungle had covered the roads leading to it.

And so when during the 19th century men of science began to take an interest in such questions, Vilcabamba was already a mysterious and shadowy place whose very existence was open to doubt. The chronicles themselves were buried in the then-impenetrable archives of Spain. (Some of the most important sources relating to Vilcabamba only came to light during the 20th century.)

At first, Choquequirao (see below), a ruin perched on a mountain spur high above the Apurimac River was thought to be the site of Vilcabamba the Old, as it had come to be known. Later this was amended to a belief that this had been merely an outpost of the Inca state. Hiram Bingham visited Choquequirao in 1909 and pronounced it an unlikely candidate.

Machu Picchu, the city Bingham discovered in 1911, was, in retrospect, an equally unlikely candidate *(see Chapter Five)*. Remarkably, in the same year of his discovery of Machu Picchu, Bingham actually did find the ruins now thought to be those of Vilcabamba, at a place known as *Espiritu Pampa* (Plain of Spirits). But perhaps because this site was more spread out and more deeply buried in jungle than Machu Picchu, he uncovered only a small part of the complex, and dismissed the ruins as insignificant. Intoxicated with his magnificent discovery on the Urubamba River, he pronounced Machu Picchu to be the site of Vilcabamba the Old. Such was his reputation that this flimsy claim stood unchallenged for the next 50 years.

Then a revisionist explorer arrived in the person of Gene Savoy. This flamboyant American moved in with everything from dollars to more dollars – plus a lot of grit and determination – and took large expeditions into Vilcabamba in 1964 and 1965. In 1911 Bingham had established beyond doubt the location of Vitcos, Manco's fortified city near the Choquechaca bridge. The real argument revolved around the probable location of the last refuge. Machu Picchu, Choquequirao and Espiritu Pampa were all about the same distance from Vitcos. But nothing else about the former two ruins seemed to fit the contemporary descriptions. Savoy believed that Espiritu Pampa was the real location of Vilcabamba, and when his party cleared the ruins the evidence began to pile up.

Savoy's hypothesis has eloquent and authoritative support from John Hemming. In *The Conquest of the Incas* Hemming makes a convincing case for Espiritu Pampa as Vilcabamba the Old, noting that these ruins are much larger than Bingham realized (they cover about 500 acres), and that new sources have emerged to which Bingham did not have access. Hemming demonstrates that everything about Espiritu Pampa – and conversely, nothing about Machu Picchu – conforms to contemporary accounts of the city and its setting: altitude, topography, rivers, climate, flora and fauna, and the locations of several important landmarks on the route to Vitcos. Excavations have confirmed the site was burned, just as Vilcabamba the Old was. Finally, perhaps most conclusively, Savoy found Spanish-style roofing tiles at the site. Bingham noticed these, too. But roofing tiles were never seen in Peru until after the Conquest (the Incas only used thatch) and certainly were not found at Machu Picchu. Vilcabamba was a post-Conquest Inca city, probably the only one to have existed in Peru. And we now know that the city at Espiritu Pampa was at least partly built after the Conquest, whereas there is no evidence for this conclusion at any other known ruin site.

The Vilcabamba region has retained an aura of rebellion and lawlessness through modern times. In the 1960s a sort of "Che lite" guerrilla movement appeared here, fomenting ultimately successful demands for land reform among the local campesinos. In the 1980s revolution returned in more radical form, when the feared "Shining Path" terrorists – whose tactics were anything but "lite"– began to appear in the area around 1983. For a while Vilcabamba was off-limits and overrun with soldiers and police.

So-called "narco-terrorist" Shining Path remnants occasionally appear in the remoter areas of Vilcabamba where few tourists go, but the troubled times are over, and for the most part the area is safe.

To visit the Vitcos/Huancacalle area, take transportation from Santa Maria (see Transportation, p. 22). To visit Espiritu Pampa only, take road transportation through Quillabamba, Kiteni and San Miguel to arrive within about a 15 minutes' walk from Espiritu Pampa (see p. 22).

NORTHERN VILCABAMBA

The area known as Vilcabamba forms a roughly square block of territory bounded in the south and west by the Apurimac River, in the east by the Urubamba. The SE corner is walled in by the massive glacial ramparts of the Cordillera Vilcabamba. And the northern sector is ringed by the dense jungle lowlands beyond the Cosireni River. Check with Maratón (see p. 39) for detailed maps of the region. The IGN maps for the area are called "Pacaypata" and "Machu Picchu."

Quillabamba
(210km / 131mi)

This beautiful high jungle city has great weather, swimming pools, fresh local produce and an abundance of parks and green spaces; a welcome break from the chilly climes of Cusco. It also provides access to Megantoni National Park, a biodiversity hotspot and wildlife corridor between Manu National Park and Vilcabamba. Museo Amazónico Andino de Quillabamba, (crnr. Jr. Timpia and Av. 25 de Julio, tel. 281251, Mon-Sun 9am-1pm, 3-6pm) has English signage and three exhibition rooms. The first showcases the biodiversity of the regional flora and fauna; the second has a collection of stone, ceramic and metal pieces found during excavations at Vilcabamba, Espiritu Pampa and Choquequirao; and the third has displays and re-creations of clothing and cultural practices of the native communities still living in the area. There are also displays on the *Qhapac Ñan* (the Inca road network – *see p.188*) and how the Andean and Amazonian communities interacted with each other through it.

Rosaspata (Vitcos) and Ñustahispanan
(Yurac Rumi) (235km / 147mi)

You need two or more nights in the Huancacalle area to visit *Vitcos* and *Yurac Rumi*. The ruins of Vitcos – known nowadays as Rosaspata – stand on a bluff on the south bank of the Vilcabamba River, roughly equidistant from Huancacalle and Puquiura. The excellent plans in Vincent Lee's *Forgotten Vilcabamba (see Bibliography)* may be used to tour this site and others, including Espiritu Pampa. The best way to visit the site begins from Huancacalle (5.5km/4.3mi round trip), where you cross two footbridges just upstream from the village; ask the locals for directions. After crossing the second bridge take the trail up the slope ahead of you to the crest, where you follow a gentle downhill slope to the *Yurac Rumi* (White Rock), at the site known as Ñustahispanan, once the holiest shrine of Inca Vilcabamba.

This huge granite boulder is some eight meters high by twenty meters wide and was once white, hence the name, but is now dark with the lichen and algae that cover its surface. A spring rose – and still rises – beneath it, and some of the superb stonework carved and laid around the emerging springwater water can still be seen. The rock itself is elaborately carved into intricate geometrical forms, with mysterious knobs and recesses over much of its surface. The Incas built shrines and a reflecting pool on the east side of the rock, to replicate its image in the water. Just downstream lies a beautifully carved ritual bath with two water spouts still running.

Spanish missionaries who contrived to enter Vilcabamba during the rule of Manco Inca's son Titu Cusi were incensed by this shrine, claiming the Inca priests called up images of demons in the mirror surface of the pool. Once they had acquired a sufficient group of converts they had the audacity to desecrate it and burn the adjacent buildings.

The Spanish later buried the reflecting pool and razed the buildings facing the *Yurac Rumi* from the east side, also diligently destroying and scattering a complex of fine stone buildings which stood on the west side of it. Remains of this complex and adjacent buildings on the north side can still be seen, together with smaller carved rocks including a recessed seat facing the winter solstice sunrise.

For a full look at the former Inca site, follow the Inca roadway down the charming valley below the east side of the mountain, where you will find more stone carvings and a superb series of terraces. At the north end of these the road ascends to the site of Manco Inca's former palace. A shorter route follows a narrow footpath through woods, ascending from the north side of Ñustahispanan and traversing the east slope of the mountain, about 40 minutes on foot, until you reach the ruins of Vitcos.

The impressive Inca layout and stonework here suggest that Manco's palace was originally an imperial stronghold, built during the Inca occupation of Vilcabamba before the Spanish conquest. It became the capital and heart of the Vilcabamba state during the early years of the Inca resistance, when Manco was leader. But Spanish forces overran Vitcos twice in the late 1530s, and one last time in 1572, demonstrating the vulnerability of this fortification. The murder of Manco by renegade

Spaniards in 1544 took place right here in the broad plaza below the knoll where the main complex of buildings still stands.

A large ceremonial platform stands a few hundred gently ascending meters to the south and offers splendid views in all directions, with the Pumasillo branch of the Vilcabamba Range filling the southern horizon on clear days. Trails descend westward from both this platform and Manco's palace to the Vilcabamba River, where you find footbridges enabling you to return to Huancacalle.

Explorer's note: Punkuyoc (a.k.a. Incahuasi) is another very interesting ruin in the Vilcabamba region, about one day's long, climbing walk north of Yupanca. Nowadays a road passes within about 6km (4mi) of the site, so access is much easier than it used to be. It is a small ruin, but very well preserved, and the location is spectacular, with a view due south to Vitcos in the distance. If the weather is fine, all the peaks of the Cordillera Vilcabamba are visible from here. The Cobos family (*see below*) can supply guides.

Espiritu Pampa
(Vilcabamba the Old) (350km / 220mi)

Figure about three to four days (plus two days' return journey to Cusco) for a trek to Espiritu Pampa. Take supplies, and basic camping gear. You can hike as an independent trekker, but will have an easier time of it if you hire guides and mules in Huancacalle. The Cobos family members Jorge and Fredy are the best known guides in the area. Inquire at Sixpac

"The Bowl of the Resistance" – imagery from a ceramic found at Espiritu Pampa.

Manco Hostal (*see p. 62*). The trail is impassable in the rainy season.

The walk to Espiritu Pampa (Plain of Spirits) takes about three days from the roadhead at Huancacalle. The ruins themselves are extensive and very interesting, and nowadays they are kept clear enough of forest growth that you can see all the important features of the site. They include well designed Inca layout, some classical buildings of well-cut stone, walkways, water channels, and a massive *huanca*, or sacred "ownership rock" in the main plaza. From 2008-2010, Cusco archaeologist Javier Fonseca excavated several of the main Inca buildings here and found copious amounts of Inca pottery, including a superb find: a large bowl decorated with a polychrome painted scene of Inca troops doing battle with mounted Spaniards – a striking artifact from the time of the Inca resistance, and the first discovery of its kind. Fonseca also made a groundbreaking and totally unexpected discovery close by the Inca site: a pre-Inca settlement complex, complete with burials and the dazzling silver accoutrements of Wari chieftains, far beyond the previously known limits of the Wari empire (c.A.D 600-1000).

A road now reaches Espiritu Pampa, where a sizeable village has sprung up in recent times. Rides to Chuanquiri or Kiteni are reliably available on Wednesday, Saturday and Sunday (less reliable but not impossible on other days). From either spot, you can catch onward transportation to Quillabamba or, possibly, direct to Cusco. Total time back to Cusco is at least a day and a half, with an overnight stop.

Source: Lic. Javier Fonseca/drawing by Arq. Betsy Apaza

SOUTHERN VILCABAMBA
Saywite (120km / 75mi)

Saywite (SST) is a beautiful site ringed by mountains, cultivated slopes and long east-facing views down the Apurimac Canyon. It is 25km (15.6mi) beyond the town of Curahuasi (locally renowned for its anise-flavored liqueurs) on the road to Abancay and just before the *Ramal de Cachora*, the turnoff to Cachora and the start of the Choquequirao hike. The star attraction of Saywite is the magnificent, intricately carved boulder at the front entrance. The boulder depicts what appears to be a miniature city plan with houses, stairways, water channels, platforms, terraces, and caves. Nestled among the city structures are zoomorphic carvings of monkeys, snakes, pumas, and marine animals. The boulder was of course defaced by the Spanish conquistadors, making it difficult to determine exactly what it represented. Archeologists speculate that it depicted the four quarters of the *Tawantinsuyu,* as it has animals from all the regions and the large ridges in the center seem to represent the cordilleras of the Andes.

Try to make time to visit the rest of the site. Just to the east lies an *usnu* (ceremonial platform) with upper and lower sections; the upper one contains an east-facing doorway/niche at the edge of the building complex which aligns exactly with the June solstice sunrise.

Follow the pathway along the northern edge of the *usnu* to descend a long staircase next to a series of baths. The trail brings you to a large boulder with a full-length fracture running through it and many finely carved benches and steps. On the south face there is a narrow, bifurcated water channel leading into two rectangular niches, probably used for channeling liquids during divination rituals. Stop and consider the difficulty of making such a narrow channel without the benefit of steel chisels.

To the south of the fractured stone lies another large platform with a wide flight of stairs leading up to it. Local folklore claims that the doorway to the left of the stairs at one point led into the center of the platform but was filled in by archeologists.

The final site of interest here is another carved boulder to the east, visible from the top of the platform above. The boulder displays the familiar step symbol with a perfectly carved rectangular hole through it, plus a number of benches. This entire boulder may be an echo stone (*see p.234*) for a mountain to the WSW.

Choquequirao (Cradle of Gold)
(165km / 103mi road plus trail)

History. This magnificently situated ruin was never lost to knowledge, and therefore never "discovered." A 16th century Spanish document unearthed by ethnohistorian Erwan Duffait listed royal properties of the emperor Topa Inca, among them a place called Chuquicarando that matches topographical and other details for Choquequirao. The earliest unequivocal mention of it as Choquequirao appears in a report by a Spanish mining prospector dated 1710.

The place became almost a legend during the 19th century, when it was mistakenly thought to be Vilcabamba the Old, the elusive last refuge of the Incas. It was mentioned by the Peruvian chronicler Cosme Bueno in 1768 and rediscovered by the French Comte de Sartiges in 1834. Thereafter it received occasional visits from treasure hunters and explorers. The French consul in Peru, Leonce Angrand, visited and did the first known drawings of the site in 1847. Hiram Bingham went there in 1909 – his first taste of an Inca "lost city," two years before his momentous scientific discovery of Machu Picchu. Even today its remoteness ensures that Choquequirao receives only a modest flow of adventurous trekkers, but it has become easier to reach since the mid-1990s, when a footbridge was constructed over the Apurimac River below the ruins (formerly one crossed on an *oroya*, a steel cable and basket). After Bingham, no serious documentation was done until the 1990s when architect Roberto Samanez mapped the main sectors of the site.

The buildings around Choquequirao's central plaza represent extremely fine ceremonial and high-status residential architecture. There is a chain of ritual baths, an enormous, curving bank of fine terraces, numerous intriguing outlier groups of buildings and a vast area of irrigated terracing on a nearby mountain slope, evidently designed to feed the local population. As recently as 2002, an astounding series of terraces was discovered on the site's west slope featuring white-stone llamas and geometric patterns. Nothing quite like them exists elsewhere in Inca design and construction.

The importance of Choquequirao has been widely underrated, partly because of its remoteness but perhaps essentially because the stonework seems unimpressive compared to that of the well-known high-status sites. This may be because the type of stone available here is a frangible metamorphic rock which cannot be worked into the subtle interlocking shapes possible in granite and andesite.

When one looks at the style and quality of construction, and the layout of the settlement at Choquequirao, to say nothing of its sheer size, one's perceptions shift. Choquequirao *was* a major Inca site. Its utterly spectacular location, on a ridge spur almost 1,800m (5,900ft) above the roaring Apurimac River, reminds one of Machu Picchu itself. And it is especially striking that the Incas built first Machu Picchu high above the Urubamba River at the north end of the mighty Vilcabamba mountain range, and then Choquequirao, high above the Apurimac River, at the south-west extremity of that same range. Together they make a matching pair of Inca ceremonial settlements, paying architectural homage in the inimitable Inca style to one of their greatest mountain ranges and the two most powerful rivers of their heartland.

Treks that pass through Choquequirao and end at Machu Picchu (*see p.310*) provide a magnificent sense of the landscape connection and the family resemblance between these two famous sites.

Like Machu Picchu, Choquequirao has its network of outlying sites. In 2001 and 2002, a National Geographic Society-sponsored project led by this author located a complex of supply sites at the area known as Qoriwayrachina, centered around the mountain known as Cerro Victoria, about 6.5 air km (4mi) north of Choquequirao. In 2001, several large ceremonial platforms were located, including one atop Cerro Victoria itself, along with terracing systems, an Inca administrative center set down amidst a pre-Inca people who were evidently conquered or otherwise incorporated into the imperial system, and another Inca/pre-Inca administrative site at Cota Coca on the banks of the Yanama River. The Inca infrastructure included storehouses, access roads to the area's rich silver mines, and a massive and vital 8km (5mi) long aqueduct located in 2002, which watered the entire complex of sites, from a glacial lake to the east at 4,900m (16,000ft). With a warm valley area on the Yanama River at around 2,300m (7,500ft), doubtless providing coca and other tropical products, through corn and potato growing sites on the mountain slopes above, all the way to mountain llama and alpaca pastures at around 4,500m (14,800ft), and with rich silver mines in the bargain, the elite inhabitants of Choquequirao overcame challenges of remoteness and severe terrain to achieve the Andean ideal of access to a broad swath of vertical ecology, obtaining most of what they needed close at hand.

Taken together, Choquequirao and its hinterland represent, just like Machu Picchu, a massive investment of time, labor, plus design, engineering and architectural skill; another large, mysterious, remote settlement that nobody in their right mind would build, but the Incas did.

The place is all the more enigmatic because it is not mentioned in any of the recorded incidents and invasions of the 40-year period of the Vilcabamba resistance. Bingham and others ruled it out it as the last refuge of the Incas, which in any case has now been incontrovertibly located at far away Espiritu Pampa. Today the available archaeological and archival evidence for Choquequirao, the remotest of the major Inca sites, suggests that its construction began under Pachacuti but was vastly expanded and completed as a royal property by his son, the emperor Topa Inca.

Choquequirao will not be remote much longer. A proposed cable car across the Apurimac canyon from Kiuñalla on the south bank is in the works. How soon this costly human conveyor belt will begin rolling is anybody's guess, but the future promises hordes of visitors *à la* Machu Picchu. If this site is on your bucket list (and it should be!), visit sooner rather than later.

GETTING THERE. There are currently two ways in, both on foot. Many travel operators (*see p. 41*) plus hotels in either Cachora or Huanipaca can help you organize these treks. A recommended independent guide and *arriero* living in Cachora is Edwin Palomino (tel. 983-767079). The website for Villa los Loros lodge near Huanipaca (*see p. 62*) has excellent maps and advice for independent hikers.

To fully appreciate the site you'll want at least a full day there, ideally two. This means a five-day trip at a minimum (two days in, one at the ruins, then two days out). A four-day tour – which is the standard budget offering – means hiking exhausting distances and elevations each day and seeing little of the ruins when you actually get there. To trek that distance for a superficial, half-day glimpse of the site seems crazy; the trek across the Apurimac Canyon is utterly magnificent, too, and you might want time to appreciate that. So if you must economize, do it yourself and take five or six days: rent necessary camping gear in Cusco (*see p.36*), take public transportation to Cachora (*see p.23*), and hire pack mules and *arrieros* there. The routes are easy to follow. A longer, eight-day route continues past Choquequirao and can connect with Machu Picchu. See Trekking on **www.peterfrost.org** for descriptions of the treks to the site.

IN THE RUINS. Arriving at Choquequirao on foot from the east, you come to the *Great Terraces* (1), an imposing set of four massively constructed walls, 350m (1,150ft) long and each about six meters high. At the foot of these lies a raised stone roadway, the *Avenue of the Cedars* (2). *Exploring Cusco's* 5th edition stated "...it is lined on the left with tall Andean cedars..." A splendid row of these trees in the mahogany family (*Cedrela angustifolia*), considered endangered, stood alongside the terraces, and

I speculated they were descendants of trees planted by the Incas. Not long afterwards, some unprintable functionary at the site felled them all for use as construction timbers. I maintain this name *in memoriam,* in protest, and in hopes they might someday be replanted.

The avenue exhibits typically exquisite Inca architectural sensitivity to landscape, as it leads you and your eye in a gentle curve towards the *Usnu* (site 17), a ceremonial platform on a levelled-off hilltop overlooking the site. The *Lower Plaza* (3) stands at the west end of the terraces. This has imposing structures on three sides: the *Main Fountain* (4); an odd-shaped and enigmatic structure with large niches, most likely an *Ancestor Shrine* (5) for the display and veneration of important mummies on ceremonial occasions; and the *Great Hall* (6), whose doorways look out towards the Apurimac and has been heavily reconstructed. The hall was probably used for banquets, because right behind it are the *Kitchens* (7), rough structures identified from potsherds and mortar stones as service and food preparation areas. A *Hall of Niches* (8), on the west side of the plaza appears to have held high-status or ceremonial significance, because its niches are triple-recessed and edged with puzzling ring stones. The first enclosure of a high-status residential group, a *Two-story Residential Complex* (9), also fronts onto the Plaza. Some of the inside walls of these buildings display traces of a clay stucco that once covered them entirely.

Follow the *water channel* (10) up the hill, passing the narrow set of ascending terraces known as the *Giant Stairway* (11), at the head of which you see the *Colcas* (12), twin rows of large buildings once used for storage. You come to the *Upper Plaza* (13), a smaller and perhaps even more exclusive area than the lower sector, where there is a well-made *Upper Fountain* (14), and the *Niche House* (15), a small, odd-shaped building containing the aforementioned niche, which was large, and most likely housed an important mummy during Inca times. The trail to Pincha Unuyoq (*see Outlying Sites, p.314*) begins from the Upper Plaza, but a round-trip visit from Choquequirao takes a full day. Trekkers continuing north towards Yanama will pass the site along their route.

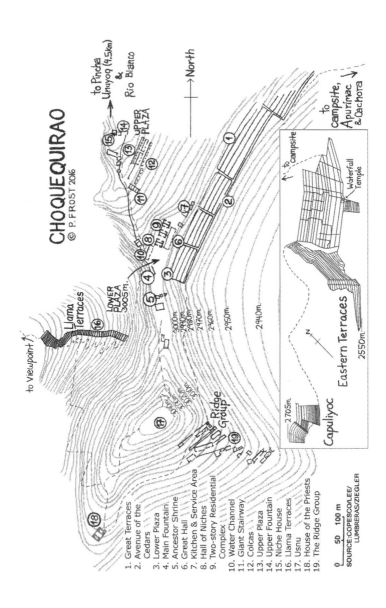

CHOQUEQUIRAO
© P. FROST 2016

→ North

to Pincha
Unuyoq (4.5km)
&
Rio Blanco

to
campsite,
Apurímac
& Cachora

to campsite

Waterfall
Temple

Eastern Terraces

Capuliyoc

2705m.

2550m.

to Viewpoint

Llama
Terraces

Ridge
Group

LOWER
PLAZA
3005m.

UPPER
PLAZA

3000m.
2940m.
2980m.
2970m.
2960m.
2950m.
2940m.

3200m.
3100m.
3000m.

1. Great Terraces
2. Avenue of the
   Cedars
3. Lower Plaza
4. Main Fountain
5. Ancestor Shrine
6. Great Hall
7. Kitchen & Service Area
8. Hall of Niches
9. Two-story Residential
   Complex
10. Water Channel
11. Giant Stairway
12. Colcas
13. Upper Plaza
14. Upper Fountain
15. Niche House
16. Llama Terraces
17. Usnu
18. House of the Priests
19. The Ridge Group

0   50   100 m

SOURCE: COPESCO/LEE/
LUMBRERAS/ZIEGLER

You will need about half a day for the above explorations. The rest of the day can be spent visiting highlights to the south and west of the main site, starting at the trail that begins on the west side of the Lower Plaza and descends steeply to the extraordinary *Llama Terraces* (16). This trail and visit are fairly strenuous, involving a long, steep descent, and a hard climb on the return journey.

The amazing Llama Terrace complex displays large scale figures and geometrical patterns created by inlaying white stone into the darker stone of the walls. The highest terraces feature chevron and checkerboard patterns (don't miss these in your eagerness to see the llamas!), while the lower area constitutes an immense sweep of descending terraces prominently featuring 22 white stone llama figures with a single human figure at the bottom, herding them up the slope. To get the best view of these continue down the path at the bottom end of the terraces about 20 minutes to the viewpoint (*mirador*).

The terraces were an astonishing discovery made by the late Cusco archaeologist Percy Paz in 2002, showing that major finds can still be made at well-known sites. They have since become one of Choquequirao's many claims to fame. Their technique of grand scale marquetry in stone is seen nowhere else in Inca architecture. The figures, patterns and surrounding stone wall construction style most resemble the work of the Chachapoya people of Peru's northern Andes, who, as it happens, were conquered by Topa Inca, reputedly the builder of Choquequirao. Some scholars speculate therefore that this, along with some other construction and design at Choquequirao, was done by Chachapoyas forcibly relocated to the Cusco region by Topa Inca as payback for their fierce resistance to the Inca conquest.

The archaeologist Patrice Lecoq, who conducted investigations at the site in the mid-2000s, proposes an astronomical significance for the arrangement of figures and symbols.

An uphill trail forking to the right is the most direct way back to the ridgeline and the next two points on the circuit, but it has been overgrown and inaccessible in recent times. Check the current situation. Otherwise, return to the Main Plaza the same way you came then head south and up to the *Usnu* (17), and artificially leveled hilltop ceremonial platform. This great spot for photos of Choquequirao's main ruins also commands the entire horizon – featuring the snow peaks of Panta to the west, Ampay across the Apurimac to the south, and nearby Marcana to the NE – and offers stupendous views of the Apurimac on both sides of the ridge. It was undoubtedly chosen by the Incas for just that reason, as a place for for celestial observation and ritual activities which could be viewed from the both the Upper and Lower Plazas. Continue south down the increasingly knife-edged ridge to a small, delightful pair of matching structures sharing a central patio, the so-called *Priest's Houses* (18), which were certainly very exclusive residences, having the finest view up and down the Apurimac of any building in the entire site – and considering their proximity to the Usnu, the name seems like a reasonable speculation. One can easily imagine Inca priests preparing themselves here for rituals and appearing suddenly, as if from nowhere, on the Usnu.

Backtrack a short way uphill to pick up a small trail traversing off to the right across the slope to meet a secondary east-west ridge where you find the *Ridge Group (Pikiwasi)* (19), documented by Vincent Lee in 1996. It has been cleared, and provides a sense of how the lower status people at the site might have lived. The buildings are more rustic than most others at the site, yet the layout still displays an overall plan, with public space and private dwellings.

A visit to these ruins completes your tour of the entire upper area and western slope of Choquequirao. You can continue on without backtracking to pick up the trail leading downhill to the campsite.

Outlying Sites. A further half day is required to visit the *Eastern Terraces* (*see map box*). The trail descends through forest from the lower end of the campsite area and continues onto an Inca stairway which emerges by the *Waterfall Temple* (*Casa de la Cascada*), for which this sector is named. This small but delightfully located cluster of structures features a ritual bath and is oriented to give a perfect view of a plunging waterfall in the nearby ravine – yet another example of Inca architectural sensitivity to landscape. The rest of the area consists mostly of massively built terraces, impressive enough in themselves, featuring large and intricate drainage and irrigation channels. Energetic explorers can ascend southwards from here up the trail to the hanging terraces of Capuliyoc. From there a trail which completes a circuit returning to the campsite exists but may be overgrown or inaccessible, in which case you will have to backtrack.

A northbound trail from the Upper Plaza (*see p.311*) leads to a huge fan-shaped area of terracing spread down a ravine, known as *Pincha Unuyoq* (Water Gushing Forth), which contains some curious structures in the Inca fountain tradition – clearly not residential, but having some connection to Inca ritual activities – which are oriented towards Wiracochan Ridge, off to the west beyond the Yanama River. Percy Paz, who worked here, suggested that the terraces were used for growing coca.

Those taking a trek northwards from Choquequirao will pass this way. If not, you need a whole day round-trip from Choquequirao to visit this site; certainly a worthwhile extra day if you can spare it, and its views of the northern branch of the Cordillera Vilcabamba and down into the Yanama River canyon are magnificent.

GLOSSARY

abra — mountain pass

altiplano — high plain

andesite — hard local basalt, used extensively in the building of Inca Cusco

Antisuyu — eastern (rainforest) quarter of Tawantinsuyu

apu — peak sacred to both Incas and modern Quechua people

arriero — wrangler

ayllu — Quechua kinship group or community

Aymara — people and language of the Titicaca region

ayni — Andean system of reciprocity

campesino — rural worker; small farmer

cancha — courtyard enclosure

chacana — step-symbol; Andean cross

chacra — cultivated land

chaski — Inca message runner

chicha — Andean corn beer

Chinchaysuyu — northern quarter of Tawantinsuyu

choque — unworked gold ore, nuggets etc.

chronicles — 16th- & 17th-century Spanish accounts of the Conquest

chullpa — pre-Hispanic burial tower

colca — Inca storehouse

Collasuyu — southern quarter of Tawantinsuyu

Contisuyu — western quarter of Tawantinsuyu

cordillera — mountain range

Coya — Inca queen, principal wife of the emperor

criollo — Spanish-descended, traditional or local, typically referring to music, food and people

cuyusmanco — Inca architectural style, a long, rectangular hall with a very wide opening at one end

hacienda — Spanish country estate, usually also a farm

huanca — Standing stone, which both "owns" a place and represents the human owners in their absence

ichu — highland bunch grass

intiwatana — literally, "for tying up the sun"; a modern name for stone pillars characteristic of Inca ceremonial sites kallanka — Inca architectural style, a large hall with many entrances, used for assemblies and transient lodging

Manco Capac — mythical founder of the Inca royal line of kings

Manco Inca — (a.k.a. Manco II) son of emperor Wayna Capac, and later leader of Inca rebellion

mestizo — person of mixed racial and cultural descent

mit'a — Inca system of drafted labor

orejón — Spanish name for an Inca noble, after the huge earplugs they wore; literally, "big ears"

Pachamama — Earth Mother in traditional Andean religion

pampa — any flat area, from soccer pitch-tiny to altiplano-huge

panaca — royal Inca lineage group

pirca — style of Inca stonework using uncut field stones

pucara — fortified area

puna — treeless grasslands of the high Andes

Qhapac Ñan — main north-south Inca highway; more generally, the Inca road network

qori — gold worked by human hands

quipu — Inca recording device made of knotted cords

runa — Quechua word meaning "people," or "humans"

Sapa Inca — Inca Emperor

soroche — hypoxia, altitude sickness

tambo — lodge house and transit point of the Inca highway system

Tawantinsuyu — "Four Quarters Joined Together"; the Inca empire

usnu — tiered platform for elite Inca ceremonies and reviewing of processions

waca — huge variety of objects, landscape features and phenomena imbued with supernatural power

Wari — powerful pre-Inca culture which dominated the central Peruvian Andes from roughly 500 to 900AD

Wiracocha — (a) Inca creator god and culture hero; (b) name of a late Inca king; (c) honorific used by modern Quechua speakers, connoting "sir" or "gentleman"

SELECT BIBLIOGRAPHY
(For a more detailed bibliography see **www.peterfrost.org**)

Incas, Exploration & History

Ancient Cuzco – Brian S. Bauer, U. of Texas Press, 2004. A comprehensive overview of the Cusco Valley's history, from 7,000 B.C to the fall of the Inca empire in 1532.

At Home With the Sapa Inca – Stella Nair, U. of Texas Press, 2015. A close look at the little-studied Inca palace of Chinchero.

The Conquest of the Incas – John Hemming, Mariner Books, (1970, last updated 2003). A major contribution to modern scholarship on the Incas, and an extraordinary story brilliantly told.

A Culture of Stone, Inka Perspectives on Rock – Carolyn Dean, 2010. An extended meditation on the meaning and use of stone in the Inca world.

Encyclopedia of the Incas – eds. Gary Urton & Adriana von Hagen, 2015. The A-to-Z introduction to the Inca empire, with numerous leads for further reading.

Forgotten Vilcabamba – Vincent R. Lee, Sixpac Manco, 2000. The explorer and Inca scholar's anthology of his investigations in Vilcabamba, with maps and illustrations.

The Great Inka Road – eds. Ramiro Matos, José Barreiro, 2015. A collection of essays and photographs that bring to life the astounding Inca highway network.

The Incas – Terence D'Altroy. Blackwell Publishing, 2002. A thorough summary of Inca society and culture.

Lost City of the Incas – Hiram Bingham, Phoenix Press, 2003. Classic account of Bingham's explorations. Outdated theories, but a great read.

Machu Picchu, A Civil Engineering Marvel – Kenneth R. Wright & Alfredo Valencia Z., ASCE Press, 2000. A close look at how Machu Picchu was built and engineered, and why it has held up so well.

Machu Picchu, Exploring an Ancient Sacred Center (4th ed.) – Johan Reinhard, Cotsen Institute of Archaeology Press, 2007. An accessible scholarly treatment of

Machu Picchu's role and meaning in the Inca world, from a leading expert on Inca archaeology.

The Stone and the Thread: Andean Roots of Abstract Art – Cesar Paternosto – U. Texas Press, 1996. A fascinating and unusual perspective on Inca stonework and textiles, by a modern art historian and artist.

Plants and Wildlife

Field Guide to the Birds of Machu Picchu and the Cusco Region – Barry Walker, Lynx Ediciones & Buteo Books, 2015. The best portable guide to the birds you might see here.

Flowers of Machu Picchu – Gino Casinelli, Daniel Huamán Chang, Gráfica Biblos S.A., 2006. A brief field guide to 96 of the region's most distinctive flowers.

One River – Wade Davis, Simon & Schuster, 1996. The life and times of legendary ethnobotanist Richard Evans Schultes and his students, beautifully and evocatively written by one of the latter.

Plants of the Gods, 2nd edition – Richard Evans Schultes *et al.,* Healing Arts Press, 2001. A global overview of medicinal plants, encompassing both psychoactive and therapeutic varieties.

Ayahuasca: Soul Medicine of the Amazon Jungle – Javier Reguiero – iUniverse, 2014. A practical guide to ayahuasca, including its traditional and modern uses, history, and how to get the most out of it.

Trees and Bushes of the Sacred Valley – Gino Casinelli, Lettera Gráfica S.A.C., 2006. Brief, informative descriptions with color photos of the area's most important trees and bushes.

Travel and Guidebooks

The Machu Picchu Guidebook – Ruth Wright, Alfredo Valencia Zegarra, 3D Press, 2011. A very complete tour of Machu Picchu, with background and the latest research.

Trekking Peru – Robert and Daisy Kunstaetter, The Mountaineers, 2017. Includes 7 treks in the Cusco region.

Turn Right at Machu Picchu – Mark Adams, Plume Books, 2011. A popular and entertaining account of the author's travels in the footsteps of Hiram Bingham.

INDEX

Areas or features within major sites are only listed under that site's name, e.g. "Agricultural Sector" is listed under M for Machu Picchu.